THE HAPPIEST PRESCHOOL

How to Create a Classroom Culture of Caring,
Cooperation, Creativity, Learning, and Emotional Health

A MANUAL FOR TEACHERS

MARTHA HEINEMAN PIEPER, PH.D.

KELLY PEREZ, SMART LOVE PRESCHOOL DIRECTOR

SMART LOVE PRESS LLC
CHICAGO

The Happiest Preschool: A Manual for Teachers

Library of Congress Control Number: 2024901709

ISBN: 978-1-7330897-2-2

Production Advisor: Vincent Mallardi, PBBA

Acknowledgments

This manual has benefited enormously from the comments and suggestions of readers of early drafts. You are too numerous to name, but know that you have provided invaluable insights into how to make the manual more accessible and helpful to teachers.

— **MARTHA HEINEMAN PIEPER**

Love does win and thank you to all of the people in my life who had the courage, strength and resilience to demonstrate it. I am forever grateful.

— **KELLY PEREZ**

Dedication

To the teachers and children, past and present, in the Natalie G. Heineman Smart Love Preschool. You made this book possible and embody its heart and soul.

Also by Martha Heineman Pieper, Ph.D.

Intrapsychic Humanism: An Introduction to a Comprehensive Psychology and Philosophy of Mind (Falcon II Press, 1990)

Smart Love: The Comprehensive Guide to Understanding, Regulating and Enjoying Your Child (Smart Love Press LLC, 2011)

Smart Love Solutions in Early Childhood: A Handbook for Parents, Teachers, and Caregivers (Smart Love Family Services, 2011)

Smart Love Solutions for School-Age Children and Teens (Smart Love Family Services, 2012)

Mommy, Daddy, I Had a Bad Dream! (Smart Love Press LLC, 2012)

Jilly's Terrible Temper Tantrums: And How She Outgrew Them (Smart Love Press LLC, 2017)

Addicted to Unhappiness: How Hidden Motives for Unhappiness Keep You From Creating the Life You Truly Want, and What You Can Do, 2nd ed. (Smart Love Press LLC, 2019)

Table of Contents

The key to a happy preschool is a welcoming, developmentally informed, consistently positive relationship with your students

INTRODUCTION

This manual offers new ways to think about the role of the preschool and kindergarten teacher in the lives of children. We describe in detail how taking a positive and developmentally informed approach to children's emotions, behavior, and learning process will make your teaching more enjoyable and more effective. Adding these skills to your existing repertoire and teaching experience will foster happy, creative, curious, compassionate, and positively engaged students. They will acquire a stable desire to learn that doesn't depend on the subject matter. They will enjoy the process of learning, not just the outcome. They will be enthusiastic about focusing on and trying new things, and they will develop social-emotional understanding and competencies. Your practice as a teacher will offer a model of care and engagement that will become a real bond and a benefit to all.

This positive classroom approach is based on Smart Love®[1], an original and empirically tested psychology that includes unique insights into child development and leads to an optimal approach to children's social-emotional needs and motivated learning, classroom management, and the role of the teacher. As you read further and incorporate the topics into your teaching practice, you will see the applicability of the S.M.A.R.T. acronym: Stay Positive, Model Kindness, Acknowledge and Accept feelings, Loving Regulation, and Time With. This approach has been used successfully for more than 13 years in the *Natalie G. Heineman Smart Love Preschool*, and our hope is that it will be adopted wholly or in part by other preschools and kindergartens. The *Smart Love Preschool* has toddler classes, playschool for twos and threes, preschool for threes and fours, and kindergarten. Because the Smart Love principles apply equally to all of these ages, unless an example is specific to an age group, we use "preschool" to stand for all the ages and classes.

This manual illustrates Smart Love principles with examples collected by our teachers. While children's names and identifying information have been changed, and examples have been edited for clarification, the examples provide depth to the topics covered and accurately reflect the Smart Love approach. Some of the examples throughout the book are in the form of professional development conversations with the authors taken from questions posed by teachers. We know how difficult the life of a teacher can be, and also we want to help teachers learn the Smart Love approach, so our teachers get a half day per week to learn, ask questions, and generally get help and support with interactions they felt were important. After some examples, you will see clarifying comments for teachers that Dr. Martha Heineman Pieper or Director Kelly Perez have made on the exchanges with students that teachers have submitted.

Any and all of the strategies presented in this manual can enrich a preschool, regardless of its affiliation. Smart Love is transformative of the preschool and kindergarten culture and inspires children to:

- **Accept and value all of themselves;**
- **Retain and enhance their curiosity;**
- **Love learning;**
- **Learn through play;**
- **Be creative in fantasy play, art, music, drama, and projects;**
- **Cooperate with and show compassion and care for teachers, classmates, and themselves;**
- **Regulate themselves without any type of discipline or coercion;**
- **Embrace differences in race, culture, appearance, and language;**
- **Demonstrate unforced social-emotional learning;**
- **Move on to the next grades as eager learners who make positive contributions to any classroom culture.**

The Basic Smart Love Principles

First and foremost, children learn social-emotional lessons most effectively by *imitation*. Research has consistently shown that imitation is inborn and is the most powerful learning engine for children.[2] Newborn babies who have never seen a face will stick out their tongues in imitation of their mother sticking out her tongue.[3] How we treat our children is how they will come to treat themselves and others.

You will be most effective as a teacher when you model helpfulness, acceptance of all feelings (positive, angry, sad, anxious, joyful, enthusiastic), compassion for yourself and others, and caring responsiveness to requests of any kind. Ideally, you will learn to welcome and respond positively to shared feelings and never lecture, regardless of the content of children's communications. As a result, your students will come to understand that they need not hide any feelings from themselves or others, nor do they have to try to make feelings go away with "coping mechanisms." Rather, they will learn that feelings are not actions and can thus be embraced and understood within a caring relationship. In our experience, this is the most robust way for children to develop self-regulation without any accompanying feelings of anger toward themselves and others.

Secondly, knowing what behaviors are age-appropriate will allow you to avoid asking children to behave like miniature adults. For example, preschool children are too young to want to share consistently, or even at all. Not only should sharing not be required; there should be many duplicates of the most engaging toys. Genuine sharing comes from the desire to foster a relationship.

Third, when children's behavior needs managing, you can use the S.M.A.R.T. approach rather than any form of discipline (including time-outs or restrictions of activities), distractions (including breathing exercises, mindfulness, or self-isolation), disapproval, or rewards. S.M.A.R.T. means that you respond to anti-social or out-of-control behavior only with kindness and understanding. This positive approach will cement the children's relationship with you and increase their understanding of themselves. For example, if a child pushes another child you might say, "I can't let you push, but I can see that you really wanted to stand where Andy was. He's in that spot for now, but would you like to come and stand by me?" This kind but firm approach is what we call Loving Regulation, and it lets you offer your caring relationship with the child as a substitute for unacceptable behavior, whereas traditional corrections too often deprive children of closeness to their teacher.

Furthermore, if you keep classroom rules both in accordance with developmental phases and to a necessary minimum, there will be fewer moments when regulation is needed. Also, you can make children partners in creating the rules. If it's unsafe to run on the bridge in the playground, ask where they think they might run? Instead of making a list of what children can't do, see if you can make one of what they can. There are numerous examples of how to use the S.M.A.R.T. practices throughout this manual. Children imitate this approach and become able to respond to differences of opinion in the classroom calmly and with a burgeoning understanding of the other's perspective. S.M.A.R.T. principles foster a true sense of community among children because they ensure that children are understood for who they are and not for who we think they should be.

Finally, we know that the most important goal of all education, most especially at the preschool and kindergarten level, is not to teach content, but to preserve and enhance curiosity and a love of learning. Children learn best through play, with teachers who build on their interests and who encourage and enhance their creativity. Play is defined as activities chosen out of interest and solely for enjoyment. Young children do not learn well through drilling or forced attention of any kind. They do not benefit from scaffolding, that is, helping children acquire a skill and then removing help when children are themselves capable of enacting that skill. We have found that scaffolding punishes children for success in learning because sometimes asking for help may simply be about wanting/needing closeness with a teacher when children are tired, not feeling well, or have had a disappointment of some kind. Similarly, at this age, formal tests are counterproductive. Children's learning is dynamic and fluctuates with time of day, family stress, health, and peer interactions. All evaluation can best be done under the radar and with the recognition that conclusions are not static.

Children preserve their curiosity and love of learning by involving themselves in activities that interest them. If you propose a project they aren't attracted to, you will enhance their progress by substituting one that engages them. You partner with children in their activities, which gives you a unique opportunity to inject learning content, as well as listen to confidences. There are certainly academic goals for preschool children, but it is best if children meet and exceed them only in ways they enjoy. When we hear, "What if you are giving children unrealistic expectations of school? What will they do later when they have to do assignments and activities that don't interest them?" we respond: "When children leave preschool and kindergarten enthusiastic and curious about learning, they will be better prepared to sustain those qualities if later grades don't provide the same excitement." [4]

At the end of the day, the core S.M.A.R.T. concept is that when you respond to children's needs compassionately and positively, children acquire the inner resources to function flexibly and effectively in the real world. And best of all, your teaching experience is significantly more satisfying.

Preschoolers With Emotional Challenges

Sometimes, you may encounter preschool and kindergarten children who have significant emotional issues. They appear consistently unhappy or seek out conflict with peers or teachers. The Smart Love understanding is that these behaviors are symptoms of what we call an "addiction to unhappiness"[5] rather than of willfulness, manipulation, lack of coping skills, or an expression of unmet needs. The reason we use the word "addiction" is that it refers to a learned need for painful, uncomfortable, self-defeating, or self-destructive experiences. Because of children's predisposition to imitate, if you respond to anti-social behaviors with disapproval, discipline, or isolation, you reinforce negativity, which, in turn, unintentionally gratifies the child's need for unhappiness. You can help children understand that when they or others act in anti-social or provocative ways, it is because they are unhappy inside and need help, not because they are "bad." And when you respond with a S.M.A.R.T. strategy, children who are angry or upset will learn to turn to you for kindness and support rather than seek out conflict in the classroom. You can also help children identify the stresses that are causing them to feel unhappy or look for conflict. If children's symptoms are severe or persistent, you may want to help parents obtain psychological help for their child, something we discuss in a forthcoming chapter.

Try It Out!

If, as a student or teacher, you have been learning or using a different approach from the one described in this manual, we know that if you choose to adopt and integrate any of these ideas into your classroom, you and your students will benefit and thrive. Our teachers come to us using a variety of traditional models, but they soon see the value in the Smart Love approach and are thrilled at how much more enjoyable teaching becomes. We hope that you, too, will come to the same conclusion and will try some of these ideas in your classrooms.

CHAPTER 1

Social-Emotional Learning
the Smart Love Way

We all know that preschoolers feel things very keenly. They can be joyful, enthusiastic, loving, and caring. But when things don't go as they wish, they can also melt down, cry, scream, be sad, and get very angry. An important part of social-emotional learning is accepting and owning the entire spectrum of human emotions. Sometimes you may not see what triggered a meltdown, but when you welcome their feelings, you can help children think about what is upsetting them. For example, you might ask, "Did something happen that you didn't want to happen?" or "Did something you wanted to happen not happen?"

Social-emotional learning in a Smart Love preschool stems entirely from the children's imitation of the social-emotional model provided by you. The ideas and examples in this chapter illustrate the extent to which children absorb, and are responsive to, your capacity for kindness, understanding, and acceptance of all feelings. As a Smart Love teacher, you will never use the pressure, disapproval, sanctions, distractions, or rewards that characterize the attempt to teach social-emotional lessons elsewhere.

Social-Emotional Learning in Other Contexts

Social-emotional learning (SEL) is currently a big focus in preschool education. The failure of the extensive testing and academic emphasis of the *No Child Left Behind* initiative led many educators to realize that focusing only on cognition with young children doesn't work – they get bored, turned off school, and they lose curiosity. The result was a new emphasis on social-emotional learning.

Despite undeniable good intentions, we find that most social-emotional learning approaches lack the all-important modeling of kind and accepting responses by teachers. Too often, SEL devolves into techniques for neutralizing or suppressing upset feelings, or for conflict resolution. Conflict resolution usually takes the form of lectures about sharing, being nice, cooperating, and taking the other child's point of view. Children who are angry or upset are taught coping mechanisms, including meditation, self-isolation, and breathing exercises/mindfulness. These widely used techniques are often in the service of distracting from feelings and enforcing behavior that is not even age appropriate. Unfortunately, lecturing children about being nice to others breeds resentment that resurfaces when teachers aren't around, and teaching coping mechanisms conveys that upset and angry feelings are unwanted, and that children should learn to suppress them rather than acknowledge and understand them in the context of a caring relationship.

In our approach to social-emotional learning, when there are conflicts in the classroom and children are upset or angry, if you use the S.M.A.R.T. principles described in this book, the relationship with you is always there for comfort and understanding, and is never negative, didactic, or pressuring. Rather than focusing on ways to help children get over upsets – which gives the message that you don't want to hear about dysphoric feelings – the consistent social-emotional message you want to convey is, "Come to me with all feelings – sad, angry, anxious, upset – that is the *best* way to feel better." Once a child comes to you with their feelings, you can begin to connect with the feelings rather than distract from them.

The S.M.A.R.T. Difference

We can't repeat it too often: A child's relationship with you is the most important determinant of the quality of social-emotional learning, because social-emotional learning occurs most comprehensively by imitation. Since the 1990s, the neurological foundation for imitation has been identified.[6] The human brain has multiple inborn mirror-neuron systems that cause humans to comprehend and imitate the actions and intentions of others. The Smart Love approach is based on the reality that children will imitate how they are treated.

The S.M.A.R.T. acronym represents the behaviors you want to model:

 **S**tay Positive: You remain positive regardless of what children are doing or saying. Children will trust you with their self-doubts and concerns because they won't fear negative consequences.

 **M**odel Kindness: You respond positively to all requests to play or to help. Children imitate you, and a culture of kindness and cooperation is created in the classroom.

 **A**cknowledge and Accept Feelings: You welcome all feelings, and help children understand that feelings don't have consequences, and so are different from actions. There is no attempt to suppress feelings through coping mechanisms or distractions. As a result, children learn that they never have to be ashamed or rejecting of how they feel, and they become comfortable with all of themselves.

 Loving **R**egulation: Loving Regulation is the Smart Love approach to managing children's behavior. Loving Regulation means that you regulate behavior when necessary, but in a positive way, and without attaching negative consequences. The focus is on helping children understand what led to the behavior that needs regulating. This models a way to connect when others don't do as we wish.

 **T**ime With: When children are upset or out-of-control they are never isolated. If they pose a problem to themselves or others, you may have to pick them up or take them out of the classroom for a time, but you will always go with them to help in a caring and understanding way. The message is that the relationship with you is always there to help them feel better and rejoin the group when they are able. Importantly, when a child is removed from the classroom for one-to-one support, the other children are told that you are helping the child feel better. This prevents children from believing that punitive responses happen when a teacher takes someone aside.

How to Have Children Come to You With Angry, Upset, and Sad Feelings

Like many things that can sound good on paper, we understand that inviting children to share their feelings in a real and ongoing way might seem challenging in practice, even as we accept that social-emotional learning is as important in the preschool classroom as learning academic skills. So how do you invite and handle the intensity of children's feelings in your classroom setting? When you remain with children and help them understand their feelings, children will learn from you both to embrace their full range of emotions, and also that the best thing to do in a crisis is to turn to the relationship with you for help and comfort. But getting children to unlearn emotional habits, or to form a trusting relationship with you, takes a little time. It also takes the awareness to react less to the "surface" of your students' emotional expression and more to their need to connect. Here are some ways to think about this that can help you begin this process in the classroom.

Angry Feelings Are Not Actions, and Angry Actions Result From Unhappiness

As a teacher working from S.M.A.R.T. principles, you personify the important message that all feelings are morally neutral and welcomed. Many children enter preschool believing that anger is both dangerous and bad. This mistaken belief is often reinforced when anger and upset feelings are seen as undesirable in themselves, regardless of whether they translate to actions, so children aren't helped to distinguish between feelings and actions. When you Acknowledge and Accept children's angry feelings, children learn the social-emotional lesson that anger alone doesn't hurt the object of the anger, and it doesn't make the angry child a bad person.

You can further your students' social-emotional learning by showing them that even when angry feelings do result in anti-social actions, these actions result from feeling unhappy inside and needing help. You can say, "I've been hearing some children saying that other kids are bad. But children that don't follow the rules are unhappy inside, or they are unhappy in that moment. That's something school is helping them with. Being unhappy inside is not the same as being bad."

If a child asks why another child is aggressive, you can say, "There are children who get confused and think if they are unhappy, they will feel better if they make other kids unhappy." You can Model Kindness and explain that the best thing for a child who is having a hard time or feeling out of sorts over something is to bring their unhappiness to you, and maybe ask for a hug or another form of comfort.

Anti-social feelings and actions are sometimes misread as manipulative, or as the desire for attention. Children who are aggressive are too often disapproved of or isolated, with the result that they have to deal with their feelings on their own, and are thus deprived of the relationship with you. So when children get the message that angry or upset feelings are a cause for shame or blame, they become reluctant to turn to you for comfort and help, and they become secretive about negativity toward others, and deny it or deflect it when asked.

Adults sometimes feel concerned that offering the understanding that "bad guys" are unhappy inside will cause children to think doing "bad" things is OK . But you are not saying that *doing* "bad" things is OK – rather, that children who do "bad" things need help and positive attention. The answer is understanding why they did it, not punishment.

One extension of S.M.A.R.T. principles is that because you are trying to help children understand the distinction between being "bad" and being unhappy, we recommend reframing play that involves labeling you or others as bad in any way. Even in fantasy, we believe it is crucial to continue the effort to show that feelings are to be connected to and not punished.

> **TEACHER:** One day a child brought plastic handcuffs to school and said I was bad and had to wear them and go to jail. I agreed to act as the outlaw, but said I didn't deserve to wear handcuffs because, "Even if I did things that I wasn't supposed to do, that's because I'm really unhappy inside. I need some help. What do you think might make me happier inside?" Accepting the premise of unhappiness and leaving the "bad" label and the idea of punishment behind, the children suggested hugs, candy, and going to the playground.

Children who have been conditioned to think they are bad when they behave in an angry way can react with fear of punishment even to your caring response. These children may run away, hide, or become paralyzed. You can offer an entirely different way of relating when you show them you understand their fear that you will retaliate for their aggressive behavior, and you Model Kindness and emphasize that you are not upset with them and only want to help them figure out why they were angry.

> **TEACHER:** At lunch, we were all pretending to be different animals and characters. Tom told us Spiderman breaks houses and tears up roads. I said, "Sounds like Spiderman is angry. What do you think – why does he break houses and tear up roads? Maybe he's feeling unhappy?" When Tom got up from lunch, he started pulling me to the ground pretending to be Spiderman. I asked, "Tom were you trying to give me a hug?" He said, "Yes," and I said, "Okay, we can hug but I can't let you pull me down." He ran to the basket of blocks, dumped them out, and curled up inside. I said, "It looks like you feel badly because I said you couldn't do something, but you aren't in any trouble, and you will feel better if you stay with me." He did come out and play for a short time, but very soon it was time to go home and he began to kick at me. I said, "Tom, I can't let you kick me. I'm going to pick you up now." I picked him up and said, "I know when we're having fun at school it can feel hard to go home, but you're coming back tomorrow." He sat in my lap and said, "Yeah, I will see you tomorrow!" After this Tom was much more available and we put on his snow clothes together.

It is a good idea to automatically track the classroom schedule, as children often become upset or angry around transitions. This is how the teacher thought to suggest that Tom's anger had to do with going home when he wanted to stay at school. Connecting children's upset to unwanted events is an important way to further their social-emotional understanding. Sometimes offering a suggestion for what might be behind their surface behaviors allows the child some space to consider if it's accurate.

Thus, rather than react to unwanted behaviors as meaningful in and of themselves, you can begin to teach children that the feelings that led to the behavior are welcomed. Slowly you see that children who get angry or upset learn that it is better to come to you than to fall apart alone. This social-emotional achievement is much preferable to believing that feeling overwhelmed is blameworthy and will result in disapproval or sanctions.

Conflicting Feelings Are Acknowledged and Welcomed

As the adult who spends a great deal of time with your students, you are in an excellent position to help them recognize that they can have several distinct feelings at the same time. This is a sophisticated social-emotional understanding that you can help children develop. At first, preschoolers usually insist that they feel only one way – for example, happy – which admits of no other feelings, such as sadness. This lack of awareness can result in seemingly paradoxical behavior when they unknowingly switch from one state of mind to another.

> **TEACHER:** Today during arrival Elaine seemed unusually distracted. I asked if she would like help with her jacket or boots. The first time I asked, she was unresponsive, so after I helped another child, I went back and asked again. She remained silent. I began to say "Elaine" in a soft voice to try to get her focus. I asked again if she needed help and she began to talk to me about something else. After she finished, I said, "Thanks for telling me that. It looks like it's time to change into your inside shoes and take off your jacket." After this she still did not do either, so I asked if she would like help pulling off her boots. She responded, "I can do it," so I said, "Let me know if you need help," and began to assist another child. Soon, she and I were the last ones in the hallway. I said, "Elaine, can I help you with your boots or jacket?" She responded, "Why did you help all the other kids before you helped me?" Confused by this, I let Elaine know that I am always here to help her, and if she needs help she can always ask me or another teacher.

> **DR. PIEPER:** This ambivalence is not uncommon at this age. Children want to do things themselves, but they also want to feel helped and cared for. You could help identify her conflicting feelings by saying, "I understand you are feeling upset that I helped the other kids first, but I think first you wanted to do it yourself, and then a little later you decided you wanted help, but by that time I had helped others. It's hard when we want two things at once!"

With your gentle assistance, children become more comfortable with the notion that they can integrate opposing feelings. In the next example, a child was able to recognize and express conflicting feelings about being at school:

> **TEACHER:** During lunch the children were talking about how they loved playing at school when Kandy said, "Well, there's a part of me that likes school and a part of me that doesn't like school." I responded, "I wonder what part of you likes school and what part doesn't?" She said, "I like school because I have fun playing, but I don't like school because I don't like leaving Mom and Dad." I said, "Kandy, you are completely right! You can still have fun and miss them at the same time."

Knowing that negative as well as positive feelings can be voiced, accepted, and understood is an important part of social-emotional learning.

> **TEACHER:** While reading one of the "Fancy Nancy" stories, there was a part where Nancy describes feeling jealous of her younger sister. I asked the children, "I wonder what it means to feel jealous?" Tabatha spoke up. "I feel jealous sometimes! I felt really jealous and mad at Momma when my sister Josey was in Momma's tummy, because I wanted to be close to Momma." I responded, "Thanks so much for telling me, Tabatha. That sounds really hard when you want to be with Mom and your sister is with mom too!"

What is impressive here is how comfortable Tabatha felt sharing her anger at her mother and sister in response to the teacher's question about jealousy. Clearly, she has learned that feelings are not actions and that she can be both excited for a new baby and also be angry or jealous. Often in the classroom, one set of feelings tends to be what you see, and it takes slowing down and inviting conversation in order to get the full picture. This is a key practice: taking time and not summarizing anyone's feelings until all the parts are heard. At that point, it's easy to draw the lesson that feelings are welcome even when they seem contradictory, and that they are all part of a person and not threatening just because they are seemingly at odds. This ability to slow down and take an inclusive view becomes increasingly habitual.

Learning That Asking for Help Reliably Results in Support

Children are often afraid that requests for help will be met with refusal. This is an unfortunate consequence of misconceptions about what it means to be independent. Dependence is inevitably a characteristic of childhood, and refusing help when asked simply makes children feel unsupported. It does not make them independent in a positive sense. The key concept is that children ask for help both when they can't do something, but also for legitimate emotional reasons. Telling children that they don't need help because they are able to do something ignores age-appropriate emotional needs for adult caring and involvement.

In the S.M.A.R.T. approach, we encourage you to Model Kindness and show children that you are happy to hear and respond to their desires, even if it's something you know the child can handle. No matter how slight the need for help, responding positively sends the message that any request is legitimate. Consequently, when the classroom culture becomes all-accepting, children learn the important social-emotional skill that everyone deserves to be treated well and have their wishes heard.

> **TEACHER:** Sylvester is a new three-year old at summer camp. He is actively engaged and likes participating in group fun. Every time it is Sylvester's turn to wash his hands for snack he will say, "I don't know how to wash my hands." We always say we would

be happy to show him how and help him. I said, "It seems you like it when I help you. It's not that you don't know how, and I'm happy to help you. You don't have to say you can't do it. All you have to do is ask a teacher to do it with you." Sylvester smiled and held out his hands to wash them with me.

When children enter school believing they aren't supposed to ask for help, it can take sensitive and careful exploration to bring out the desire behind the camouflage.

TEACHER: Lloyd is new to the preschool and has had some trouble with transitions. Today he told me he did not want to go in the back yard and that he wanted to go straight to the front yard (meaning he wants to go home). I said "Well, I was hoping you would help me make a list of things we could check on outside. Remember when we did that last week?" He replied enthusiastically, "Yes!" While we were making the list he admitted, "I didn't actually want to go home. I wanted to make a list." I responded, "Thank you for telling me! Sometimes it feels hard to ask for what we want, and you might feel like you want to go home. But I always love to play with you, and you can tell me what you'd like to play." Lloyd had a super easy transition outside after this.

In the above example, notice that the teacher didn't confront Lloyd about his desire to go home, even though that was the explicit request. Instead, she remembered what had engaged him the week before (making the list), and she guessed that maybe he was afraid to ask for what he really wanted.

Even children who have been in the Preschool for a while, and can ask for what they want fairly fluently, may have desires that in their experience are not usually granted. For example, children often want to change, take off, or put on different clothes, and for some reason they have difficulty making those requests. Part of social-emotional learning is accepting and acknowledging one's wishes and believing teachers want to grant them whenever possible. As the person with an intimate experience of each student, you can grow adept at seeing where a request may be masked by another behavior.

> **TEACHER:** Today washing his hands for snack, Easton put his sweatshirt under the water. I said, "We need to change your sweatshirt because it is too wet, and when we go outside you will be cold." Easton happily agreed to change his sweatshirt. When we got to his cubby he said, "Please don't put another sweatshirt on me, I don't like them." I responded, "If you want to change out of your sweatshirt you can always tell a teacher! We will change you into something comfortable because we want you to feel good at school." Easton smiled and looked relieved.

What's important to consider is that the "surface" action – getting the sleeves wet – might be where the child could expect to be criticized. Slowing down and following the child's lead allows the unarticulated request behind the action to emerge. Preschool teachers are busy with many tasks and children at once, so we encourage this small change of perspective wherein you can see a behavior or a sudden change of mood, and, before reacting to it, ask yourself, is this behavior masking a need the child can't say but that I could uncover? When children learn the social-emotional lesson that requests for help are always welcomed, they learn to become more direct and self-assured.

> **TEACHER:** At extended day while we were getting out our cots, Cassie asked me if I could help her with her sheet and blanket. I said I would love to. Cassie said she wanted help again because she remembered it was fun doing it together yesterday, when we both searched for two corners of her blanket and used teamwork to place it on her cot. Cassie said excitedly, "We can look for the corners just like we did yesterday!"

In her note on this activity, the teacher commented, "It's so awesome that Cassie assumed I would agree to help and that we were able to have a spontaneous fun experience together." You may have been told that granting requests without questioning their validity will make children dependent. In actuality, when you consistently respond positively to requests, the culture in the classroom becomes one of helpfulness and children absorb and exemplify it. Rather than becoming dependent, they take on your role as active and welcoming helpmate.

Fears Should Be Acknowledged, Comforted, and Handled

A key component of social-emotional learning for preschoolers is the ability to recognize fearful feelings, to share them with you, and to receive comfort and understanding.[7] It can be very difficult for children to admit to feeling scared and to concede that being frightened by scary video programs, games, movies, or books is not really enjoyable. This is especially true when children are scared by media that their siblings or friends like reading or watching.

> TEACHER: While Aubrey was painting at the easel, she repeatedly said she was painting the flying monkeys from *The Wizard of Oz*. She told us that at home she watches *The Wizard of Oz* over and over again. I said, "Those flying monkeys can be scary and maybe you like to paint them because then you can be in control of them. You can paint them how you want and change and erase them when you want. But we think *The Wizard of Oz* is too scary for children your age and we will talk with your parents and see if they can't find movies you would like but not be scared by."

This teacher later explained to Aubrey's parents that her repeatedly painting the flying monkeys was a sign she was overwhelmed and overstimulated by *The Wizard of Oz*. The teacher explained that sometimes children want to experience scary stories and characters over and over as a way of trying to master their fear. But at this age, children cannot reliably distinguish between what is real and what is not, and so it's preferable not to expose them to scary entertainment. Her parents responded that they had never thought about it that way and agreed to find more appropriate content for Aubrey. Within a week, Aubrey's painting turned to more enjoyable subjects. Note that Aubrey did not stop focusing on scary characters because a teacher made her feel there was anything wrong with it, but because once the scary movie was removed, her interests moved on.

Preschool children may also tell you that they like playing scary video games, and you can try diplomatically to convey that these are for older children. Too often adults take children's denials at face value, and children continue to feel scared. Feeling frightened is an emotion preschoolers dislike and try to avoid, especially if they think that admitting fear would make them seem "babyish." Even when children can't admit to being afraid, you open the door to social-emotional learning when you gently disagree.

> **TEACHER:** Colby said, "I'm a zombie and I'm going to eat your head." I asked, "I wonder what a zombie is?" He explained it was a creature in his video game and told me zombies eat brains. I said, "That's scary! Sounds like it might be a game for older kids." He told me he was good at the game even when he played with older kids, so I said, "Oh maybe there's a part of you that likes to play the game, but maybe also a part that is scared?" He responded, "My brain likes the game, but my body doesn't so much." I said, "Well I wonder if any part of you doesn't like it then maybe you'd be happier not playing it." He repeated how the game works and what he does when he plays. When he was finished, I let him know that it sounds to me like a game for older kids. He said again that he's good at it and we kind of went through the whole cycle again. I was wondering what else I could say to help the conversation progress? Or should I just keep repeating?

> **DIRECTOR PEREZ:** Be clear and definitive that this is a game for older kids and that it's not good for him to play it. Tell him you know it doesn't feel good to feel scared, and there are games for kids his age that are fun for both his brain and his body that he can be good at too. The part of him that feels scared makes it hard to have fun, and there is a part of him that doesn't want to be scared and just wants to have fun.

Like scary video games, scary books have no place in a Smart Love preschool, and you might consider what materials are available in your classroom. Many children come to school having been read stories that have frightened them and given them nightmares. All books should be screened for frightening or upsetting content, and children should not be allowed to bring scary books from home for you to read. While children may resist the notion that they can be frightened by a storybook because they think it is shameful to be scared, sad events do affect them and make them gratuitously unhappy. For example, even though *Bambi* or *The Lion King* eventually has a happy ending, children are still worried, frightened, and have nightmares from the part of the story in which Bambi's mother and Simba's father are killed. When children persist in arguing for a book or video, it is a good moment to convey that you are rejecting it because you believe it is best, but that you do not expect or insist that they will agree with you.

> **TEACHER:** Greyson brought *The Lion King* book to school. I said, "You can read that at home, but it's on the list of books that are too scary for the children at the preschool." Greyson retorted, "It's not scary. You are stupid!" I said, "I think you are calling me stupid because I said something you don't agree with. Teachers and students can disagree, and friends can disagree, and that doesn't mean they are stupid – it just means we don't agree." Greyson insisted, "Well I think it's stupid we can't read the book." I said, "I know you feel that way, and that's OK, but the teachers have to make decisions about what's best for the students and you don't have to agree."

Another social-emotional lesson in the above example is that children may become angry when teachers don't do as they wish, but when teachers Stay Positive, the relationship with them is unharmed and preserved.

Another fear preschool children have involves dying. They don't understand the concept of death, but they perceive that adults become very sad when anyone dies, and they adopt this concern and apply it to themselves. Moreover, when family members or others close to children die, adults often say, "They were sick" or "They had an accident" or "They got old." Children can conclude that because they also get sick, have accidents, and are getting older, they are about to die as well. For this reason, it is a good idea to try to differentiate the cause of death from anything children can apply to themselves. For example, "Grandpa was very very old, and his heart was very tired and stopped working. Your heart is young and just fine."

The following exchange between a teacher and Dr. Pieper shows the importance of being available to hear all worries, including about dying. It can be painful to see children cry and be upset, and we may want to make them immediately happy again, but that focus sends the message that feeling sad is unwanted, or that they should hide those feelings. The social-emotional lesson is always that they can fully possess all their feelings, even when they are painful.

> **TEACHER:** Yesterday on our walk we came across a tiny mouse who had died. Luna immediately burst into tears and wanted to help it. She was concerned for its well-being, mother, and friends. It became clear that at some point in the past she must have heard someone talking about "passing away when you get older," because she immediately brought this up about the mouse. I told her she was young, and she didn't have to worry. Understandably, she seems to be quite emotional about this. To be honest, I'm not exactly sure how to help her navigate these big issues and feelings.

> **DR. PIEPER:** Explain the difference in life expectancy between mice and people: Old for a mouse is young for Luna, so she doesn't

need to worry about growing up. But don't try to take away her sadness so she knows it's OK to feel that way. In fact, you could say you were sad, too, seeing the mouse that died.

In the midst of a busy event like walking with the class, it can be hard to give a sad child your full attention when you have other children to take care of. You can always revisit the topic at your first opportunity, or take a moment with the child if you can. The payoff is that they, and the other children, will feel the continued invitation to share deep fears that are triggered by even small upsetting events.

Missing Loved Ones Can Be an Opportunity to Connect With You

Another emotional sharing you want to encourage with your preschoolers is when they feel upset at school because they are missing family members, especially if there are problems at home. Social-emotional learning occurs when you help acknowledge those feelings and find a way to communicate with their family. Unfortunately, children who are missing their parents at school are often made to wait until the end of school to get in touch with them. Expecting children to be patient or "get over" missing family members can be traumatic. Children need help and support from teachers right away, and sometimes if that comfort is not available they can regress and, as a result, feel even more ashamed and miserable.

TEACHER: While waiting for his mom during dismissal, Ted said, "I didn't like the school I went to before." I asked, "Why didn't you like the school?" He recalled, "I would cry all the time for Mom, and I would feel so sad. One day I was so upset I had a poop accident." I responded, "I'm so sorry that happened to you. Any time you feel upset, a teacher should help you with those feelings like we do here, not make you feel worse. And when you ask for your mom, teachers should make sure they have her connect with you, like we do here."

As a teacher using S.M.A.R.T. principles, you can help a child write letters, email, text, or call parents or family members when the child is missing them and wants to communicate.

Teacher: Angie went three times to the hall to hug her stuffed bear. I asked why she needed to hold her bear, and she replied that it felt hard in the classroom. She said she was missing her mommy. I told her that I knew it could be upsetting to want to see her mommy when she's at school. I added that her mommy is always thinking of her, too. After this, she said that she was also missing her grandpa. I asked, "Where is Grandpa right now?" She let me know he was in Oregon, and she misses him and likes when he visits. I asked if she would like to make something for him, and maybe Mommy and Daddy can mail it to him. She was super excited by this, and we went into the classroom where she made a valentine for her grandpa.

Crucially, because this teacher didn't try to divert Angie's sadness about missing her mother, Angie was able to get to the real loss that was bothering her, namely, missing her grandpa. Again, slowing down and asking questions of the student that go beyond the behavior being presented is a key to introducing these practices into your teaching. When children who are missing parents want to go home early, if you are receptive and don't dismiss those feelings, you can be creative in helping children choose to stay. In other words, always offer your relationship with the child as a way to help with unhappiness. Relying on relationships to feel better, along with getting to the real feelings, are the key ingredients of genuine social-emotional learning.

Guilt or Fear of Punishment Need Not Apply!

Because practicing S.M.A.R.T. principles allows you to manage students' behaviors without shame or recrimination, children become more willing to share their "misdeeds" and mistakes. Slowly but surely the tendency of preschoolers to hide their dubious actions begins to wane. What seem like horrendous transgressions to preschoolers (taking a cookie to eat before dinner!) are really quite normal, but when adults punish any broken rule, no matter how small, children respond by becoming furtive. Loving Regulation, in which you use kindness to connect with the feelings behind a rule-breaking action, teaches children the social-emotional lesson that no matter what they have done, they will always feel better if they don't conceal it but share it with a caring adult. In this example, a child had violated an actual law:

TEACHER: Five-year old Karl was sitting in his cubby. I asked if everything was OK. He shared that he had taken something from a store, and he knew it was wrong. He was scared the police would take him to jail. His mom did not know about this incident, but he wanted her to. He appeared extremely anxious. I said, "It seems like you have been holding that inside and feeling badly about it." Karl said, "I can't stop thinking about it." I said, "I'm glad you told me so I can help you. The police won't take you, but we need to tell your mom so she can fix it with you." When his mom came, I told her what happened, and that she should be proud of Karl for sharing. I suggested they go back to the store. If he was too frightened to go in, his mom would return it for him. Karl looked so relieved. To his mother, I quietly suggested she arrange with the store in advance to be positive about his returning it. I also suggested that she might think about ways in which Karl might be feeling emotionally deprived and as a result seeking material objects as a way to feel better. I suggested that initiating or increasing "special time" with parents is always a good way to help children feel more fulfilled.

Some teachers might have been tempted to remonstrate with Karl about the theft itself. But if you keep in mind the primary goal of maintaining the relationship, you'll see that there's a reason the child is able to talk to you, sometimes even before talking to the parents. This doesn't put you in competition with parents, but allows the child an extra place to feel seen and safe. The consequence of becoming judgmental in that moment of confession would be that the child might have nowhere to turn if there were a next time. Involving the parents is tremendously important because you can model kindness and suggest ways to help the child with the feelings of deprivation that drove the theft.

Other Sorts of Upsets Offer Lessons for Self-Acceptance and Growth

In addition to the specific situations described above, there is a wide array of other reasons children get upset at preschool, a few of which we will discuss here. The fundamental approach remains the same: When you Acknowledge and Accept children's feelings, Stay Positive, reframe their problems, help identify the source, show concern, and offer attractive solutions – and even humor – you are modeling the most effective social-emotional lessons about unhappiness. We know it's not easy to be faced with multiple classroom conflicts and tears, but by using S.M.A.R.T. responses you can stay connected to the students rather than trying to "manage" them into line.

For example, because preschool children dislike being copied by other students, they can quickly become upset and feel intruded on, and suddenly peaceful playtime becomes a storm. Rather than discipline the child who is copying and upsetting another, you can make clear that copying is a sign of affection, offer to let children copy you, and make a game of it.

TEACHER: Sandy yelled at Jade, who was following her and doing what she did. "Stop copying me! I don't like that." Jade kept copying her. Sandy looked like she was going to cry. "Stop it! I mean it!" I intervened and said, "She is being like you because she likes you and wants to be like you! Would you like to copy me? There's nothing wrong with copying. It shows you like the person." Sandy and Jade agreed to follow and copy me. I began to do funny movements and the two girls copied and giggled.

Hurt feelings from another child's actions also lead to emotional upset in the classroom, and you can acknowledge the upset feelings while also offering the relationship with you for comfort.

TEACHER: Two-and-a-half-year-olds Jasmine and Lionel were building butterflies. Lionel started walking through the room flying his butterfly into other kids' faces. When he flew it into Jasmine's face, she batted it away. Lionel responded by pulling her hair. This was understandably upsetting to Jasmine, who immediately yelled, "I want my mommy!" I said, "Yes, you want your mommy, and we can tell her about this at the end of the day when she picks you up. Mommy isn't here at school now, but I can help you while you are here. Do you want to sit on my lap?" Jasmine climbed into my lap and continued to cry. Jasmine asked, "Is my hair all gone?" I reassured her, "No, it got pulled, but you still have it all." Jasmine kept crying while leaning on me. I said, "No one should ever hurt your body at school." Jasmine sniffled and calmed down and went back to playing.

The teacher listened to Jasmine's sadness and worries before she reassured her that she was OK, which communicated that her sorrow was important and deserved attention. Another teacher went to Lionel and said that she knew he had gotten upset when Jasmine batted his butterfly away, but that he needed to find a different way to express being upset other than pulling hair. She said he could have told Jasmine that he didn't like what she did, or he could have found a teacher to talk to.

Children will often be preoccupied and upset about concerns and disappointments at home. You can ask if they would like you to talk to their parents about these feelings, but if a child says "No," you should respect that, and simply be positive that they are sharing their feelings.

TEACHER: After winter holiday, Adam looked sad. I asked him what was wrong. He said he had gotten a present, but it was too complicated to put together. I asked, "Can your mom or dad help you?" Adam said, "No, my mom says she's not good at that, and my dad didn't have time to play with any of our toys." I said, "I can see you are upset. That is really too bad, but it's good you can tell me. Would you like to email your dad and tell him how you are feeling?" Adam continued playing with a fake shooter. "No, that's OK. Boooom." He was making increasingly loud noises. I said, "I see you feel angry about this, and it's understandable. I hear your loud noises and maybe you have talked about it as much as you want for now, but we can talk more about it any time."

When children enter school unhappy about something that happened earlier at home, if they feel comfortable confiding in you, they are much more able to move on and enjoy their day. Even though the beginning of the school day can be hectic, it's a good idea to observe each of your students to see if something is bothering them. Remember that signs of unexpressed feelings often look different from a child's usual appearance on arrival. If you realize a "surface" action seems to be "speaking" in this sense, this gives you the chance to begin a conversation. This is because upset feelings are often expressed nonverbally.

Another type of upset can manifest as elective mutism. Children who are habitually silent will usually begin speaking if they aren't pressured, and often when you Model Kindness, the other children pick up on your response and are helpful. Not all children develop in lockstep with peers, and speech can be an area fraught with social pressure. In many schools, a "deficit" involving speech gets communicated to parents and the child is referred out to a speech therapist. If you can help the child feel competent in other non-verbal ways, and demonstrate this with the other children, the quiet child will make gains on their own timetable. The following two examples involve Chloe, who initially didn't speak at all.

TEACHER: During extended day, some girls wanted to create a play. Annie and Chloe were going to do one together. Annie told

Chloe she should sit in the middle and be the main princess and sing. Chloe sat in the middle and stared into the "audience" (Esther and me). Annie explained that a play means there is talking, and that Chloe should talk. Chloe still sat silently. Before I was about to get up and help, Esther went to Chloe and said, "If you don't feel comfortable being up here you don't have to. Listen to your body, right?" Chloe nodded and sat down to the side. Esther went back to her seat, and Annie and Chloe's play continued with them pretending to be sisters who went on adventures in the forest, but only Annie spoke.

In the next example, Chloe ventures a word and the teacher responds to what she says, without too much focus on Chloe.

TEACHER: Annie, Chloe and I worked on an I-Spy board. While spying for farm animals, Annie spied a bunny and told me her favorite animal was a bunny. I wondered what Chloe's favorite animal was. She stared at me, and I let her know that she didn't have to say anything, but that Annie and I would love to hear what her favorite animal was, and she could let us know when she was ready. Annie began listing other animals that were her favorites. "Wow!" I said, "You can have lots of favorite animals just like you can have lots of favorite friends." Chloe said, "Bunny." Annie said, "It's a match! I know three people who love bunnies! My cousin, me and Chloe!"

Chloe continued to venture a few words until she began to talk quite normally. Many children come to school with inhibitions like Chloe's. An understanding, non-pressured approach allows them the space to want to participate and be like the other children.

Differing opinions in the classroom can lead to angry arguments, so handling verbal conflicts offers good practice in S.M.A.R.T. principles. Slowing down, Modeling Kindness, and Acknowledging and Accepting the feelings behind the behaviors, will result in helping children begin to develop an understanding of other perspectives.

> **TEACHER:** Larry and Nolan were pretending they were on a firefighter boat. Larry had asked Jason if he wanted to sleep or drive, while someone else napped. Nolan answered, "I'll drive the boat – wait what do you want?" Larry said, "It's OK, I'll take a nap first." Nolan replied, "OK, thanks!"

Nolan has absorbed from the teachers the important lesson that others may have different wishes, and that friendship means recognizing them and taking them into account.

Introducing the All-Powerful Self

You may not have heard of the all-powerful self, but if you know any preschoolers, you have no doubt encountered it. The all-powerful self is a normal developmental phase that occurs sometime after two years of age.[8] It embodies children's unrealistic beliefs that they have enhanced powers, both physical and cognitive. All children go through a period in which their inner well-being depends on getting what they want when they want it. Their all-powerful self also convinces them that they can fulfill any and every wish. It tells them they are strong enough and wise enough to do what adults can (including cook on the real stove and drive the family car), and that no one has the power to interfere. This unreasonable certainty is adaptive. If you think how many attempts young children must make to learn life's most basic skills – to tie their shoes, learn letters and numbers, hold and carry objects, ride a bike – you can see that the belief in their invincibility likely keeps them from giving up.

In other contexts, manifestations of the all-powerful self are misunderstood and responded to negatively as signifying grandiosity and needing reality corrections, such as, "You don't know what you're saying" or "You aren't as strong as you think you are." This disapproval is unfortunate because it engenders unnecessary and off-balance power struggles. Of course preschoolers often don't know what they're talking about, and of course they can't lift the heavy grocery bag. But the all-powerful self is simply a consequence of immature cognition, and it will be outgrown naturally as the child's cognition matures. Children eventually realize they are not really faster, taller, stronger and smarter than everyone they know. For example, an adolescent who as a child claimed to run "faster than a cheetah," may tell her parents how much she admires a classmate who is a champion runner.

When you understand that this is a normal, adaptive, and time-limited phase, you can relax and not feel you have to correct irrational beliefs. In fact, it is a mistake to puncture children's fantasy of omnipotence. There is no reason to clash head-on with a trait that will be outgrown on its own, especially when children have no ability at the moment to know that the powers they believe they possess are not real.

Even though you need to let this phase extinguish itself naturally rather than interfere, you can diplomatically help children find better ways to feel good about themselves.

> **TEACHER:** Manny is a three-year-old who regularly challenges his classmates to races, saying, "I'm the fastest! I'm taller than you. I'm the tallest!" or other such statements. As Manny is one of the younger children in the class, this usually results in the other children winning the race or demonstrating that they are in fact taller, which will either upset or stimulate him to continue to insist that he won or is bigger. This irritates the other children, who get upset with Manny if they are not already upset with him after his initial challenge. When Manny begins running races with other children, I let him know that it might not feel good if he doesn't win, and to think of other kinds of play that is fun for everyone. I gently suggest, "There are different ways to feel good. You can feel good by being the tallest, fastest, etc., or you can feel good by trying your best."

As a teacher, you value facts, and it may feel contradictory to refrain from correcting the inaccurate claims of the all-powerful self. Our teachers are often uncertain about what to do and ask for help.

> **TEACHER:** Neddy's need to be at the top is pretty important to him. I have noticed this many times before, but since he turned

six, I have noticed this even more. At lunch, the teachers were talking about how they liked sushi and where it came from. Linda chimed in that she liked sushi as well. Bob said that his dad went to "Japanese" (aka Japan) before he was born. Upon hearing this, Neddy interjected that he went to Japan and saw a ninja! Linda asked, "You saw a ninja?" She could hardly believe it. No one was sad or upset, so we just didn't say any more about it. I feel like Neddy does this all the time. Is this just his way of connecting? Why does he feel he always has to one-up everyone on their experiences/stories?

DR. PIEPER: This is Neddy's all-powerful self. The notion that no one can have been anywhere he hasn't been is at play here. Just leave it alone. Reality is going to interfere with it soon enough. These overblown claims about himself are different from normal misconceptions about facts, which can be gently corrected.

This example illustrates that the all-powerful self's extravagant claims about worldliness are very different from normal misconceptions about facts, which you do usually want to correct gently, as discussed in the next section.

Helping Children Learn Despite Their All-Powerful Self

When a student asserts incorrect facts with absolute certainty, keep in mind that the goal of preschool is to preserve curiosity and the desire to learn, so you can point out the correct answer to other children while at the same time avoiding dashing the student's commitment to the wrong answer.

TEACHER: The other day, Jasper pointed to a compass on the globe ball and said, incorrectly, "That's Chicago." Raven, a new student, said, "No, it's not. That doesn't say Chicago." Clearly, she knew how to spell Chicago and was right. I wanted to help Jasper save face, but also to recognize that Raven was correct. "Yes, Raven, Chicago is actually right here," and I pointed to it. Jasper insisted, "No, this is Chicago." Again, Raven said it wasn't. So I said, "Well, Raven, it's OK for Jasper to say that's

Chicago if that's what he is thinking." Jasper said, "I'm not saying it, it's true!" I said, "I really hear how much you want to be right and it's important to you. On the other hand, I know you also want to learn. Let's go to the map over here where we can find Chicago." After we looked at Chicago on the other map, I asked Jasper if he wanted to go back and look for Chicago on the globe and he said, "No." I said, "That's fine. Maybe another time."

The teacher did a nice job of supporting the child who had the correct answer without clashing head-on with the child whose all-powerful self made him cling to the belief that he was correct.

In the next example, a new teacher made the mistake of directly contradicting a child's assertion of an incorrect fact, and the child's all-powerful self reacted strongly, rejected the conflicting knowledge, and lost interest when the teacher continued the discussion.

TEACHER: Len and April told me they were cold while we were outside. I asked who they thought was colder, them or penguins. Len replied, "Us because penguins have fur." I said, "Actually, penguins have feathers, because they're birds." Len argued, "No, they're not birds because they can't fly." I told him that not all birds can fly, and penguins are one type of bird that doesn't fly. Len insisted, "That's not true and I know more than you." I said, "Oh, OK, I wonder what makes you say that." He told me because he's five and he knows a lot because he's been around for five years. I told him if he wanted to, we could look it up and double check, but he was not interested in looking anything up.

DIRECTOR PEREZ: From the outset of the conversation, you could offer to go look things up. This allows a way under Len's all-powerful "radar" to share the information. Keep offering to look different things up, or find out more from some source outside of the conversation, such as "Let's look up how animals that live in cold stay warm" or "Let's look up if penguins have fur since they look so smooth" or "Let's look up if penguins are birds." After you confronted Len directly, it makes sense he can't change gears to go along with looking it up. In this situation, timing matters.

Teachers with more experience would not have directly contradicted a factual error but would have said what an interesting idea the child had and would he like to look it up and learn more about it.

The All-Powerful Self Can Cause Children to Distort Reality

Losing at games can be hard when children's all-powerful selves have an age-appropriate belief that they can control every outcome. Using the S.M.A.R.T. acceptance of all feelings, you can gently recognize that losing is hard.

TEACHER: Silas and two other children were racing trucks. One of the boys declared, "I won!" when his fire engine reached the finish line first. Silas appeared upset and insisted, "No, I won." The other boy stated, "No you didn't, I won!" And a back and forth ensued. Silas moved his dump truck close to the finish line, put it over, and declared, "I won!" Jeff said, "You won 'cause you started at the end." I said, "Maybe Silas won the dump truck race, and you won the fire engine race." Both boys seemed to agree. I said to Silas, "I can see how much you wanted to win, it was really hard when your dump truck didn't get there before the fire engine."

Without an understanding of the all-powerful self, some schools classify children who have tearful and upset reactions to losing as needing to learn to be a "better sport." You can see there's a more creative way to work with this all-powerful phase.

Children in your class may even take blame for something they didn't do out of a general conviction of controlling everything. Without an understanding of the all-powerful self, it would be easy to see their behavior as extreme and worrisome.

TEACHER: I leaned against a shelf and a block fell and hit me in the head. I said, "Ow," and got a cold pack. Pierce said, "I'm sorry. It's my fault." I said, "Oh Pierce, it wasn't your fault. Blocks just fall sometimes. I can see that you're blaming yourself, but I leaned against the shelf and it fell." A little later he climbed into the mirror cube by himself and curled up in a ball and stayed there. I said, "I can see you are still feeling badly. Are you still feeling it's your fault? Did you see me lean against the shelf? That's what made the block fall." Pierce asked, "Are you sure it wasn't my fault?" "I'm very sure!" Pierce climbed out and joined the class.

A child's all-powerful self can also react dramatically when material objects don't obey. When you understand what is happening, you can acknowledge the hurt feelings rather than assume the child is being overly reactive to everyday mishaps.

TEACHER: Jameson screamed and got up to leave when his tea set capsized. I said, "Jameson, I can see that you're upset that your tea set fell over, but look, we can pick it up and put it back right where it was." Jameson was on the verge of crying, so I asked, "Would you still like to play with your tea set?" He said, "Yes" and started playing again but immediately said, "This is a stupid toy!" I said, "I wonder how you're feeling?" He said, "I'm angry!" I said, "Sometimes we feel angry when something doesn't go our way. But when we can fix it we might feel better." After a few minutes I said, "I wonder how you're feeling now, Jameson?" And he said, "I feel OK."

Children can likewise grow upset when the thing that doesn't "behave" is somewhat removed from them. Without an understanding of the all-powerful self, their behavior can seem quite out of proportion. In the next example, the teacher creatively restored a child's sense of control and, therefore, his equilibrium.

TEACHER: Antonio and Justin noticed that the clock wasn't working. Antonio went to see it more closely. He noticed that the second hand was stuck between the numbers nine and ten. He said, "I want the ten to be where the six is." Before I had a chance to say anything, he started to breathe more heavily, and his anxiety almost brought him to tears. He asked, "Can we open the clock to move the numbers?" I told him that I knew it was upsetting for him to see the broken clock, but that we couldn't remove the clock from the wall, and someone would be in to fix it soon. I asked him if he wanted to make his own clock so that he could put numbers wherever he wanted. His face lit up and we got drawing supplies and cut round paper for clock faces. He was content to draw clocks, seemingly forgetting about the broken one on the wall.

When you are aware that children's all-powerful selves feel hurt whenever things don't go as they wish, you can find fun ways to soothe the disappointment without confrontation.

SUMMARY

You Are the Gateway to Social-Emotional Learning

As the examples in this chapter illustrate, you have everything you need to develop enduring positive relationships with your students. You can simply model the helpfulness, cooperation, and interest in children's communications and feelings that you want children to adopt. The social-emotional learning that arises when children imitate your S.M.A.R.T. responses is freely chosen and durable.

CHAPTER 2

S.M.A.R.T. Management for a
Healthy Happy Classroom

As you learned in the previous chapter, developing S.M.A.R.T. practices encourages children to come to you with their feelings. You also engage disruptive behavior with thoughtful and caring responses, and help children understand and accept all of their strong feelings. When you think about managing your whole classroom, the Smart Love focus is on creating an enjoyable learning environment where children can make decisions, be spontaneous and creative, interact enjoyably with peers, express themselves, enhance their curiosity, and learn through play. This classroom culture allows children to thrive and reach academic benchmarks while having fun and preserving their enthusiasm for learning.

So how does a classroom managed and running on Smart Love principles differ from other preschools? First and foremost, you see teachers actively playing with students and working on projects, not just reading or lecturing or observing. You hear loud enthusiastic voices with no one saying, "Use inside voices." You see children engaged in projects they chose that are not imposed. You see children making choices about whom they want to play with, or not play with, without requirements about including others. If a child is unruly, you see a teacher go with them out of the room and stay with them until they are ready to come back in. No time-outs or isolation. You see teachers focusing on the feelings that lead to anti-social behaviors rather than lecturing about the behaviors themselves. You see children who aren't ready to use the toilet wearing diapers or pull ups and teachers changing them when necessary. You see normal resistance about things like washing hands met with creative fun solutions rather than threats or disapproval. You see no rewards or incentives such as crowns, extra privileges, or gold stars. You see transitions to outside and back inside with teachers and children singing and playing games like I-Spy. No quiet lines. You see children learning writing, arithmetic, reading and other academic subjects because they are relevant to activities they have chosen. In the beginning of the year you see parents of children who aren't ready to have them leave remaining on-site. You don't see worksheets, formal group time, or teachers testing students on what they know. You don't see teachers insisting on manners or telling children to cooperate and play with others. Overall, you see a place of care, excitement and unforced cooperation and kindness. Let's look in detail at how this is achieved.

Advantages of Loving Regulation

Loving Regulation (the "R" in S.M.A.R.T.) is a key concept that distinguishes the S.M.A.R.T. approach. In a difficult moment, or when a meltdown occurs, Loving Regulation allows you to lower the pressure and be understanding. Sanctions such as time-outs, restrictions of privileges (no recess), making children listen to lectures, and other disapproving requests (forcing children to apologize, and so on) only convey the message that *might makes right*. These responses are not a good model for future relationships. When you are pressed for time, sanctions may seem the quickest solution to classroom disorder, but even in the short run they are less effective than Loving Regulation because children imitate them, feel alienated from you, and apply them to others in the classroom with whom they disagree.

Loving Regulation Teaches Children to Turn to You

Traditional behavior management alienates children from teachers because the teacher stands apart from the child and dispenses disapproval or sanctions. It can be hard to find the motive to Model Kindness when children are hurting other students. But when you show children your genuine interest in hearing about the causes of their behavior, children have the space to reflect and learn.

> **TEACHER:** Gianna, Ayla, Harper, Rose and Esther were playing mermaids running around the playground. Gianna shouted, "Ouch, Rose, you can't pinch me!" Rose looked surprised and began to cry. I asked Gianna if she was OK, and she said yes. I brought Rose to the bench and offered her a tissue. "Rose, I wonder what happened with Gianna? You know at school we can't pinch anyone and no one can pinch you." Rose said, "I was trying to tell my body to stop pinching Gianna, but I couldn't stop. I was just doing it." "Oh Rose, thanks for telling me. That sounds so hard. When you get that feeling like you want to pinch someone, come to a teacher and we can help with those feelings."

In this instance, if Rose were given a time-out or sent to the principal she would feel shame or defiance, and she wouldn't have the relationship with the teacher available to help her recognize her conflicting feelings about pinching, and she wouldn't have a positive action plan for how to handle her feelings next time.

> **TEACHER:** Cooper yelled that a tow truck was missing from the classroom. I told him that I would look after school. I asked if he wanted to play with the firetrucks instead. He insisted that he wanted to play with the tow truck right now. I let him know that I had to stay in the classroom to help another teacher, and asked if there was any other toy he wanted to play with in the meantime. He shouted, "No!" and started throwing all of the toys around him and grabbed toys from the cabinets and threw them on the floor. I told him that I thought we should go for a walk, and we went in the hall. I said, "It seems like you are very frustrated, and it can be really hard when we don't get what we want to play with, but I can't let you throw toys around in the classroom because it might hurt you or the other kids." He fell into my lap and started to cry a bit. I hugged him and told him that I was here whenever he feels frustrated or when things feel hard. Later he told me he was frustrated. He said that some kids were yelling at him, and Tom was making him mad. I said, "It's great you can tell me when you feel upset. When it's not fun to play with your friends, you can play with me or by yourself for a little while."

Behavior change is a choice, and over time you will help children progress socially and emotionally because Loving Regulation – in combination with the other S.M.A.R.T. principles – shows them that a meaningful, caring relationship always feels better than their first negative response.

Loving Regulation Shows You Can Disagree and Still Be Friends

You will often confront the situation in which children become aggressive when other children don't play the way they want. They may even turn on you when you step in to defuse the situation. If you can look past your own reaction to their anger, Stay Positive and focus on helping them, usually their anger will abate, they will reconnect with their affection for you, and they will reunite with their friends.

TEACHER: Meg was upset when other kids didn't play the way she liked. I brought her to the office while she was trying to hit and kick me. I kept her at some physical distance, and she screamed she wanted to go home. I said, "Let's send an email to Mom and Dad." She leaned hard on me and continued to say she wanted to go home. I said, "I can see how upset you are." She ran into the hallway and tried to go out the inner door. I explained, "In order to get Mom or Dad to come to school, we have to let them know, and standing out in the hallway and trying to push the door open won't help." Her demeanor quickly shifted, and she asked, "Did you see my new bracelet?" She took it off and snapped it on her wrist. I said, "Wow, it was straight and now it's around your wrist." She suggested, "Let's write the email." I asked, "OK, to whom?" She said, "My mom, but wait, she might be working at home and I can't disturb her." I said, "What does that mean?" She said, "It's like, you know, you can't interrupt her." I said, "Do you think she would want to know when you're upset?" She agreed. "Yes, let's send it." I said, "Maybe it's hard to know that Mom is working at home while you're at school, but you know that we're here to help you feel better. What would you like it to say?" Meg said, "Say Lois and Nan wanted to play my game a different way. Then Lois said she was never going to play with me again. I want to go home." She looked at me and said, "I'm never going to play with them again either." I said, "That was hard when they didn't want to play the way you wanted. Well, Meg, if they don't want to play your game your way, you don't have to play the game with them. We can find someone else, or a teacher will." I asked, "Can I tell you something?" She said, "Yes." I said, "It seems like it's been harder this week when you're playing, and when something happens you want to go home. If you go home, it won't help the next time something happens, and I know so many children will miss playing with you." She suggested, "Maybe we can have a girl chat like we did the last time when we came in the office and worked it out." I said, "It looks like they are outside now. Would you like to do it there?" She said, "Yes." We went outside and I asked the girls if we could talk with them. I said, "Meg, did you want to say anything?" Meg replied, "It hurt my feelings when you said you would never play with me again." Nan said, "I didn't say that, Lois did." Lois said, "I wanted to play your game but not that way and then you yelled and that's why I said that." I said, "It's OK to be upset with someone and tell them you're upset and why, but we can't yell at them or say things that hurt their feelings." Meg said, "I know I say I'm never going to play again, but then we feel better and we do." They began chatting, and I said I was going back inside and reminded them that should anything arise, they could come to my office if they wanted to.

As the above example shows, Loving Regulation can take time and effort, but the payoff is that children learn they can be angry with friends and teachers and still reconnect and remain close.

Loving Regulation Shows Behavior Management Doesn't Equal Punishment

Because many children are used to being punished or isolated when they do something against the rules, they can interpret your use of Loving Regulation as disapproval. This gives you a chance to help them gain the understanding that they do not have to feel alienated from you when you have to help them control their behavior.

TEACHER: Santiago was throwing blocks, and I took him to a corner and asked him to sit next to me. He looked very sad. I said, "Sitting next to me is not a punishment. I really like to sit next to you, and I'm trying to help. This isn't saying anything bad about you." (At home his parents tell him that there are elves who watch him and count when he is "bad.") "Your mom told me about the elves. That is not happening at school. There are no elves here counting up your behaviors. School and home are different. Maybe you are feeling I'm mad at you, but I want to sit next to you and help you." Santiago looked relieved and went back to playing after a bit.

The problem with traditional discipline is that it actually *does* convey disapproval, so children have trouble learning that the relationship with their teacher is not disrupted when their behavior has to be corrected.

Loving Regulation Helps Understand What Leads to Behavior

Most children who melt down cannot articulate the trigger, but, as in the next example, when you are understanding rather than disapproving, and suggest a cause, children are often able to connect the dots. It is usually helpful to think about what changed for the child immediately before the meltdown. In the next example, it was the fact that other children were diluting Eliana's alone time with the teacher.

> **TEACHER:** Eliana was excited about re-enacting the story "The Mitten." Other children walked up and joined. Eliana wanted me to hide the mole and then they would search for it. We did this a few times, then Eliana stomped off and said, "I don't want to be with any teachers or kids, and I don't like school!" I said, "Eliana, can you tell me why you're so upset?" She just repeated she didn't want to be by a teacher. I had a feeling it was because she wanted our game to be exclusive, so I mentioned that to her. She wouldn't say at first, but there were about four other children around. Once they dispersed, I gave her some space and said, "I'd like to help you, but I'm not sure why you're upset. Is it because you wanted to play this special game with me, and then other children joined in?" She said, "Uh-huh." I said, "That's fantastic that you could understand why you were feeling upset!" She accepted that explanation and calmed down and did some ballet.

Eliana's feelings of wanting the teacher to herself were Acknowledged and Accepted at face value without shaming her or lecturing on social responsibility toward others.

Each of the S.M.A.R.T. strategies plays a part in helping children come to you with their feelings, but Loving Regulation can be considered the most overarching of them when it comes to managing classroom behavior.

A Classroom Without Rewards

S.M.A.R.T. principles are incompatible with rewards. You may have been taught that rewards such as gold stars, privileges, and praise for achievements are good ways to motivate children and, on the surface, this seems logical. However, there is much research demonstrating that rewards backfire and are counter-indicated as motivators. [9]

There are also many intrinsic reasons not to use rewards with your students. Effort, not success, is the real goal of learning as an ongoing process, and you want to send the message that effort is rewarding in itself. In a classroom where there is a constant economy of incentives, rewards become the focus of children's efforts rather than the pleasure of learning or getting along with classmates.

Rewards as a way of stopping unwanted behavior ("Sit down and be quiet and then you can ...") are about compliance, and it is better to show your students that a positive, understanding relationship remains available to help them no matter what they are doing. Minimizing rules, as we will discuss, provides an atmosphere where compliance itself becomes less necessary.

The problem with all rewards, whether they are used as incentives or re-enforcement, is that they devalue the activity they are supposedly incentivizing, whether that be sharing, listening to the teacher, learning math or reading, cleaning up, or using the bathroom. In other words, rewards convey that an activity is not sufficiently important to be engaged in for itself.

Rewards also create hierarchies in the classroom, and often upset and discourage children who aren't getting them. This can have far-reaching consequences as this can make some children feel they aren't "as good" as others. Also, some children learn to act badly to get rewarded for behaving better later. In some cases, rewards are not given to individuals but are proposed for the entire class if they follow the rules (i.e., no pushing or yelling), but this only creates peer conflict and negativity when some children won't or can't go along and thus prevent the rest of the class from getting the reward.

It can be hard to believe that a classroom can be run without rewards. However, when you structure materials so that children's learning follows their interests, their motivation becomes intrinsic rather than extrinsic. Also, when behaviors that need correction are met with S.M.A.R.T. strategies, these are often felt as rewarding in themselves. For example, Time With can turn into a wonderful opportunity for connection, even if it starts as a way to moderate a challenging moment.

There Are Only Three Classroom Rules

One of the factors that contributes to teacher burnout is having to spend a lot of class time enforcing rules. Teachers are instructed to make children sit down and do worksheets, walk quietly, use inside voices, socialize, use materials a certain way, and take turns using the bathroom. In contrast, in a Smart Love preschool, there are only three rules! Infractions of these are always responded to with Loving Regulation or another of the S.M.A.R.T. skills. Of course, any behavior that is a health and safety risk is stopped immediately and is viewed as an indication that a child requires extra attention and care. When you see a child break a school rule, it is crucial to respond calmly, and focus on the motivation rather than the transgression, so that children will not feel they have to hide their antisocial desires. For example, if a child grabs another's toy, you can say, "We need to give it back, but I can see how much fun you thought it would be to play with it. Come with me. I'm sure we can find another fun toy." When rules are minimized, your interactions with your students will be immensely more rewarding.

 ## RULE #1:
Children Cannot Hurt Themselves or Others

When children push or shove others, you can use Loving Regulation and step in immediately – but without recrimination – to defuse the situation. Children may resist this rule in the moment, but it makes sense to them. When you tell children they are not allowed to be physically or emotionally aggressive toward others, deep down they understand because they know that they would not like to be on the receiving end of physical or emotional aggression.

TEACHER: Four children were doing superhero moves, but weren't hurting anyone, so I didn't say anything. The intensity level began to rise, so I asked the kids some questions about who they were playing and who they were saving versus who they were fighting. I tried to enhance their play and draw out some of their ideas. Larry said, "I'm Batman and Eddie is Clark Kent." I think once Larry acknowledged Eddie, that made Eddie more enthusiastic, and he started really hitting other kids, so I intervened and said, "OK, I can tell that you're excited, but when we play superhero, you can pretend to be stronger than everyone else, but we can't actually tackle and hit." Eddie said OK, but continued to grab his friends a little too aggressively and they reacted with equal force to push him off. I stepped in to stop them. Larry said, "We're just playing superheroes." I said, "I know, Larry, but I'm afraid someone is going to get hurt, even though you are only playing. Is there a way you can play superhero without really hurting each other?" Larry said reluctantly, "I guess so." They moved into another room and dispersed.

The teacher enunciated the rule and, when that didn't work, she used her physical presence to defuse the situation, but in a way that neutrally conveyed the reason behind her intervention. Some schools don't allow superhero play because they worry about it escalating, as it did here. However, children play superheroes when they are by themselves, so it is better for them to be superheroes in school where a teacher can step in and help them understand where the boundaries are.

In a situation where one child is being physically aggressive toward another, you can use Time With to help the aggressor find more constructive things to do.

TEACHER: The kids were playing hopscotch and Abel started going too fast and bumped into Petra. I told Abel he had to slow down, but he continued. I told him to come close to me. "I know it feels fun to play hopscotch, but we have to take turns because we don't want to bump into anyone. If we keep bumping into people, we'll have to stop and take a break." I also had a book I brought, and we started looking at it. I asked Petra if she was OK. He didn't bump her hard, but I could see she was uncomfortable. She said, "Yes," and I told her that it's never OK for someone to push you or bump you, and she can tell a teacher. She nodded and went back to hopscotch. I went back to Abel. He loved the book about cars and trucks and began naming them. After we read the book together for ten minutes, he went back and played comfortably near Petra.

The usual disapproving or controlling responses to this kind of pushing behavior would cause a play-destroying intervention that can take the joy out of kids' games, and result in compliance that is in effect only when adults are around.

In the next example, the teacher follows the principle of immediately stepping in with Loving Regulation to stop one child from pushing another. Rather than disapproving, she simply Models Kindness and offers to engage with him in a cooperative activity.

> **TEACHER:** Marshall and Dion were playing at the water table. Marshall started pushing Dion to the left with his body, trying to crowd him out. I said, "I see there is some pushing here. Can I help?" Dion pointed to Marshall. I asked, "Do you like it when Marshall pushes you?" Dion shook his head and said, "No." I said to Marshall, "It's important that Dion said he doesn't like it, so you need to find another way to play with him." Marshall pushed again. I said, "I see you can't stop pushing right now, so let's go over here and build with the blocks." Marshall came with me, though reluctantly.

In this example you can see how the teacher made a decisive change for the child who seems unable to make a good choice by Staying Positive and not attributing to him any type of willfulness or bad attitude. You will see, if you begin applying these practices, that your patience increases and children's misbehaviors become much simpler and more satisfying to creatively redirect.

> **TEACHER:** Everett had just sat down on the blue rug. Evidently, Marcia had been in a nearby spot but had walked away. When Marcia walked back over, I thought she was going to sit near Everett. Instead, she hollered, "Hey, I was sitting there!" I said, "Oh, I hear you, Marcia. You were sitting there and then got up and think that no one else can sit there. But when you get up, that means someone else can sit there. I can see you're upset, but there's

lots of room right next to him." Marcia started to sit down, but then nudged him with her arm. Everett said, "She pushed me." By this time, I had gotten in between Marcia and Everett. I told him, "I know. That looked like it hurt. Are you OK?" He said, "Yeah, but she pushed me." I said, "Marcia, remember we talked earlier? We can't let you push anyone." She said, "But I was sitting there." I said, "I know, and I can tell you are upset. It looks like it might be too hard for you to sit here right now. Let's come away for a while." I took Marcia's hand, and she walked with me to the snack area and sat down in a chair at the table with other children.

Notice how the teacher took Marcia out of the situation, but stayed with her and Acknowledged and Accepted her upset feelings.

One common preschool behavior that violates the rule about not hurting others is throwing sand, water, or toys. Sometimes S.M.A.R.T. means that you need to take children who are throwing things out of the situation. But you will go with them (Time With!) and help them get in touch with what is bothering them.

TEACHER: Ernie told me Morris was throwing sand at him. I told Ernie I was sorry to hear that, and that it was good he could let me know. I told Morris I could not let him throw sand at people, and that if it was too hard to play in the sand, we could play somewhere else. After a couple of seconds Morris threw sand at Ernie again. This time, Ernie, with a very stern voice said, "Please stop that. I don't like it." Morris asked, "Why doesn't that feel good?" Ernie just looked at me. I told Morris, "At school if someone doesn't like something, we stop doing it. I am here to make sure everyone is safe and having fun. Sand can get in his eye and that doesn't feel good." Morris again asked Ernie why he didn't like the sand being thrown at him while he continued to throw sand at him, but I blocked it. I told Morris that it looked like he was upset about something and asked if he would like to share with me what was going on. He said, "I just want to know why he doesn't like sand thrown." I asked Morris to come with me because it was too hard for him to play in the sand right now, and we could try again later. He went to play by the cars, and I asked him if he was angry about anything and he said no. I didn't want to mention lunch, which is the reason I think he is angry, but in future, I will see if he will share what he is feeling.

DIRECTOR PEREZ: After the first time you sense he isn't going to stop throwing sand, and is stretching things out, you could say to Morris, "It seems too hard to play here without throwing sand. Let's go find another place." To find out why Morris is angry, you can ask: "Maybe someone did something you didn't like, or you wanted them to do something they weren't doing." Yes, Morris has to go home while Ernie gets to stay for lunch. I'm sure this could contribute to throwing sand at Ernie. Morris has asked his parents to let him stay, and they told him maybe, and they left it at that. I have talked with them, and they are still on the fence about it. To Ernie you could also say, "Good job telling Morris how you felt, Ernie. It's not OK for anyone to throw sand on you."

Again, the temptation, reinforced by what you may have been taught, is to lecture children about not hurting others, and to talk them out of the choices they are making. But using S.M.A.R.T. practices, you can turn throwing things into a constructive activity that might engage other children. In the same sentence as saying what can't happen, offer a fun alternative that makes for a transition away from the behavior that needed regulating.

TEACHER: Rob and I were playing with a clock puzzle when he started throwing the number pieces. I let Rob know that we could spin or slide the number pieces, but I couldn't let him throw them. I modeled spinning the number pieces and tried sliding them across the floor. Rob's face lit up and we started sliding the pieces back and forth to each other calling out "I'm sending you the four!" Rob slid a piece toward another teacher. I said, "It looks like you want more people to join the game. Let's show her how to play." We showed the other teacher how we were playing it, and then Bella and Andrea asked to join the game too. We created a big circle then slid the number pieces back and forth to each other calling out the number and whom we were sending it to. "This feels fun to play a game all together!"

As you can see, when children are entertaining themselves by throwing things that could hurt others, a positive solution is always preferable to sanctions.

TEACHER: I noticed Andy was starting to throw toys, so after I told him I couldn't let him throw things and wondered if he was upset about something, I asked him to help me put a puzzle together. He responded, "You need help? You are silly. This is how you do it." I said, "Thank you, Andy, for helping me with the dinosaur puzzle. The spikes are a bit tricky!" He gave me a thumbs up and walked away like a cool cat!

By asking for Andy's help, the teacher engaged the constructive and mature part of him seamlessly and without lectures, which made him forget about throwing blocks.

In the next example, Juliana is imitating the teacher by thinking of positive ways to help another child (remember that *modeling* is the "M" in S.M.A.R.T.) rather than labeling her misbehavior as "bad."

TEACHER: Addie was yelling for her mommy and throwing her backpack. Another teacher removed her from the group and went with her to the corner. Julianna asked me what was upsetting Addie. I said that it was feeling hard for Addie because she was missing her mommy. Juliana suggested that we get a picture of Addie's mommy and she could look at it when she's thinking of her. I thanked Juliana and said that when Addie was feeling better, maybe we could share that idea with her.

In the following interaction, when the teacher stepped in to defuse the situation without recrimination, the children were able to adopt a kinder approach with each other.

> **TEACHER:** Carl and Larry could stay outside as long as they played well. We were joking around in the sandbox, and Carl started throwing sand. I said, "Carl, I can't let you do that," and Larry said to Carl, "Remember, Carl, just playing or we have to go inside," and Carl stopped throwing sand immediately. I said, "Thank you, Larry, for that reminder and for being a good friend."

The temptation might be to solve the breach of the rules by responding immediately and negatively to Carl's sand throwing and sending him inside, but the teacher's neutral but effective response gave the boys the space to make a good choice that allowed them to keep having fun outside.

RULE #2:
No Grabbing

Because this is an age when children want what they want when they want it, if they see a desirable toy, they may go for it without thinking about who has it or what the consequences will be. You will find that this rule is especially challenging to regulate with the twos, who just see possession as an obstacle to be overcome. With them, Loving Regulation takes great diplomacy.

> **TEACHER:** Blakely is three and Robin is two. Blakely was playing with the kitchen and pretend food items when Robin grabbed some of them. Blakely said "Hey, I was playing with that!" I told Robin that Blakely was playing with the kitchen toys and got his attention with some trucks. Robin slowly turned his attention toward the trucks, but I think he had a hard time understanding, because he looked a bit confused. Luckily Blakely walked over and gave Robin some items so he could play as well. I was wondering if you would handle this situation differently. It seemed a little more difficult because of the difference in age. Robin was a little

confused about why he could not play with what Blakely was playing with at the time.

DIRECTOR PEREZ: This is an example of trying to upstream the problem if you can see it coming. If Robin is approaching Blakely and you think he may take something, try to get between him and Blakely. If it's after the fact as it is here, after Blakely says, "Hey, I was playing with that," you could say, "I'm sorry that he took that, Blakely," and turn to Robin and say, "I can see you want to play with what Blakely had, but if it's in her hand, that means she is playing with it and we can't take it." Before asking Robin to return the item, be sure you have something in your hand (preferably something you know he would like) ready to be offered when you ask him to return the toy. "Can you give that to me, Robin?" and open your hand and give Robin the opportunity to hand it to you. If he doesn't, you can say, "I know it's hard when you want to play with something someone else has, but we're going to give it back to Blakely, and let's see if we can find another one, or something else to play with until she is finished." Then say to Blakely, "Will you let us know when you're done with it?" And then engage Robin with another toy you know he likes. At just a little over two years old, he is learning how to engage in play. Best to go under the radar not to dampen his optimism about his choice of play and peers.

Every preschool teacher knows that children can get upset and grab when other children have something they want. You can help by acknowledging that wanting something you can't have feels hard and frustrating, and by offering to help find other things to play with. In the next example, you will see that there were no lectures, such as, "You have to learn to take turns when you want a toy, and you can't just grab!" or disapproval. You can Acknowledge and Accept all of a child's feelings even when you have to regulate their behavior. You may have to remove a child temporarily, but you will go with them, which is the S.M.A.R.T. principle of Time With.

TEACHER: I took Chloe out of the classroom because she tried to take part of the dollhouse away from Ayla. I let Chloe know I couldn't let her take the toy away and we could play another way, but she continued to hold on to the toy. I said, "I see it feels too hard when Ayla doesn't do what you want. That happens sometimes, and it can be upsetting. Why don't you come with me, and we will find something fun to do." But Chloe would not release the toy. I let Chloe know she could come with me or I was going to pick her up. She refused, and I gently took the toy and gave it back to Ayla. I picked Chloe up and went out into the hallway where she started screaming that she wanted me to go away. She tried to kick me. I said, "I see you are angry and upset and that is OK. But I can't let you kick me, and I'm going to stick with you until you feel better." I held her so she couldn't kick. It seemed Chloe was stuck, so I said I was going to take her to go see something special in the office. Once there, I set her down and I looked for a clipboard and paper. I could see her feelings change to interest. After we did some tracing in the office, Chloe had the idea to trace her stuffed animal. After we traced it, she felt ready to go back into the classroom without confronting Ayla.

Notice that when you understand children's aggressive feelings, they will often allow you to find a constructive way to help them.

TEACHER: I was helping Angela use the blood pressure cuff on the dolls. Alice sat down close to us and asked what we were doing. I told her Angela was checking the babies' blood pressure. She observed for a while, but suddenly reached over and snatched the cuff from Angela. I said, "I can't let you take the cuff Angela is using, but we can find you another one. It looks like you would like to play with a cuff, too. Let's give this one back and there is one by the doctor's coat." We went to get it and I asked if she would like to use it on the babies, or would like to do something else with it. She said, "On the babies."

The teacher didn't tell Alice she was breaking the rule not to grab, but simply offered her another way to have something she wanted, all the while using Loving Regulation to return the cuff to Angela.

Children may adopt your modeling of Loving Regulation and offer a substitute when another child grabs from them.

> **TEACHER:** Tania had a ladder piece from a fire truck in the dollhouse. Henrietta came toward her and grabbed the ladder. Tania said, "Hey, I was playing with that." Henrietta said, "I'm going to play with it." I told Henrietta that Tania was using that at the moment, and that maybe we could play with something else while we wait until she's finished with it. Henrietta said she wanted to play in the dollhouse. I suggested that maybe she could ask Tania if they could play together with the ladder in the dollhouse. Henrietta agreed. Tania disappeared for a moment and then had in her hand a new ladder. She told Henrietta she could play with the ladder she had just brought if she could get hers back. Henrietta switched ladders with her and told her, "Thank you!" and asked if she could play with her. Tania said, "Sure!"

The temptation when you see a child grab is to say, "Hey, give that back!" but these examples show that when you solve conflicts by offering fun engagement with you, children will copy you and come up with their own resolution when another child grabs from them.

 # RULE #3:
No Damaging the Classroom

Children at this age enjoy activities that can interfere with the integrity of the classroom, such as drawing on walls or putting water and sand on the floor. These behaviors make the classroom unsafe or unattractive for other children. You may have to be creative in using Loving Regulation to get children to take care of the classroom. Again, you don't want to give lectures about keeping the classroom nice for everyone, but rather you can state the rule neutrally and help a child move on.

TEACHER: Today while I was playing trains with Tom, I saw two-year-old Nash sift sand onto the floor by the shoe cubbies. I said in a friendly tone, "The sand needs to stay in the sandbox." Nash said, "It is snowing," and showed me the sand on top of the postal truck. I said, "Yes! That does look like snow, but it needs to snow inside the sandbox – let's make that happen." Quinn was already getting a dustpan and brush. Quinn and I cleaned up the mess together, and Quinn said, "Nash doesn't understand yet about the sand." I said, "I know, he's learning." Nash managed to keep it snowing on the postal truck in the sandbox.

Like the teacher, Quinn did not focus on the fact that Nash was breaking the rule, but rather that it was understandable given his immaturity. This is a nice example of how children will adopt your Stay Positive and Model Kindness approach to regulating behavior.

When children do things that mar the classroom in some way, Loving Regulation means that you stop the behavior, but do not force children to fix the problem themselves. In that way you create the space and the alliance to try to help children understand what drove them to break the school rule.

TEACHER: Rob was painting pictures. Later in the morning, he walked by the easel, took a paint brush and threw it on the floor. I said, "Rob, we can't get paint on the floor." He said, "No, it was Kevin." I said, "Kevin is over there. I was just with him. He didn't do it." Rob retorted, "It was ... (and he rattled off the names of six other children)." I said, "I know you threw it, I can see fresh paint on your hands. Let's go fix it." Rob insisted, "No!"! I gently led him over and cleaned up the paint while he watched. "I can see that when you are feeling badly inside, one way you try to feel better is to throw paint on the floor, and then we have to stop playing and clean it up. But a better way is to come and talk with us about it." He didn't say anything, but he didn't throw anything else on the floor.

By neutrally stating the rule and then explaining that throwing the paint brush on the floor was a reaction to being upset, the teacher helped Rob understand that he wasn't in trouble and didn't have to keep insisting that someone else had done it.

Unnecessary and Inappropriate Rules

When kindergartens and preschools are thoroughly rule governed, there exists an atmosphere in which children are frequently in the wrong. The misconception is that a multitude of rules makes for an orderly classroom, and that without them there would be chaos. In reality, the opposite is true. Most rules are neither necessary nor age-appropriate, and when children understandably have difficulty abiding by them, they get in trouble, are sanctioned, and much of class time is spent with teachers trying to create and maintain "order." Teachers feel bad when the amount of time they have to spend enforcing rules means that there is less time for teaching and connecting.

Children who have been to other schools, where there are many rules and traditional discipline, are very aware that the atmosphere can be unpleasant. Strict rules are an accepted part of most preschool culture and are almost never reconsidered. We believe that the following rules are **not** necessary for children's well-being at school, and that they interfere with children's spontaneity, enthusiasm, closeness to teachers, friendships, and joy of learning.

Bathroom Restrictions

Many schools mandate that only one or two children can use the bathroom at a time, and that before they go, they must ask or raise their hands. We designed our space so that the bathroom is within a room in the classroom, and children can go any time. Even if your school bathroom is removed from the classroom, there is no reason why more than one child shouldn't be able to go. Because they hate to stop playing, children often wait until the last moment to tell teachers they need to use the bathroom, so it is important not to limit access by imposing a timetable.

You may have children who pretend to need to use the toilet in order to accompany other children. The Smart Love approach is to be accepting of this subterfuge and let them join in, rather than to reprimand them for "faking."

> **TEACHER:** Almost every time I take kids to the bathroom, Allie says she has to go, too. Rarely does she actually need to use the toilet, and she tells me when we get there, "Tricked you!" or, "I just wanted to come for the trip." I say, "Or maybe you weren't sure or maybe you just wanted to be with everybody?" She laughs.

Remember, you never want to confront children with their untruths, but rather help them understand the reason they are hesitant to admit what they really feel or want.

Also, we think there should be no rule that children have to use the toilet by a certain age. Hopefully, you are or will be in a preschool that uses the Smart Love approach to toileting in which toileting is entirely optional and there are no restrictions on the use of diapers or pull-ups. Helping children who are reluctant learn to use the toilet is an important part of every preschool curriculum. In fact, the Smart Love term for this milestone is *toilet choosing* rather than *toilet training*.

Unfortunately, many preschools only accept children who already use the toilet, and other schools will call parents to come and change their child because children aren't allowed to wear a diaper or pull-up to school, and teachers won't get involved in changing diapers or pull-ups. As a result, parents feel the need to pressure children to use the toilet by age two or three in order to make it possible for them to go to preschool. The pressure to conform to this schedule causes children unnecessary grief over an accomplishment that is inevitable and should be freely chosen.

Children who have been pressured to use the toilet often feel shame that they aren't ready or make mistakes. You can step in and try to help them understand that there is no universal timetable, that each child is different, and that it is a choice that will happen naturally in the future.

> **TEACHER:** Eleanor said, "I am a big girl. But I still poop in my diaper. I'm afraid to go on the potty, so I still poop in my diaper instead. I'm silly. Isn't that silly?" I said, "Some kids go in diapers or pull-ups, and some kids go on the potty. You know what, it's really OK to take your time. It's not silly. You have your reasons and when you are ready to do it, you will do it."

You can feel comfortable accompanying children to the bathroom when they need help, and changing children if necessary. Some teachers resist this, and feel it is not their job. However, given the ages of your students, you inevitably take on some parental responsibilities, such as helping with clothes and wiping noses, and assisting children with toileting is no different. Because children almost always need to use the bathroom while they are at school, it makes sense that part of a teacher's job is to assist children who need help with that process.

TEACHER: Ralph, who is just three, let me know both times he had to go to the bathroom. The first time he pointed at the bathroom and said, "Potty!" and ran right into the bathroom. I followed him and helped him with his shorts. He sat down on the toilet and forgot to push his penis down, so he got a little wet. We changed his shorts and underwear and headed back out to play. The next time he had to go he was outside, and he said, "I have to go pee-pee!" I said, "Thanks for telling me Ralph. Let's go inside." We went inside, and this time while I was helping him with his shorts, I asked him if he would like to sit or stand while he goes potty. He said stand, and this time he got it into the toilet without getting himself wet. I asked him if it felt better to stand or sit and he said, "Stand!" And we went back to the classroom after Ralph washed his hands.

You can gently help children who are thinking about using the toilet to try in stages, including pretending to use it. The child in the next example had always worn pull-ups and had never been willing to even sit on the toilet.

TEACHER: Last week when I told Justine that it was time to go to the bathroom to change her pull-up, she asked me excitedly if she could sit on the toilet. This was the first time she had asked, and I said, "Yes! Of course!" We went to the bathroom, and I helped her take her shorts and pull-up off and she sat on the toilet. She asked if I could read her a book, so I went and chose *The Potty Book* and read it to her while she was sitting on the toilet. When she got up, she told me that she peed and pooped (there was nothing in the toilet). I said, "OK! Can I help wipe you?" as I was getting out a wet wipe. She said "No, it's just pretend." I said, "OK, thanks for telling me. Do you want me to wipe you anyway?" She said, "No thanks." I asked her how she felt, and she smiled, balled up her fists and jumped a little bit. I asked if she was feeling pretty excited and she said, "Yes!"

In the next two weeks this child very proudly began to use the toilet for real and would smile and say it felt "great."

You may need to stay with children for support when they are transitioning to using the toilet.

> TEACHER: During lunch I noticed Lainey dancing around on her chair. I said, "It looks like you might need to use the potty." She responded, "I do." She asked if she could bring a doll, and I said, "Sure." While we were in the bathroom, she told me that it feels better to use the bathroom than to wet your pants. I said, "It sure does!" She asked me if I would hold her hand and the doll while she used the potty. I said, "Happy to!" She used the potty and jumped up to wash her hands.

This is a reminder of why you want to Model Kindness when you get requests for help and never tell children, "You don't need me," or "You can do it yourself." Children who ask for help feel they need it, whether or not they could do the thing themselves.

Taking Turns Talking or Using "Inside" Voices

The role of preschool is to encourage children's enthusiasm, not dampen it. So if a group of children all want to talk to you at once because they are excited about an idea, you can use Loving Regulation and ask them to go one by one so you can respond to each of them, but you can do this in a positive way that makes clear you endorse their enthusiasm and that they are doing nothing wrong. Many schools make an issue of "interrupting," and children are made to feel that there is something amiss with their enthusiastic wish to contribute.

Similarly, many classrooms have rules about using "inside" voices, and children who are understandably loud and excited are sanctioned. Teachers who come to a Smart Love preschool from other schools sometimes need advice when children are loud.

> TEACHER: I'm looking for something general that I might say to a group of children who all want to do something, or get picked at

the same time by shouting "Me, Me, Me!" It has seemed to get quite popular in our group, and often the whole group will be shouting it very loudly. I'm not sure how to regulate this. Please advise.

DR. PIEPER: This is classic for this age. Just ignore the loud voices. Smile and tell them, "It's great that you all want to participate! We're going to take turns. I'll pick someone this time and someone else next, until everybody gets a turn." We don't want to dampen their excitement by making them speak softly. Assure them that everybody will get a turn, but acknowledge that, "It can be hard to have to wait."

Loud voices are an appropriate aspect of preschool culture and are usually an indication of enthusiasm and enjoyment.

Being "Orderly"

An almost universal rule in preschools is that children have to line up and be silent during transitions between spaces. This is not an age-appropriate expectation, and it is hard on children, who constantly have to be reminded to be disciplined and not to talk. There is absolutely no reason why going inside or outside should not be made playful, and why children should not be vociferous. For example, you might help children transition by composing a "train" of children, and children usually enjoy this, as there is an engineer and a caboose. Moreover, if they are ready to go out before the "train" leaves, they can go by themselves if there is a teacher ahead of them. Transitions are hard enough at this age, and the Smart Love approach is to keep children happy and occupied.

TEACHER: As we were getting ready to go outside, Kerry was confidently telling the children that today she was 4! Linda said, "But I'm older than you. I turned 5!" I replied, "Linda you are 5, and Kerry is 4, and then she'll turn 5 like you, then 6, then 7." I began creating a song as I continued to count up. The other children waiting to go outside began counting and singing along. Wanda said, "Wait, what about half birthdays!" So we began singing the song including half birthdays. When we were finished singing the song, we were already outside, all feeling confident about how old we are and will be in the future.

When children can talk and sing with you during transitions rather than having to be silent, they will be cheerful and you will feel positively engaged.

Sitting Quietly

If you have had to corral preschoolers for group time, you know that it can be like herding cats. And once you get them in a group, they tend to fidget, talk, shove each other, and generally act in ways that require you to exert your authority and reduce their enjoyment. Often group time becomes about enforcing the idea that everyone should be interested in the same thing simultaneously. As a result, children whose interest is not engaged often become restless, bored, and generally find it hard to sit for extended periods of time. Frequently, children are publicly reprimanded for this age-appropriate behavior. Then they are doubly upset if their classmates agree with their teacher's negative response and turn critical as well.

A better plan is to avoid formal group time and let groups develop naturally. For example, groups that form around snack and activities are fun and educational and do not become power struggles about sitting quietly. The so-called advantages of formal group time, such as being able to listen to others, sit quietly, share views, develop social graces, stay on task, and follow directions, are actually learned best in active, real-life engagement. When children choose to come together in groups, they see the reason for the skills groups are meant to teach.

You can take advantage of moments like lunch, when children are naturally together, to suggest inviting group activities.

TEACHER: During lunch we have been staying together at the table reading Richard Scarry's *Busy, Busy Town* and *What Do People Do All Day?* Because of the variety of pictures on each page, there is much for the children to discuss. Both today and yesterday we stayed at the lunch table for about 40 minutes completely engaged in conversation regarding how others spend their day and how we spend our day. Each page offered different scenarios about workers and their jobs. This group of four children were not only interested in the story about others' day-to-day lives, but also wanted to know more about each other as well.

If the teacher had insisted that these children sit down in a formal group and discuss the book, their participation would undoubtedly have been much less spontaneous and durable.

Sharing

As we have described, teachers are frequently expected to enforce social behaviors that are not appropriate for preschoolers. One of the most common mistakes is to insist that children this age share toys. With a Smart Love understanding of child development, you know that it is normal for preschoolers to resist when it comes to sharing anything desirable, and you would not insist or pressure them to do so. Instead, you would reduce opportunities for conflict by having duplicates of attractive toys or activities, and use S.M.A.R.T. practices to offer comfort to all parties should conflict arise.

> **TEACHER:** We have pretty much two of everything in the kitchen, but sometimes one child will want to use all of one thing. Three-year-old Aster was having a milk stand and another child wanted one of her foods. I could see how involved Aster was in her play: creating the store, selling the milk ... etc., so when another child wanted to take one of the cartons, and Aster became upset, I let the other child know that Aster was still using those things, but that when she was done, I was sure she would love to share with her. I also helped the other child set up another stand selling different kinds of fruit.

Not only did the teacher avoid derailing Aster's enthusiasm for her project by forcing her to share, but she helped the other child develop her own project.

These sorts of creative solutions require quick thinking and are rewarding, and over time the children trust that conflicts will be resolved without bad feelings, leading to a sustained positive classroom atmosphere.

You may have encountered skirmishes over possession with twos and threes because they tend to value toys more than friendships. Forcing them to share by lecturing them about social mores, or using other forms of social or physical coercion, may result in compliance, but will almost certainly breed resentment, and certainly does not foster the desire to share when enforcers are not around. In fact, quite the opposite usually occurs. At this age, even having duplicates of popular toys may not be sufficient to head off conflicts between little ones.

> **TEACHER:** In the two-year-old class, Terence, who has a new baby sibling, has a problem with needing to have all of the duplicate toys at once. His mother jokingly refers to him as being a "hoarder." When he sees another child with a toy or finds a group of toys, he becomes protective. He insists on holding all of them and will not let the other toddlers near his collection. We understand this reaction to the upset he feels at the attention the new sibling is getting, and we have allowed him to keep all the duplicates until he feels more comfortable. We just redirect the other toddlers to different toys and activities.

By avoiding a power struggle with Terence, teachers gave him the space to realize that he didn't need to grab all the toys because they would be there for him when he needed them, and that no one would force him to give up toys he was playing with at school. This also showed other children that if they ever felt the desperate need to hold on to a particular toy, teachers would respond with understanding.

Children are not ready for unforced sharing until friends become more important than toys, and this typically doesn't occur until children are four or five years old.

> **TEACHER:** Nan was making a ring with string and beads, and she asked me if I could tie the string. After I tried tying and

taping it, we realized it was too small and the beads began to slip off. She got upset that it was not working. I got her a new string, saying, "I'll make a longer string so we can put more beads on it." This ring worked out and fit her finger. She wore it the rest of the day and told me she wanted to make a new one tomorrow. Lottie overheard and asked Nan if she could have the ring that she was wearing now. Nan was excited about this and said, "Yes, you can!" and proceeded to put the ring on Lottie's finger. I followed their conversation with "I wonder how it feels to give Lottie your ring?" and she responded "Good!" I was impressed that Nan offered the ring that she had put so much effort into.

Older children who have matured enough to want to share often set an example for younger children. Kindergartners, for instance, often share with friends, and a younger child will observe and be impressed by the generosity. This illustrates the value of a classroom with mixed ages. At the Smart Love preschool, ages are mixed in the morning and the kindergartners have their own class in the afternoon. You will find that once children understand that sharing won't be forced, a child wanting something another child has, while knowing there will be no demand that the other child share, will often come up with a creative solution.

TEACHER: Cindy was upset because Felicity collected all of the kittens from the sandbox. Cindy said, "Felicity always finds all the kittens faster than me and that's not fair." I said, "That can feel hard when your friend finds all the kittens first. I wonder what we could do so it feels fun for you both, because I know how much you like to play kittens together." Cindy said, "I'll think about it, but now I don't want to play with her." A little while later Cindy said, "I got it! Before you close the sandbox each day you should hide the kittens under the sand so nobody can see them. That way we'll all have a chance to look for them when we get to school." I said, "That's a great idea Cindy! Then finding the kitties will be fun for everyone."

Children who are forced to share at home often take toys they want while lecturing other children about the necessity to share. When you see that happen, you can use Loving Regulation both to help children understand they don't have to share, and also to show the children forcing others to share that they are creating a diminution of fun with their friends. When children make dysfunctional social choices, you can guide them out of the dilemma they have created.

> **TEACHER:** Bob and Cory often play together with the trains. Recently, it has become increasingly hard for Bob when he doesn't have all of the trains, or all of the tracks. He will say to Cory, "If you don't share them with me, I'm not your friend anymore," which makes Cory upset and worried. Cory will proceed to give him whatever he requests, even if he doesn't want to. I have often heard Cory say, "Here Bob, you can have all of them, just be my friend, OK?" You can see that he still wants to play with the trains but is worried about upsetting Bob. I said to Bob, "You think the way to get all the trains is to say you won't be Cory's friend, but I think you might be very sad if he really wasn't your friend." I said to Cory, "You don't have to share the trains with Bob. He is saying he won't be your friend if you don't give him all the trains, but it's not clear that would really happen, and anyway you could also keep your trains and find someone else to play with."

Sometimes when children really have trouble standing up for themselves, you may need to actively model how to respond. You can do this, however, without shaming or lecturing the child who is dominating.

> **TEACHER:** Riley and Carmelita play a lot with one another. I have noticed, though, that they have a lot of negative interactions. Usually Carmelita makes Riley give her a toy she wants, or acts too rough. When Carmelita says, "I want that," Riley gives it to her and looks sad. I said to Riley, "If you feel upset when Carmelita asks for your toy, you can tell her that you want to keep it. You

don't have to let it go. Maybe you believe that if you want to be friends with Carmelita, you can't say what you want, but that is not how friendships should work." Riley is getting better at standing up for herself, but it takes me saying something like, "Carmelita, Riley is still playing with this toy. If she wants to keep it, let's play with this other one that Riley isn't using." After I say that, Riley will nod and agree.

By talking to Riley about standing up for herself the teacher also conveys to Carmelita that she shouldn't be disregarding Riley's wishes.

When children want what other children have and are refused, you can show the child who is disappointed that you understand how they are feeling, and then help them find a substitute.

TEACHER: Shelly brought ballerina shoes to school along with a dress that was admired by all the children. Iris saw Shelly's shoes and immediately wanted a pair. Shelley said they were hers. I agreed that those shoes belonged to Shelly but told Iris that I could make a pair for her if she liked. Iris enthusiastically agreed. She picked out white and pink felt pieces. Once they were on, she went onto the rug where Shelly was rehearsing *The Nutcracker*. As Iris came in, Shelley said, "Those aren't real ballerina shoes." I said, "They are very real – we just made them!" Shelly didn't say anything else, and they both kept dancing.

You will find that when children mature enough to make the unforced choice to share, they really enjoy the good feelings that follow.

TEACHER: Nancy was wearing the necklace she made yesterday and talking about making one for Jess. She worked hard and was thoughtful about which beads she wanted to use. Zelda also noticed Nancy's necklace and told Nancy how pretty it was and that she would like one, too. Nancy said, "I can make one for you!" Nancy asked Zelda which color string she would like. They ended up making necklaces beside each other, and you could tell Zelda felt so happy. Nancy also made a necklace for me, and she was excited because I said I was going to wear it every day!

Sometimes a child's desire for peer relationships inspires them to share toys even if they previously were not willing. Your role in facilitating this is to support the friendships and provide the necessary encouragement. As with all developmental trajectories, the important thing is that you never pressure or shame a child who doesn't feel like sharing. Give them the space to make a genuine choice of friends over possessions and the problem works itself out.

Including Others

Another nearly universal but unnecessary preschool rule is that children cannot exclude others who ask to play with them. The Smart Love understanding is that when we impose social niceties, we create subterranean resentments rather than true prosocial sentiments, and there is no guarantee that children will remain nice to each other when no adult is in sight. At a Smart Love preschool, children do not have to play with others – they can choose to play by themselves and tell others that is their choice. This derives from the same logic as not enforcing sharing. If you allow children the freedom to decide when and with whom they want to interact, they will view their choices positively and make them based on pleasure rather than pressure. So what can you do as a teacher aware that feelings can be fragile when it comes to peers and play? You can help children ask other children if they can join in their play, and if refused, you can offer alternatives.

TEACHER: Landon was playing Legos by himself while watching Valentina and Lettie build with the large blocks. I said to Landon, "It looks like they're having fun playing together. I wonder if you'd like to play with them, too." Landon replied, "I wonder what they're building." I replied, "I was wondering that too. What should we do?" Landon said, "We could ask them. Let's check!" and went over to the girls. "Hey guys what are you building?" "We're building a kitty house," Lettie replied, "and we want to build it by ourselves." Landon looked at me and said, "They're building a kitty house, and I want to build a stage." I said, "It's good you asked. Let's find blocks so you can build what you want to build." Landon built his stage next to the kitty house, and when Lettie and Valentina were finished with their kitty house, Landon asked to use their blocks to make his stage bigger. Lettie said, "Yes, we're done playing. You can use our blocks."

The teacher was matter of fact about the right of the girls to choose not to play with Landon, which allowed Landon to shift to playing with the teacher. If, as often happens, the girls had been told they were not being nice, this

would have given Landon the message that he should take the rejection personally.

Often when children don't want to play with other children, teachers use some form of conflict resolution to get them to play together and think of that as social-emotional learning. However, more durable social-emotional learning occurs when we do not pressure children to play together. The idea is to help children think of solutions rather than impose them, and also not to take others' social choices personally. In this way, children can remain friends with a child who doesn't want to play, and the child who wants to play alone realizes there is pleasure to be had that way, as well as from joining others. This models a good balance for future happiness.

> **TEACHER:** Simone and Nancy were chatting when Leona asked if they wanted to play with her or Mary. Simone said she would just play with Leona, and then she noticed that Mary was upset. Simone said, "Mary, just because we are not playing right now does not mean we're not friends." I added, "That's right Mary. Even when you play with someone else, you and Simone are still friends, and even when Leona plays with someone else you are still friends, too! If someone doesn't want to play right now, I can play, and I'm sure we can find someone to join." Instead of Mary feeling left out, we found another game.

Because children have the right to want to play alone, other children cannot simply insert themselves, but need to ask to participate. When you see children try to participate in others' play without asking, you can use Loving Regulation and gently suggest that it is necessary to check in, and also remind them that the answer could be either "yes" or "no." Again, there is no implication that children are not being friendly or nice if they choose not to play with another child, which gives children the space to change their minds on their own.

> **TEACHER:** Cindy built a complex marble run. Essie (it was her first day of school) came over and took a marble from the base and

put it at the top of Cindy's marble run. I said, "Essie, it looks like you want to play marble run. Let's ask Cindy if you can play, too. She might say 'yes' or she might say 'no.'" Essie asked if she could play and Cindy shook her head no. I told Essie, "It looks like Cindy doesn't want to play right now, but maybe later. Let's see who does want to play right now." We asked Kathy and Sandy, who were playing at the farm, and they said, "yes." Later Essie went back to Cindy, who was still playing, and asked if she could play now, and Cindy smiled and said, "Yes." Nice closure for both of them.

In the same vein, you can help children learn that they need to ask before they "help" another child with an activity rather than make assumptions or unilateral decisions about how to engage with them.

TEACHER: Sal and Millie were taking care of animals by using tape to bandage them. Sal carefully put a piece on a dog's neck, then Millie took the tape off. Sal said, "Hey I wanted that tape there." I acknowledged that they were having fun playing together and said it sounded like Sal wanted to keep the tape on the dog's neck, and so what did Millie think about asking before she took it off. Sal piped in, "You have to ask because you don't know what I am thinking of on the inside." I said, "Thanks for telling us, Sal, that you can't know what someone is thinking inside their mind so it's always good to ask them." Both girls agreed. I helped Sal put the tape back on the dog's neck and found another dog for Millie to put the tape on and off. The play was preserved and continued.

Millie's acceptance of the need to ask Sal before removing the tape was not out of enforced social politeness, but out of the recognition that others' wishes would have to be taken into account as well as one's own. Children even learn that they need to ask if someone wants a gift they want to give. Knowing to ask other children if they will accept a gift demonstrates a high level of social-emotional learning because children this age naturally assume that others will want what they want to give.

TEACHER: Astrid was making special mail for everyone. She made pictures and then rolled them up. Before Astrid gave the special mail to each child, she would ask if they were accepting deliveries. She said to Peach, "It's OK if you say no, but are you accepting deliveries at the moment?" Peach said, "Yes!" When Astrid brought one over to Elsa, she let her know that she had taken a picture of Elsa and her family playing at the park together and asked if she would like it. Elsa was so excited, she ran over to me and said, "Look! Astrid took a picture of me and my family at the park!"

When children do take others' rejections personally, you want to notice their unhappiness and offer to play with them. Your positive relationship with a child is always the best antidote to their feeling hurt.

TEACHER: Amy was playing by herself in the sandbox and looked unhappy. I asked if anything was wrong. She said, "I'm not playing with anyone because no one wants to play with me." I said, "Amy, I know that feels hard, and I would love to play with you if you would like." She said, "OK!" I asked her how I could help, and she said, "Well I can't get the sandcastle to stay." I said I could help with that, and we filled up a bucket with sand and I flipped it to make her sandcastle. She showed me how to use the seashells as flying cars for the kitties, and we flew them around. She started giggling and yelling, "This is so much fun!" and I said, "Yes, playing together feels fun, and I would always love to play with you whenever you'd like!" We kept playing for a few more minutes and went inside for lunch.

The S.M.A.R.T. practice here is to show children that you Acknowledge and Accept their unhappy feelings before suggesting ways to feel better. That unhappy feelings aren't welcome is the unfortunate message conveyed by coping mechanisms of various kinds. So when a child is rejected by another child, help with the feelings before you help them find someone to play with or something else to do. Once acknowledging the feelings, you can also offer yourself as a fun playmate, even to do the same activity, rather than insist that children play together. This avoids creating underground resentment and hostility toward the left-out child when no adult is there, and cements your value as the relationship to turn to to feel better. In the next example, as often happens, when you don't force children to play together, they often reconsider, change their minds, and make a different choice.

> **TEACHER:** Dutton and Holden were playing with magnetic tiles and building separate things when Holden went to build on Dutton's construction and Dutton said he didn't want him to. I said, "I can see, Holden, that you want to play with Dutton, but Dutton already said he doesn't want to play right now. It doesn't mean he's not your friend, and maybe he'll want to play later. You could play with me or someone else, but we do have to ask Dutton if he wants help before we add to his building." Holden asked Dutton and Dutton said no again. I said, "It sounds like Dutton wants to build on his own right now, but we can make something over here." Holden agreed and started building his own creation close to Dutton. Dutton went to Holden's building and asked, "Can I put this right here?" Holden said "Yes!" They continued to build with the tiles together.

While you don't want to force children to play with one another, you do want to make sure they communicate their choice in a reasonably nice way. This is in accord with the rule about not hurting another physically or emotionally. As a preschooler, understanding the distinction between telling another child you don't want to play, and telling them in a way that gratuitously hurts their feelings, is subtle and, as in the next example, probably requires a teacher's clarification. Children who refuse another child can often be softened by entreaties. But, like Ellen, they understand that they are making an unforced choice.

> **TEACHER:** Ellen arrived late and was eager to start playing. When Cathy saw Ellen, she asked her to play. Ellen said, "I don't want to

play with you right now." I heard her say it and how she said it. It was in a way that clearly hurt Cathy's feelings. So I said, "Ellen, it's OK to want to play with someone else besides Cathy, but you can say it in a way that doesn't hurt her feelings. You can let her know that you just don't want to play with her right now, but maybe you will later." So Ellen said to Cathy, "I just want to play with Merry right now. It doesn't mean I'm not your friend." Cathy was still upset and had a very sad face. She was half crying and said, "But I don't want to play with you later. I want to play with you now." I got closer to Cathy and explained that that's how it is with friends sometimes. Sometimes they don't want to do the same thing, and that's OK. Ellen said, "You can sit with me at snack and at group time, OK?" I thought this was very sweet of Ellen, but Cathy wasn't having it and cried, "But I want to play with you now. Can I please, please, please play with you? PLEASE?!" I just stayed close and in the meantime it affected Ellen. She said, "Hmmmmm" and started thinking. After a few seconds of contemplation, she said, "OK, Cathy, you can play with us." Cathy brightened and said, "OK, but I just have to finish this picture for my mommy, then I'll come play with you." She walked away toward the other room. She stopped by John first and said, "Ellen wasn't gonna let me play with her, but she thought about it, and now she is."

When one child doesn't want to play with another, you can often use play to bridge the gap between them and inspire them in an unpressured way to play cooperatively.

TEACHER: I saw Paul building with magnetic tiles. Jerry asked if he could build with him. Paul told him no. Jerry said, "But I want to build with you. You're my best friend." I came over and said, "It sounds like Paul wants to build by himself right now, but that doesn't mean he's not your friend. We can try playing together later." Paul said, "Yeah." I asked Jerry, "Can I help you build?" and he said yes and a few moments after we started building, Jerry said. "I want to connect mine to Paul's." I said, "Let's ask Paul," and he did, and Paul said yes and they started building together."

When children aren't made to play together, they learn that the choice to play should be based on enjoyment and, if playing is not feeling fun, that it's a good idea not to keep trying to fix an unrewarding friend interaction – an important social-emotional achievement.

TEACHER: Alyssa said, "I guess Ian's not my friend anymore. He was playing with Maya." I said, "Alyssa, Ian is still your friend. Even when you're not playing together, you can still be friends. It can feel hard when you want to play with him and he wants to play with a different friend. Maybe Ian will want to play tomorrow. Let's find someone who does want to play." Alyssa said, "I could play that ambulance game with Rose and David. They're my friends, too." I said, "Great idea!"

Even two- and three-year-olds eventually absorb the important life message that just because someone doesn't want to play with you, that doesn't mean they aren't your friend. You can find other things to do that are fun, and there is no reason to take the rejection personally.

TEACHER: Quinn and Sandy were building a castle. Pam asked if she could play. Sandy replied, "Not right now. Maybe later when we're done building." Pam checked in with Quinn and got the same response. Pam said, "OK, let me know when you're done," and went to play with the airport. I let Pam know that she had done a good job of keeping things fun for herself, because it could feel upsetting when your friends don't want to play. Pam said, "I know!" and went on playing with the airport.

Instead of a rule about children being forced to play together, you can Model Kindness while helping each student in the situation have a genuine experience of connecting to you and to their feelings. Children will demonstrate social-emotional learning by imitating your caring response to children who are feeling rejected by another child. And they will slowly begin to come up with their own solutions in social situations without taking the needs of others personally.

Good Manners and Politeness

As a teacher learning to practice S.M.A.R.T. strategies for a happy classroom, you want to avoid demands for social politeness. Most preschools expect standard expressions of politeness from children. Children comply, but the parroting of "please," "thank you," and "I'm sorry," is robotic. Children understand that they need to say these magic words in order to get what they want from adults. The compliance falls apart when teachers are not actively watching, and leads to resentment. Instead, you can model kind speech by saying "please," and "thank you," and apologizing for any missteps. Note that even when you model politeness, children may be slow to adopt it at the preschool age. Still, because you want their choice to be genuine, you don't put pressure on them. Eventually, because they love you and want to be like you, most children will make unforced choices toward caring speech. Here the teacher models saying "thank you" when a child shows the same kindness to her that she showed to him:

> TEACHER: I was playing with Ralph outside and he noticed a mixture of soil and water and took a shovel and began to stir it. He motioned for me to join. I saw he was kneeling on mulch, so I brought over a garden pad and asked if he wanted to use it. He said, "Yes," and knelt on it. Then he looked at me kneeling and said, "Do you want one?" I said, "Yes, thank you so much!" and he went and got me one.

Children usually come to preschool indoctrinated in the ways of saying "please" and "thank you," so it's not surprising that they can impose these expectations on classmates. When this happens, you can explain that these responses are not *required* in school, even if they are nice to say.

> TEACHER: Sally did a twirl with her skirt and I commented, "Beautiful skirt, Sally." She smiled back at me. Leticia, who was

sitting nearby said, "Say 'thank you,' Sally." Sally did not say anything, and I responded, "Leticia, that's very thoughtful of you, but it's OK if Sally doesn't want to say thank you and, actually, Sally did say thank you by smiling. There are many ways to say thank you. Just being happy is saying thank you."

The teacher helped Sally understand that "thank you" is really a communication of feelings, not just rote words. When children correct other children's manners, they are imitating behavior that is expected of them at home. In the next example, a teacher asked the director for help educating a child and making the distinction between home and school.

TEACHER: Joan, Gina, and Myra were playing underneath their fort and sharing chalk. When Joan gave Gina a piece of chalk, she said, "Don't forget to say 'thank you.'" Gina didn't respond, and Joan said, "If you don't say 'thank you' then you're bad." Gina responded, "I'm not bad!" I walked over and said, "Joan, I heard you ask Gina to say, 'thank you,' but if someone doesn't say 'thank you' it doesn't mean they're bad. I heard Gina ask you nicely for the chalk and it was kind of you to share it with her." Joan has a tendency to demand politeness from other children, and it makes others want to play with her less. I'm glad Gina stood up for herself, but it's been tough getting Joan not to enforce what she sees as correct behavior.

DIRECTOR PEREZ: Tell Joan, "Saying 'please' and 'thank you' is a choice – not something that has to happen. This is where home and school can be different – maybe at home you have to say those things, but at school you have a choice, and if you choose not to do it that is just fine."

In order to achieve genuine social-emotional learning with your students, you also want to avoid insisting on apologies for mistakes. For example, when a child bumps another child you can use S.M.A.R.T. principles to explore each child's feelings about what happened. Pressuring children to apologize results in lip service, but not true feelings of being sorry. On the other hand, you will want to model apologizing when you have the chance.

> **TEACHER:** Julie asked, "Where's the mummy book?" I said, "It's over there on the shelf." Julie said, "Mummies don't move." I said, "No, mummies can't move. They're dead." The next day Julie shared with me that she was thinking about mummies when she went home and in her sleep. I said, "I looked at the book. I don't think it's good for you or the other children, and it was a mistake that it was there. We have given it to a school for older children. I'm sorry it was here and that it upset you. That was our error." Julie said, "Well it wasn't scary to me." I said, "I have to make this decision about what is best for you and the other children, and I think it's too scary for preschool, and I'm sorry you had to see it." Julie didn't say anything but asked to read a different book.

Any chance you have to demonstrate that you made an error and are sorry models genuinely taking responsibility, and students will begin to develop a more competent sense of what an apology does. When children are new to preschool, they often resist apologizing because they fear there will be consequences for their mistakes or because apologizing is associated with power struggles with adults. After they realize that their teachers are comfortable apologizing for mistakes, they learn the important social-emotional lesson that an apology is a way of being kind and caring toward another.

Applying S.M.A.R.T. Principles to Everyday Classroom Issues

In contrast to the sanctions that many schools impose for children's everyday struggles in class, such as refusing requests, having trouble waiting, difficulty with transitions, being generally inattentive, bullying, bending the truth, being intolerant of others, and so on, you can use S.M.A.R.T. strategies to offer children acceptance and understanding of their feelings and help them make a positive choice to move on from whatever impasse they are confronting.

Refusing

Preschool children encounter numerous requests, such as washing hands, transitions, putting on indoor or outdoor clothes, and truly a hundred other things a day. All of these can and should be handled with S.M.A.R.T. practices so that they don't turn into power struggles and other negative kinds of interactions. When Loving Regulation, Acknowledging and Accepting Feelings, Time With, Modeling Kindness, and Staying Positive are all used regularly and consistently, children learn that you will remain present for them even when requests are resisted. They also see that you can make agreeing to the request fun and companionable rather than unpleasant. Here are some common areas where preschoolers may resist you, and a few ideas for how to turn these into opportunities for S.M.A.R.T. teaching practice.

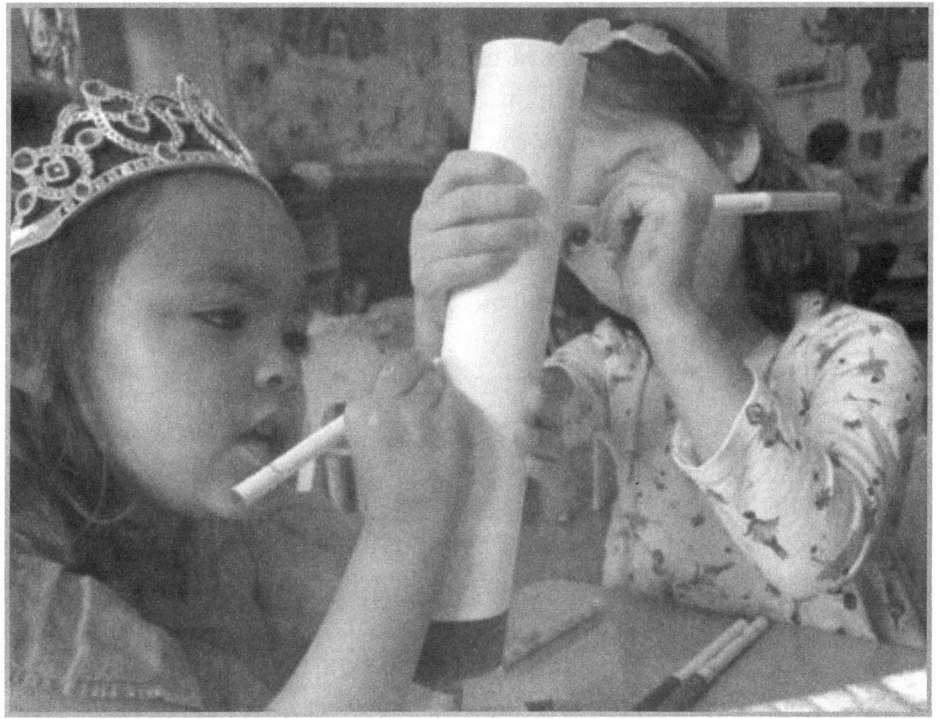

Interrupting Play to Use the Toilet

You will encounter many children who have great difficulty going to the bathroom because they want to keep playing. You may have to anticipate the need and be creative in order to encourage them to make the right choice.

> TEACHER: Roger was dancing around indicating he had to use the bathroom. Roger tends to hold it and not go, even if I ask him, until he really has to, and then we don't make it to the bathroom before he starts going. So when he started dancing, I asked if he had to go and he shook his head no. Minutes later, I noticed he was dancing again, so I said, "It looks like you really need to go. Come with me. We're going to go potty. It makes it harder to have fun when you have to go potty." I let him know that we could bring his toy train in, too. I also pretended we were on a train and said, "Wow, Roger, we're on the train, just like the one you have!" Almost every time we come in from outside, he will walk up to the toys and start playing with them instead of going to the bathroom. This time, I went in front of him. After he went to the bathroom, he was happy. I said, "Roger, you went on the potty today. I wonder how that feels?" And he happily smiled at me and giggled. He got to see how quickly he can resume playing when he goes in the potty, and he was excited to go back outside.

Because the teacher used playful methods rather than threats, such as, "If you don't go potty now you are going to wet yourself! " she allowed Roger to make an uncoerced choice that made him feel happy and in charge.

Washing Hands

Washing hands is necessary, but it interrupts play and children often resist. Washing hands often turns into a power struggle which is resolved with threats or "consequences" – "If you don't wash your hands, you can't have snack ..." However, if you give it some thought, you can Stay Positive and make it fun, which will avoid conflict and strengthen your relationship.

TEACHER: It can be hard for Carol to wash her hands. So, to upstream the solution, I invited Carol to be my hand-washing assistant to help me keep track of who had washed their hands. I gave her a clipboard with purple paper and marker. She said, "I want to help, but I don't know how to spell all the names." I said, "I wonder what we can do." Carol suggested she could write the first letter of everyone's name. I said, "That's a fantastic idea!" Carol wrote the first letter of each child's name on the clipboard when they were finished washing their hands. She said, "After I'm done washing my hands, I'll write the C, and after you're finished, I'll write the T."

This was a nice example of a teacher thinking ahead about how to avoid a refusal by offering the relationship with her to help the child do something she had resisted. Also, the teacher supported the child by choosing to use her strengths – knowing the first letter of names – rather than focusing her on what she didn't know – how to spell the whole name.

Changing Wet Clothes

Children are not crazy about interrupting their play to change wet clothes. You can find your creative ideas come in handy to find solutions that don't involve lecturing.

TEACHER: Daphne had gotten snow in her boot. She noticed her indoor pants were wet at the bottom, and she got upset. I said, "Thank you for letting me know! Would you like to change into dry pants? That might feel better." She hesitated and shook her head, but I grabbed a dry pair of pants and noticed there were flowers on them, so I said, "Wow, Daphne, I see so many flowers on these pants. I wonder which one is your favorite?" She became excited to pick out her favorite and this allowed her to come with me to change, although she kept protesting.

As in this example, you want to avoid power struggles that lead to threats and sanctions and to look for ways to use your relationship with the child to make the process of changing out of wet clothes enjoyable.

Putting On/Taking Off Outside Clothes

Changing clothes when coming in or going out is the last thing many preschoolers want to do. It is not obvious to them why it is even necessary. As elsewhere, offering fun, rather than threats ("Then you can't go in/out") is the answer, especially if you remain close with the child.

> **TEACHER:** Several kids have been bringing toys from home. But when it is time to get ready to go outside, they are focused on playing with the toys rather than getting ready to go out. I have been asking, "Would you like me to hold the toy while you put on your shoes?" I tell them I know it can be hard to stop playing when it is time to go outside, but that we can play more when we get to the garden. Sometimes this helps, but sometimes children just continue to play. How can I best help during this transition?
>
> **DIRECTOR PEREZ:** I would concentrate on ways to make transitions a little more fun. For example, maybe find a bag or a box that you could carry with the toys the children want to take outside. You can have this box available for home toys or classroom toys. If you go out with it then they will want to change clothes and come out.

When children get inside from being outside, they see the toys they want to play with and want to go to them immediately without taking off their outside clothes. Using S.M.A.R.T. strategies, you can think of ways to make taking off clothes a way to stay connected and have fun.

> **TEACHER:** Soren was distracted taking his outside clothes off. He sat down and was unresponsive when I asked if he was ready to change his shoes, snow pants, etc. I asked him what the first

step was when he took his shoes off, which one are we taking off first, left or right? I did this while pointing at his shoes, so he knew which ones I was talking about. This made him more engaged and it turned into a game. When we got to his jacket, I asked which sleeve goes first left or right? I did this with his snow pants, inside shoes and taking off his gloves. It also worked when putting his outside clothes back on to go home. He was able to lead me through the steps he takes and was excited pointing out which arm/leg/hand would go first. Making small things more enjoyable can really change how a child approaches the day.

This way of helping Soren transition was also teaching him left and right! There are children who consistently resist changing clothes, and you will need to use understanding and creativity to help them. Even though you have other children to see to, and you may feel rushed, it is better in the long run if you can Stay Positive and find ways to make it a game.

TEACHER: Paula arrived early and I said, "Hi, I am so glad to see you! Now you can take your outdoor clothes off so you can wash your hands and begin playing." Paula said, "No I'll wait for other kids." A little later I said, "Well, Paula, all of the other kids are here, so now you can take your outside clothes off and head to the sink." Paula just stared at me. I said, "Would you like some help?" Paula nodded her head, yes. I said, "Why don't I unzip your coat halfway? Do you want to unzip the rest?" Paula said, "I can't. I don't know how." I knew she did, but I said, "I am happy to help." Paula helped me take some things off. She hung her hat and coat up and I said, "Wow, you had to reach pretty far up to put that coat on the hook. You did a great job."

The above example illustrates that S.M.A.R.T. practice means you never confront children who feel they need help with the fact that they actually don't need it. In this case Paula was at an impasse about taking off outside clothes, and asking the teacher to do it was a face-saving solution.

Sometimes children refuse to put on their gloves and hats when it is cold out and they should be wearing them, but they really don't like the way they feel. Also, some children who don't want to put their gloves or hats on, take them off outside after they have put them on inside. One way to avoid a power struggle is to engage children as partners in the decision-making process about what clothes are necessary. You can creatively convert this issue into a learning experience. For example, before recess in cold weather, the children can check the outside temperature together. Help decide on a guideline: Above 40 degrees everyone can choose whether to wear gloves and hats. Below 40, everyone wears them! You can use your phone weather app to show the temperature. This also inspires further learning about what numbers are higher or lower than 40. Plus it connects the feel of the weather to the temperature. On various days you can discuss what happens when skin gets cold, and why it's important to protect your skin, or talk about how you can lose heat from your head, and how a hat helps keep the heat in your body.

Going Outside

When they are engaged in an activity that engrosses them, children often have trouble leaving the classroom to go outside and play. They may completely tune out teachers who stand apart from them and give orders, which causes teachers to resort to threats or sanctions. The better solution is to offer a positive and fun relationship activity to break the logjam.

> **TEACHER:** Toby was refusing to leave the classroom to go outside and play. I said, "I know it's hard to go when we're having fun, but we'll play some more outside." I had him come close to me to play I-Spy on the I-Spy board, but he began to run around in the hallway. I got in front of him and said, "Toby, you can help me open up the sandbox for the day, since we will be the first ones out there. Grab my hand let's go!" He grabbed my hand, and we went outside. He helped me take off the sandbox cover and asked me to make ice cream with him. I asked him how he did it. He happily showed me and began talking about his favorite ice cream flavors.

Although it is always tempting to tell children who are refusing to make a necessary transition that they just have to do it, you can see from this example how much more effective you are when you partner and are playful with children.

Cleaning Up

Preschoolers resist cleaning up almost as much as changing clothes. Taking out toys is fun, but when children want to move on to other things, putting toys back feels burdensome. And too often cleaning up is made truly unpleasant by threats and sanctions. These are counterproductive to the goal that children ultimately choose to put things away. To use the S.M.A.R.T. approach means when a child doesn't want to put toys away, you simply do it while the child stays near. Cleaning up is not a health and safety issue like washing hands or putting on appropriate clothes. Rather than get into a power struggle about cleaning up, you can ask if children would like to help, but if they refuse, it is better to do it than to start a conflict. At the same time, you can try to make cleaning up a cooperative and fun effort that children will want to choose. For example, you can call cleaning up "special deliveries," or invent scavenger hunts for special toys ("Let's find all the blue blocks!").

> **TEACHER:** I decided to start picking up for coming inside, and I asked Leilani and Helen if they wanted to help. I propped the shed door open and stayed there, gathered nearby toys and showed them what I was looking for (all the red and clear buckets, for example) and asked them to go get all the ones they could find, like a scavenger hunt. They went looking for all the matching items. Leilani gave me a good idea of how to get the children to help cleaning up, because they already do love scavenger hunts when we are outside.

Giving reasons for cleaning up is also helpful – for example, being able to find particular toys again, or freeing up the teacher to move on to another activity.

> **TEACHER:** We were inside due to weather and the students were playing with different materials in different areas. Hester used the beads and buttons in the bowls and mixed them up and left

the area to play elsewhere. I have noticed that when she plays, she will jump from one thing to the next, which I thought might be developmentally appropriate for her age. However, she leaves everything out when she is done. I was wondering what you would suggest to encourage children to clean up before they move on to the next activity.

DIRECTOR PEREZ: When you see her beginning to move on, ask if she is all finished with this one. If she says yes, you can say, "Well let's find its home so we know where it is in case we want to play with it again." If you're unable to catch this in between activities, ask her if she was finished with it and just put it away.

DR. PIEPER: Yes, it's always better not to make a big deal of cleaning up. The teacher can ask if a child wants to help, but if not, the teacher can just do it. But if the teacher says, "I would like to do the next thing with you, but I have to clean up first, would you like to help me to make it go faster?" the child is more likely to help.

When children adamantly refuse, rather than get into a power struggle, it is better to take the long view and conclude that the child may feel differently on a different day.

TEACHER: Axel asked me when snack was. I told him that we will play for a little bit then it will be time for special deliveries (cleaning up) and after special deliveries we will eat snack. He said adamantly, "I'm not doing special deliveries." I responded, "I hear you." He repeated that he was not going to do special deliveries. So I told him that special deliveries is when we find homes for toys that are out. He said again that he didn't want to do that, so I told him that when it's time for special deliveries he could be close to me while I find homes for the toys. He did stand near me while I was putting toys away. I would pick up a car and ask if he knew where a parking spot for the car was and he would put it away – however he did so somewhat reluctantly. He did eventually help with a few more toys.

In this case, Axel made progress by voluntarily putting a few toys away after he had strongly refused. This is much preferable to demanding compliance and engendering resentment and alienation.

When you make cleaning up optional and fun, you can use it for teaching purposes. In fact, when you maintain positive relationships and partner with your students, you can inject learning into almost any interaction, including the routine and everyday ones.

> **TEACHER:** Once Kirk and Tate were finished playing with the blocks and animals, I asked if they were ready to put them away. Kirk and Tate said yes, as they wanted to start a new activity. I asked if they knew the words on the animal bins and Tate responded, "Yeah, this one says 'Ocean,' this one says 'Forest,' and this one says 'Jungle!'" I said, "I wonder if you could find all of the ocean animals …" and Kirk grabbed the jungle bin and said, "I'll do the jungle animals!" The three of us categorized all the classroom animals by habitat. This brought many interesting questions to the table such as can snakes live in the jungle and the forest? Yes! What kind of animal is this? An anteater! Is this a type of shark or a dolphin?

This enjoyable learning experience would not have been possible if the teacher simply ordered the children to clean up and didn't participate.

Children sometimes help clean up even though you have offered to do it because they enjoy partnering with you and want you to be available for the next activity. Cleaning up is often presented to children as a kind of moral obligation, which turns it into a chore rather than a natural consequence of playing.

> **TEACHER:** Baylor finished playing with the magnetic tiles. I watched him use a big stack of tiles to pick up the rest and put

the box back on the shelf. This is a fun way to do it. After he put them back on the shelf, he saw Jerry picking up his tiles. He went up to Jerry and asked if he needed help. Jerry responded, "No." Sometimes Jerry says no when he means yes, and he quickly changed his mind and said, "Yes." Baylor again used a stack of tiles to pick up the loose ones. Jerry saw this and did the same thing.

Eventually, you will find that many children choose to put things away after playing without being asked. They are imitating you and not trying to get praise or rewards.

Bullying/Teasing

Bullying is currently an important focus at all levels of education, from preschool through graduate school. Unfortunately, at the preschool level, responses to bullying mainly consist of sanctions and lectures leveled at the child doing the bullying. Because young children learn most thoroughly by imitation, when we lecture or sanction the bully all we do is model bullying ourselves and, therefore, reinforce the behavior.[10]

A crucial part of social-emotional teaching in the classroom is using S.M.A.R.T. principles to prevent bullying, to teach the bullied child that they can stand up for themselves or come to a teacher for help, and to help the bullying child understand the motivation to hurt other students' feelings.

TEACHER: Carmen and I were in a conversation when Beckett stuck his head between us and said, "Hello, irritating Carmen!" She looked shocked and said, "I'm not irritating Carmen, I'm princess Carmen!" I said, "It's great you are sticking up for yourself, Carmen." Beckett went on to list the reasons that Carmen was irritating to him, while she looked taken aback. He said "You always say the same things over and over, every day, without stopping! You always do the same things, forever and ever!" (She does have a daily routine that she sticks to in preschool, which includes prancing around in a pink princess dress, and singing songs from a Disney movie.) I saw the hurt look on Carmen's face and said, "Wait a minute, Beckett. You are hurting Carmen's feelings and we don't hurt each other's feelings in the classroom. If there is something about Carmen you don't like or that is upsetting you, you can talk to a teacher, but making Carmen feel bad is not a good way for you to feel better." I said, "Carmen, I can tell that you're still feeling sad that Beckett called you irritating." She nodded. I said, "I'm glad you're telling me that. Is there anything I can do that might help you feel better?" She thought about it and replied, "Maybe we can go put on my princess boots?"

Imposing sanctions on a bullying child causes them to feel isolated from the relationship with you and emotionally shut down or resentful. However, when you take a positive S.M.A.R.T. approach, the aggressor can often preserve the emotional space to understand what is behind their hostility.

TEACHER: I heard Sheryl saying to Ted, "I'm not going to play with you today." I said, "Well, Sheryl, Ted just walked in the door. He's not playing with anyone right now. He is still taking his coat off. If he comes up to you and you don't want to play with him, you can just tell him that you want to play by yourself right now. But maybe you should wait to see how you feel in a little while." Sheryl said, "I won't change my mind!" I said, "I notice you are talking to Ted the way Lulu (Ted's sister) talked to you. Maybe you are mad at Lulu and are taking it out on Ted? They are two different people. It is true that Lulu was not nice to you, but Ted really wants to play with you. Think about whether you want to treat them the same. Just because people are in the same family that does not mean they are the same." Sheryl reluctantly agreed.

If Sheryl had been reprimanded for not being nice, and told to apologize, she would never have had the chance to understand and modify her rejection of Ted. When you help resolve conflicts by protecting the child who is on the receiving end of hostility without showing negativity or being punitive toward the aggressor, you give children the space to recover and reunite.

TEACHER: In the bathroom, Claire was washing her hands and Savannah "playfully" pushed them away. Claire did not experience this as playful and got upset. Claire said, "Go away, Savannah. I'm not your friend." Savannah responded, "What, Claire?" Claire walked behind me to hide from Savannah, who followed her. I said, "Savannah, can you wash your hands while I talk to Claire?" Claire told me, "Savannah splashed water and moved my hands." I said, "I see it must be hard to wash your hands while someone is moving them away." Claire responded, "Yeah. Go away Savannah, I'm not your friend." I said, "Did you know you could be upset with Savannah and still be her friend? I then turned to Savannah and asked, "What happened in the sink with Claire? She thinks you pushed her hands and splashed." Savannah said, "Yeah, I was having fun!" I said, "Oh, Claire didn't think you were playing. She was washing her hands and that made it hard for her. It wasn't fun for Claire – and it has to be fun for both of you." Savannah said, "Sorry, Claire." Claire replied, "Thanks." They went off to play amicably.

No one told Savannah to apologize. She did so because she wanted to continue playing with her friend, and because, as we have said, you will often model apologizing and moving on from a problem.

Teasing is ubiquitous in preschools, but it is often a prelude to bullying, and you can use Loving Regulation to defuse it. Moreover, when a younger child is being teased by an older child whom they admire, you may need to step in and help the younger child realize that the older child isn't treating them well and they should find someone else to play with – an important model for responding to teasing/bullying.

TEACHER: Brooke and Morgan were doing different activities. Brooke was telling Morgan about her upcoming fifth birthday. Morgan got excited and said she had a fourth birthday coming up. Once Brooke heard this, she changed her tone a bit and said,

"Oh well you're only going to be four and I'm going to be five, so I'm older." I chimed in, "It sounds like you're both excited for your birthdays!" After this Brooke looked over at Morgan and teased, "Well, she's only turning four." I said to her, "Yes, Morgan is turning four and that's exciting, just like it's exciting to turn five! Our classroom has kids of many ages!" Brooke got quieter after this. I started to walk away when I noticed that she leaned over and said something in Morgan's ear, and Morgan looked upset. I walked back over and sat in between them. "Brooke, I can't let you say things that upset Morgan. She is excited for her birthday just like you are excited for yours, but it is not OK to tease someone because they are different from you." I asked Morgan if she wanted to come with me to clean up the art boxes. When we were alone, I told her that it is never OK for anyone to hurt your feelings. She responded "Yeah, that didn't feel fun." She sat at a table with other children who were eating snack.

Children who passively accept bullying feel helpless. While they are still young, it is important to help them realize that they dislike being treated badly and that they can resist or move away. Mostly, with preschoolers, you can keep a keen eye for ways to help resolve teasing before it escalates, and model different approaches that keep connections and don't make anyone feel punished.

TEACHER: Beckett began bossing his brother Lucian around very sternly. He told him to guard the clubhouse while he walked around. He kept repeating, "Don't cross the line, otherwise I'll take you to jail," pointing his finger at Lucian and looking very angry. Lucian complied. I stepped in and told Beckett that it was best to ask before giving orders, and I asked Lucian if he wanted to guard the clubhouse. Lucian didn't say anything. Beckett put his hand on his shoulder and said, "Come on bud, say yes!" Eager to please his brother, Lucian did. The whole time he continued to obey Beckett's commands, he never looked happy about anything. But he also never clearly said that he didn't want to do it, and even declined when I presented other alternatives to him. I repeated, "Lucian, it doesn't look like it's a lot of fun to have Beckett talk to you like that, and you don't have to stay here just because Beckett wants you to. Would you like me to help you find someone to play with that will talk to you more nicely and be more fun." Lucian looked sad but eventually nodded.

The practice to notice here is that the teacher didn't confront Beckett, but in her focus on helping Lucian think about how he really wanted to be treated, she communicated to Beckett that there was a problem with how he was relating to his brother.

Loving Regulation is an equally appropriate response to bullying as to other behavior management issues. And when a child cannot control themselves and needs to be removed from the classroom, the S.M.A.R.T. principle of Time With means that you will go with them.

TEACHER: Carl and Larry were talking loudly and saying nonsensical sentences that occasionally had other students' names in them. Elsa and Kinsley were getting upset about this – Kinsley in particular was stomping around and sighing loudly – and I told Carl and Larry that speaking like this was hurting their classmates' feelings. Carl kept doing it, and Kinsley looked on the verge of a meltdown. So I took Carl to be with Director Perez in the office. When I came back, I told Kinsley, "Carl is having a hard time and Director Perez is helping him." She said OK and seemed totally fine – I wish I had asked her more about her feelings, but it was a hectic time and the removal of Carl from the room seemed helpful for her.

DIRECTOR PEREZ: Let's upstream this a bit. Before Larry and Carl sit next to each other, ask them if they think they can sit together and have fun without making it not fun for anyone else. If they agree, then give it a go. At the first instance of hurting someone's feelings, interrupt and say, "I can see Kinsley and Elsa do not want you to use their names in that way, it's hurting their feelings and I can't let you do that. Come with me. We'll try sitting together at another time." Then separate them. If Carl continues to escalate, take him out of the classroom. With regard to Kinsley, just let her know that it's never OK for anyone to hurt her feelings and tell her you are sorry that happened.

It is wonderful when you help children understand that social interactions should be enjoyable, and that they do not have to put up with others' behavior that feels unpleasant.

TEACHER: Jessie was hitting Denise's animal with another animal. Denise said, "Stop doing that!" but Jessie didn't stop. Denise said, "This doesn't feel fun anymore." And she stopped playing with Jessie and went to find other friends.

This outlook will stand Denise in good stead. You have a crucial role to play in this social-emotional lesson. First, you Model Kindness and intervene to help children identify how others' behaviors affect them. Then you Acknowledge and Accept the feelings of the child being bullied, and spend Time With the bully to help connect them with the cause of their angry feelings.

Touching

Children don't always understand other children's reactions to touching. Also, adults tend to touch children without asking them – they ruffle their hair, or give them a pat or a hug, and children can imitate this and treat other children the same way. This is a good opportunity to teach children the life lesson that others may feel negatively about being touched, and also that they shouldn't touch others' bodies without asking, and that others should ask before touching theirs.

TEACHER: I noticed that Bryce pats other children on their heads the way many grown-ups do to children. He's not hitting them or doing this in any mean way, but obviously he should not pat children without asking first. While playing in the sandbox, Bryce patted Paul's head and Paul yelled out, "He hit me!" Bryce said, "No, I just patted you." I told Bryce, "I know you're having fun playing with Paul, but any time you touch someone you have to ask first." Bryce responded, "But it was just a pat." I said, "I know, but some people don't like how it feels to be patted and some people do. I think the pat may have surprised Paul, so next time, just ask him if you can touch him."

You can also teach children that they need to ask about touching even when they are trying to be helpful.

TEACHER: The playschool class was mixing shaving cream, glue, and paint in a bag to make puffy paint. Kandy got quite a bit of it on her lap. Cullen noticed this and walked to the sink and wet a paper towel. He started dabbing the paint off Kandy's pants. Kandy looked at me and said, "What's Cullen doing?" I responded, "It looks like he wanted to help." She smiled and said, "Oh! Thanks Cullen!" She continued with her art. I told Cullen, "It looks like you're having fun being close to Kandy right now." He smiled and kept wiping the paint off her pants.

DIRECTOR PEREZ: Although Kandy seemed OK with Cullen wiping her pants, and it was thoughtful of him to try to help her, just stop him before he gets to Kandy's pants and ask her if it is OK if Cullen helps clean her pants. If she says no, show him something else (like a teacher's pants) he could help clean.

Showing young children that they need to ask before touching others, and that others shouldn't touch them without their permission, is clearly an important lesson, and it reinforces other permission-asking moments, such as joining play, etc.

Cooperating

Like other social niceties, cooperation should be a choice rather than something children are pressured about. Cooperation can be more fun than doing an activity by oneself, but not when it's commanded by an adult. When children are forced to cooperate, the resentment they feel is often expressed as conflict with their peers. You can facilitate cooperation in a variety of creative ways, and then reorient if a child wants to do something alone.

> **TEACHER:** Axel and Hank were playing fire engines and had stacked the police station and school on top of each other. Usually, Hank would sound the alarm and both fire engines rushed to the scene. Axel told Hank to put out the fire inside while he put out the fire outside. Hank complained that Axel was doing everything and there was nothing left for him to do. I mentioned that usually many people are needed to put out a fire. I also slipped an extra character inside the police station so that Hank had a little more to do.

Some teachers might step in and tell Axel to cooperate and let Hank do more. But by creatively elaborating the scene, the teacher helped the boys make the unforced choice to cooperate. When you model cooperation, most of your students will eventually absorb this approach and elect to cooperate with each other.

> **TEACHER:** Ayla and Celine were arguing because Ayla put the animals Celine was playing with "on pause." Celine gave her the animals and moved on to play with kittens instead, but they did not want to play together. I sat between them. While I was complimenting Celine on her "kitty castle," Ayla asked if she could play with us. Celine said that she could play if she wanted to use the kitties. Ayla agreed and all three of us played. After about five minutes, I was able to step away and they continued together. By staying close to both of them, and having positive interactions with each of their games, I slowly bridged them back together so they could continue to play without me.

Using S.M.A.R.T. practices, you can foster cooperation and downplay competition. This is another reason we prefer not to have grades, give gold stars, or compare children in other ways. Sometimes children will choose to play a competitive game, but the culture of cooperation can defuse any competitive edge.

> **TEACHER:** Gianna and Barb created a watercolor painting on one piece of paper. It was a true collaboration, each one checking in with the other when selecting colors and deciding where to put their names. To decide who should take the painting home, Barb came up with the idea to do the sticky note game. I wrote their names on sticky notes and Barb stuck them on, closed her eyes, and pointed to the one with her own name. Gianna agreed Barb could take the painting home. Then Gianna had the idea that they could make a copy! I asked Barb if I could make a copy of the painting on the copy machine, and she said yes, so everyone went home with a painting.

Asking for help often leads to cooperation, so when you give your students unconditional help they will copy you and feel unconflicted about asking their classmates to assist them, or coming up with creative ways to solve problems.

Bending the Truth

Bending the truth is age-appropriate for preschoolers.[11] They often do it out of fear of consequences, the desire to win, or the wish to have something another child has. Unfortunately, distorting the truth often gets mislabeled as lying, and children are reprimanded. As in other areas of practice and training, misconceptions about child development frequently cause teachers to respond to normal behaviors with harsh judgments. However, with the knowledge that when they are under stress all preschoolers are inclined to bend the truth, you will know to respond diplomatically and kindly. For example, when children try to put the blame on others to avoid facing what they have done, you may gently show them how to fix their mistake without confronting them. You can show a child that they can say what really happened because you will Stay Positive, be understanding, and there will be no consequences for telling the truth.

> **TEACHER:** Rosalie and Raya were playing with magnetic tiles. They usually play well, but today Rosalie tore down Raya's structure. I watched Rosalie tear the structure down and I said, "Raya, you look really upset. I saw you working hard on that structure." Raya said, "I was, and Rosalie tore it down." I said, "Rosalie we can't tear down something another child is building without permission. What happened?" She replied, "I didn't. Leigh did it." I said, "I can tell you are worried about my knowing you tore your friend's structure down, and maybe that's why you are saying Leigh did it. Were you playing with Raya?" Rosalie said, "Yeah." I asked, "Did you help her build that structure?" Rosalie replied, "No." I said, "It must be hard to play with someone and watch them build but not be allowed to build that structure with her." Rosalie said, "Yes." Rosalie asked Raya if she could play, and Raya agreed and they started playing again.

The thing to notice here is that the teacher went directly to the upset that led to the untruth without focusing on the fact of the untruth. Through gentle questions, taking the time to follow the child's lead, you can uncover the reason for bending the truth, and put things back on track without a direct accusation.

It is not uncommon for children to try and get a coveted toy by incorrectly asserting it is theirs, or that they had it first. Rather than confront a child with that distortion, you can help them recognize the wish behind it.

> **TEACHER:** Liz and Gertrude were having a conflict involving a doll. Gertrude kept repeating, "That's my doll!" and insisting that Liz give it back. I knew that it was Gertrude's doll, but when I suggested that, Liz continued to insist that it was hers, and she began to cry. I said, "I know that you want to play with the doll,

but it's Gertrude's and maybe you imagined that by saying it's yours, you'd have a better chance of getting it?" I helped Liz find another doll to play with.

If you Model Kindness and remain non-confrontational when children bend the truth to cover up an error, children may save face by quietly using your help to fix the problem.

TEACHER: Lydia let me know that she needed a blue marker. I went and got her the marker, and as I sat down, she said, "I don't know why all my markers keep disappearing." I said, "Well, after we are finished coloring, we can check that all your markers are back in your marker case with their caps on. That way they'll be there for you the next time you want them." Lydia responded, "I put them in my marker case every day after I'm done, and someone must be taking them." I know that most days Lydia leaves her markers on the table, even when we ask her to deliver her markers to their spot, because she gets excited to go outside. But I just said, "We would never let anyone take your markers out of your marker case because those are yours, but sometimes we may forget to check your markers are in their case when you feel excited to go outside. Today let's make sure they are in your case and that your case is zipped so they're ready for you tomorrow." Lydia made no response. But after school was over, when I was going through the children's art boxes, I noticed that all her markers were zipped in her case in her art box.

Lydia never admitted to her false accusations, but quietly took the teacher's suggestion to make sure her markers were put away for the next day.

Transitions

As you certainly know from your training and teaching practice, transitions are difficult for preschoolers. It is hard for them to abandon an activity they are enjoying and go somewhere else. Despite the age-appropriate difficulty preschoolers have going from one place to another, teachers are often required to maintain a developmentally unrealistic level of order and control. The result is scolding and sanctions until both teachers and children feel frustrated and irritated. Once you recognize the need to ease expectations for preschoolers, your approach will change. You can make transitions fun rather than rule driven, and you can rely on S.M.A.R.T. techniques to encourage reluctant children to switch gears more readily. Here we discuss some of the most common transitions that you encounter in preschool teaching.

Home to School

You can make the first days at preschool as easy and pleasant as possible by putting aside rules about parents having to leave after a certain time. In fact, we think it's best to encourage caregivers to stay until their child is comfortable having them leave. It will be obvious to you when children are ready for their parents to leave because they will go nearly the entire morning without having to touch base. When children reach this level of comfort, they will often tell parents, "You can go now!" If parents have to work and can't stay, perhaps you can encourage a family member or friend to fill in. If not, even a one-minute video call, in which children can see their parents' faces and hear their voices, would help. And you would know to be especially attentive to that particular child's feelings about the transition to school.

Even after children are well settled into preschool, the transition from home to school may be difficult, and you will want to do everything possible to make that transition easy and enjoyable. In our preschool, for example, one teacher is always in the vestibule to greet children and parents. Another teacher is in the classroom sitting on the floor ready to welcome. And teachers arrange an immediate fun activity in anticipation of children who may have a hard time.

TEACHER: Colette was crying when her mom handed her to me at drop-off. I told her I was happy to see her, and I could see that she was upset. I said we could go on a little playground tour. I had already hidden small animals around the playground in anticipation that someone would need extra help. While I was carrying her around, I asked if she could see a red bunny on the playground, and then a yellow bird, and a puppy on the bench. Some of the animals were hidden by sitting on something that was the same color, so it took some concentration. The task was interesting and challenging enough that she stopped crying because she was focusing on the little animals and enjoying the care she was getting. Eventually she got down to look for more animals and made no more mention of missing her mom.

When you are helping children separate from parents, you want to remain available to hear feelings of not wanting to leave parents before you engage them in fun activities. You may have been told that children do better when their upset feelings are downplayed, but ignoring them simply drives them underground. Either they are expressed in new ways, or children expend a lot of energy during the school day trying to keep them from surfacing. Acknowledging and Accepting Feelings in a caring relationship means that children feel whole and understood for who they are before they are asked to move on to something else.

TEACHER: Two-year-old Lainey was having a hard time coming inside. I said I knew it was hard to see Mom leave. She looked sad and nodded. I said that it was understandable to miss her mom even while she was having fun at school. We sat together quietly for a few moments, and then I asked if she would like to play with some animals. We went to the sand and went through the animals we found and made the sounds they make. I would hold a dog and meow, and she'd say, "Dogs don't meow, they bark." She thought it was so funny! Then Murray came over and he wanted to go fishing, so I filled little buckets of water with fish and gave them a fishing rod so they could go fishing in their own lake. Lainey was happy and clearly enjoying herself.

Older children who experienced the kindness of teachers when they were transitioning into preschool often imitate this caring response and volunteer to help younger children who are struggling. This is another advantage of having mixed ages in the morning classroom.

> **TEACHER:** I realized that two-year-old Leo was having a hard time taking off his shoes. Before I had a chance to ask him if he needed help, Alina piped in, "Leo, do you need help with your shoes?" He nodded yes, and Alina scooted over to help. I said, "Wow, Alina, that was so kind of you! I wonder how it feels to help Leo with his shoes." She responded, "Good!" and she looked to see what else Leo might need help with. She said, "Leo, can I help hang your backpack?" He giggled and nodded yes. She asked him if he had his water bottle and he showed her where it was. After he had his water bottle, she said, "Look, now you're ready!"

Even two-year-olds can follow your example of caring responses to all their feelings about leaving parents, and become kind and helpful to new children who are transitioning into the classroom.

School to Home

When you make preschool fun and interesting for children, you will be amazed to see how hard it can be for them to leave. As with other upsets, you begin with Acknowledging and Accepting Feelings, and then reassure children that they will be back again.

> **TEACHER:** Today as I was taking Athena to her mom at dismissal after her first day, she let me know that she didn't want to go. When she saw her mom, she ran back inside. I followed and asked what was feeling the hardest. She was able to let me know that she wanted to keep playing, so I said that I knew it was hard to leave and that we would be thinking about her, and how much fun we will have playing tomorrow. Finally, she was able to go with Mom and wave goodbye.

You can sometimes give little take-home presents, like stickers to choose from on the way out, as a good way to bridge home and school. As in most instances of S.M.A.R.T. practice, it's important to remember to Acknowledge and Accept Feelings before offering distractions or solutions to the problem presenting itself. If you slow down and give children space to experience their feelings, they often go on to share more complex, and even contradictory, ones.

TEACHER: Carlyn was having a hard time coming with me to get his backpack to go home. Usually, I would just wait until he stopped saying no, but instead, I asked if I could pick him up to show him something. He agreed. I showed him the snow on the playground which entertained him for a minute, and I said, "OK, now it's time to grab your backpack, and we can come play with the snow again tomorrow." Carlyn excitedly said, "Tomorrow!" and we were able to move forward.

DIRECTOR PEREZ: Yes, that was good help with the transition, but it's important to acknowledge feelings before distracting. When he says, "No," you can ask him if it feels hard to stop playing outside when it's so much fun in the snow. Then doing what you did was terrific. You could also add, "I wonder if we could bring some snow inside and put some in a bucket."

When you have a squirmy two-year old who doesn't want to go home, using S.M.A.R.T. approaches may take creativity and effort, but it's ultimately most rewarding for you and the child. Even though transitions may also be a time when you are tired and feeling as though you need to move forward quickly, you will benefit from the connection between the child's feelings and your feelings, and from the acknowledgement that transitions are difficult as well. You both end up engaged and happy, whereas power struggles just result in upset and alienation.

TEACHER: Two-year-old Turner was having a hard time getting ready to go home. Once the children started throwing their lunch trash away, he got up and ran from the table, pretending to fly away from me instead of putting his outside clothes on. He dove onto the pillows and hid his face. I asked if it was hard to leave when he was having fun. Then I asked if we could fly like birds together? We ran around the classroom like birds until I checked my watch and said, "Wow it's already time to go! Let's get your outside clothes on so you can be ready to fly outside." He flew over to his cubby, and we put on his outside clothes. He asked me to pick him up to fly around the room and we flew around the room again. We saw his mom walk onto the back porch and I asked if he wanted to fly out to Mom, too. He excitedly said yes and put his arms out like wings, and I counted down from three and opened the door. He flew outside to his mom.

When your students don't want to leave, they can become angry at the adult who comes to take them away. You may have to help parents understand to not take it personally when their children don't want to leave with them.

> **TEACHER:** Stan has been having a hard time leaving school lately. More than once he has needed to be carried part of the way by a teacher even when he has a sticker to take home. Yesterday when he yelled, "I don't want to leave!" and started walking in the other direction, I caught up with him and acknowledged that it was hard to leave school when he was having so much fun playing, but that his mommy was here to take him home and that he'd be back tomorrow. Then he started shouting, "I don't like Mommy! I don't like Mommy!" and began running away. I said, "I know you love your mommy, but leaving school is really hard, and I think you feel angry at her for being here to take you home." His mother looked hurt and a little angry, so I said to her in front of Stan, "This is not personal – of course he loves you, it's just hard for him to leave school and you are the one taking him from something he likes, so he is directing his anger at you." His mother looked relieved, smiled at him, and said, "I know you love it at school, and you will be back tomorrow." He got in the car.

Here the teacher helped the mother think about what was behind her son's rejection, which also gave her a good model for how to respond at times at home when he felt angry over restrictions. You can teach parents a lot from the way they see you respond to their children at pick up and drop off.

Play Time to Snack and Lunch Time

Following Smart Love principles, you would never force children to eat snack or lunch. Insisting leads to a power struggle you will lose unless you threaten consequences, and then the enjoyment goes out of eating. Teachers often mistakenly assume that it is their responsibility to make children eat. In reality, when you don't make a big deal of their refusal, children often change their minds and want to eat when they see other children eating. And in any event, if children don't eat at one point in the day, they will normally make up for it later.

In contrast to what you might have learned, it is not your job to make children finish everything in their lunch, and you can accept their choices about what they feel like eating. At the same time, you can think of unpressured ways to get children to rethink their decision.

> **TEACHER:** Today at lunch, Patty said she wasn't hungry and we let her continue to play. She came to the table and said she was really thirsty. I asked her if she wanted to drink her milk or water. She chose her milk. After it was time to get ready to leave, I went to pick her lunch up and she said, "Not yet, I would like some more milk before I go, please." I told her, "Sure, thanks for telling me."

> **DR. PIEPER:** Perhaps you could be more helpful in a positive way to help her eat. For example, "Maybe a doll would like to share some of your lunch, what is your favorite food in your lunch, I hear you say you aren't hungry, but if you were what would be your favorite food?"

When children are playing, they may ignore feelings of hunger. So when it is snack time, you may want to help children realize that their toys will still be there for them if they stop and eat. However, if they refuse, there is no reason to pressure them.

> **TEACHER:** It was snack time and I asked Finley if he was hungry. He said, "Yes, but I want to skip snack because I don't want anyone to touch my toys." I responded, "Sometimes it can feel hard to leave your toys to eat snack. I'm wondering what your body is telling you?" Finley said, "My body is telling me I should eat snack, but I don't know if I want to." I said, "It can be hard to choose! You can keep playing and skip snack today, or you can eat snack now and maybe play with these toys later. What do you think?" Finley thought about it for a moment and said, "I think I'm going to play with these later and eat snack right now."

When adults try forcing children to eat, they usually lose the battle because children can simply refuse. If you don't argue when children tell you they aren't going to eat, you ensure that they won't lose face if they change their minds.

> **TEACHER:** Franklin told me definitely when he arrived this morning that he did not want to have snack at school today. I said, "OK, that's up to you." Then at snack time, I was getting everybody's snack ready, and he overheard the other kids say, "The mystery fruit is honeydew!!!" He came closer and said, "I like honeydew." I asked him if he would like to try it at the table and he said, "Yeah, I want to sit here." He sat down and ate all his snack.

Children should want to eat and enjoy it. Often children who refuse food change their minds when they see other children enjoying the food they rejected.

> **TEACHER:** During extended day, our snacks were apple and cheese with almond butter. I asked Ricky if he wanted to spread some almond butter on his apple, and he said, "No, I don't like that." I asked Andy and he said, "Yes, I love almond butter with apples!" Once he began to eat it, I asked how it tasted and he answered, "Yummy." Ricky then said, "Can I have some on my apple?" I gave him some for his apple and he said, "It is good!"

You never want to taint the pleasure of eating by taking away children's enthusiasm or choice.

Vacations and Holidays

School interruptions such as vacations and holidays can be stressful for children and cause them to feel upset, angry, or sad. This can be hard for you to focus on because you may be looking forward to some time off, and also you may not realize how much children will miss you and school. You want to help children identify their feelings about missing school and offer suggestions for maintaining contact.

TEACHER: Marion looked at me and said, "I will miss you when I go." I responded, "Thanks so much for letting me know. I will miss you when you leave school, too, and I'm always thinking of you." I told her that we still have time to play together today and that she would come back to play again tomorrow. She said, "I think I might miss school tomorrow. I think I'm going to St. Louis." I asked if she was going on a trip with Mom and Dad to vacation there and she said, "Yes." Since she seemed unsure of the facts, I asked her if she wanted me to ask her mom or dad when they were leaving. She said to ask her dad when he picked her up. Dad said they weren't leaving until the following Tuesday, so she would definitely be here tomorrow. I let him know that she was unsure when they were leaving and worried about missing school. I suggested that they could make her a calendar and take pictures on the trip to show everyone when she got back.

On their return from vacation, preschool children often have big reactions to having missed school, but they are almost never aware of the cause of their reactions. In the next example, when a teacher connected a child's angry outburst toward another child to his reaction to having been on vacation, the child immediately abandoned his anger.

TEACHER: Last week when Pat came to school, Ezra and Monty were ready to greet him and he seemed very excited to see his friends. Ezra asked him why he was in Florida for so long and he said he went swimming. I asked if he swam in a pool or the ocean, he said a pool. I helped him change his shoes and then it seemed like out of nowhere, he said to Ezra that he couldn't come over to his house, only Monty could. Ezra replied that then Pat couldn't come over to HIS house either. I said "Pat, sometimes it's hard to come back to school when you've been gone on a vacation, and you might be having some angry feelings about that." I wasn't sure if he even heard me, but I guess he did because he immediately told Ezra that he could come over to his house.

The teacher knew to make this connection because she anticipated that the child might come back to school sensitive about having been away. It is a good rule of thumb to expect some difficult moments with children who have missed school.

Aging Out

It is easy for adults to think children are happy and excited about moving on to the next grade and a new school. But children who have loved their teachers, friends, and school experience in general, and who may feel anxious about what lies ahead, can be sad about the prospect of graduating. And these upset feelings can show themselves far ahead of the actual event. So you want to be alert for these signs, and Acknowledge and Accept the sadness children feel about leaving rather than try to put a positive spin on their feelings.

TEACHER: Arlen spent time with Daisy and me in the sandbox. Inside we worked on a puzzle. At the end of the day, he said, "I'm really going to miss all of you." It was the first time he had ever said anything like that. I said, "Arlen, you are coming back tomorrow and we will all be here. We have many more days to play together."

DR. PIEPER: You don't want to give him the message that it's not OK to feel sad and that he needs to make those feelings go away by thinking of good things such as coming back tomorrow. It would be better to say, "I know you are feeling sad about going to another school next year and we will miss you, too." Then you could add, "But we will have pictures of you, and you can take pictures home of us, and we will find other ways to be in touch."

Depending on their emotional awareness, children vary in the adaptiveness of their approach to aging out, though the same child can also respond differently at different times. Sometimes, as in the previous example, children are able to be in touch with their sad feelings, but at other times they try to manage their feelings by convincing themselves they don't like their teachers or the school, and so there is no need to be upset about leaving. You can help these children understand that there are better and worse ways to handle feelings of leaving. In the next example, the same child who was able to say he would miss his teachers began to tell them he didn't like them at all.

TEACHER: Last week, Arlen started saying "I hate you" to me and the other teachers, and he told us he wants to poop on our heads. Sometimes I said, "Oh, I wonder why," and he might say, "I hate your eyeballs." In general, I'm not quite sure how to react to this. He doesn't say it with any kind of hateful feelings or rage. It's very casual. He has taken a long time to communicate his feelings and he often uses humor to share them. I'm also wondering if it's a reaction to the several weeks of strongly expressing his attachment to the teachers and the school.

DR. PIEPER: Talk to him about different ways of leaving to go to another school. Sometimes he can feel close to his teachers and other children and feel sad. Sometimes he tries to tell himself it's no loss because he doesn't like the school and teachers anyway. Help him understand that he will be happier if he stays with feelings of being attached to everyone even though it means feeling sad.

When children are truly out of touch with their sad or fearful feelings about leaving, they can express these in oppositional behaviors that need Loving Regulation and other S.M.A.R.T. strategies. In the next example, the teacher didn't keep in mind that the child would be aging out of preschool, and so didn't understand the vehemence of his reaction.

TEACHER: Jose enjoyed being back at school from vacation and playing with his friends. When it was time to go home, he had a hard time transitioning. He ran to the corner of the room and kept repeating, "I am not going home!" I reminded him that it seemed like he had a fun time at school, and it can be really hard to leave when you are having fun, but tomorrow he will come back and we can play again. He insisted, "No I won't go," and ran to another corner. He finally put his shoes on and went out the door. I was wondering if you had any advice on ways to make going home easier for Jose.

DR. PIEPER: Tell him you think he really missed being at school when he was on vacation and so now that he's back he wants to keep having fun – but maybe especially so because he will be going to a new school soon, so all the time here is special, and it makes sense he doesn't want to leave. In other words, show him his feelings are entirely understandable even though he still has to go home.

The best thing you can do for children who are graduating from preschool is to be comfortable hearing and accepting their sadness. If you try to reassure students about how wonderful the new school will be, children will feel alone with their unhappy feelings and assume they are wrong to have them.

TEACHER: Bette said, "I've quit smiling." I said, "I wonder why you've quit smiling. Did something happen?" With tears in her eyes, Bette replied, "I'm sad about school." I asked if it was because she was leaving and new kids were starting? Bette nodded. I acknowledged how sad it can feel to leave your school because you're moving. I showed Bette how many days we still have together. I said we'll be thinking of her and that we can send each other messages. Bette kept looking sadly at the calendar. Bette and I sat quietly together, then I asked if she would like to make bubbles (wash hands) with me, and she nodded.

Sometimes children blame their parents for having to leave preschool. When children are angry at parents, remember that they can then worry about whether their anger will cause harm.

TEACHER: Carine is five and has been in the school for several years. This week she had a hard time separating from her mom. Carine cried and asked her teachers to let her call her mom on the phone to make sure she was ok. I said to her, "We know you saw a movie where Cinderella's parents died, and maybe you feel angry at your mom for sending you to a new school when you like it here so much. Perhaps you worry that if you are angry, she won't be OK? But angry feelings never hurt anyone. If you want, we can call your mom, or we could email her a photo or make her a drawing." Carine decided to make her a drawing and she looked relieved and was able to return to playing.

When you realize how hard leaving is, you can help children think about how to keep memories fresh and available. You can also think of the complex layers of feelings your students may be having, and ask questions that prompt reflection. As always, this kind of reflective space can be difficult in a busy school day and in a classroom with many children. But the payoff is enormous in social-emotional health and happiness. Other children see you taking this time, and they feel valued as well because they know you are there if they need it. They also realize that the transition out of preschool is one that it is OK to have feelings about.

Frustrations

Children this age can get unhappy when materials they are working with don't "cooperate." If you feel that you are responsible for fostering adult responses, you may give children the message that they need to toughen up by telling them that "things happen," or they need to just try again or try harder. But when you understand that children's all-powerful self feels a loss when things don't go as planned, and that, in addition, children tend to personify objects so that they feel personally insulted when a toy doesn't "behave," you will be understanding and accepting when they melt down. It is important to Acknowledge and Accept children's upset feelings before suggesting solutions, so that children see that by offering concrete help you are not suggesting that they need to stop feeling upset.

> **TEACHER:** Jade built a tower that fell down. She began to cry. I came over and said, "You worked really hard on the tower. That was upsetting. It's not fun when we work hard on something and it falls down. I understand why you would feel unhappy." Jade nodded sadly. I said, "How do you feel about rebuilding it? Do you need help?" Jade nodded and she and I began to rebuild.

This is a nice example that shows you don't need to stand apart from children and give suggestions, but offer yourself as a partner to fix problems after you've acknowledged the feelings.

Sometimes children who are frustrated don't show their frustration and just give up and walk away, which is a signal to you to offer help. When you notice this, and step in with assistance, you reinforce the important message that rather than give up, it is best to turn to a relationship.

One constant frustration at this preschool age is waiting. In many schools, children spend a lot of time waiting (to talk, use the bathroom, line up to go in or out, for turns) and the assumption is that this is part of social-emotional learning. But waiting patiently is not an age-appropriate competency for preschoolers and, as in other areas, their inability to act more grown up than they are often brings them disapproval and sanctions. Try to keep waiting requirements to a minimum. When children do find it hard to wait, you want to avoid negativity and be creative about supporting and helping them.

> **TEACHER:** Brett asked me to read a story in the cozy corner. A few other children wanted to join. I opened the book and Brett said, "No, I want to play doctor instead." But Nathan, Savannah, Layla and Ayla were all waiting for the story, so I let Brett know that since more children wanted to join the story, I would read this one to everyone before we went to play doctor. He started to look upset about having to wait, so I said, "You know sometimes when I am at the doctor's office, I have to wait for the doctor to see me in the waiting room, so I read while I wait for my appointment." Brett smiled and said, "OK, let's read our story and then I'll take you to our appointment."

What a great idea the teacher had to share her own experience with waiting and what she did to make it more comfortable.

Caring and Respect for the Natural World

All preschools want to encourage young children to develop concern and feelings of responsibility for the environment. Unfortunately, this worthwhile goal is often expressed in the form of lectures, for example, about recycling and not wasting resources, with the result that children are made to feel they are always in danger of doing the wrong thing and ruining the planet. It is much better to you to engage them in active care of plants, for example, so that they have the hands-on experience of nurturing a part of the living world. Not every school has the resources for a garden or greenhouse, but even bringing a few plants into the classroom for them to take care of will be meaningful. They really embrace their responsibility as caretakers.

> **TEACHER:** Turner and I were looking at the new plants. I touched one of the plants because it still had some dirt on it. Turner saw it

and thought I was trying to pull the plant out. He tried to stop me and said, "No! We don't pull out the plants! We have to let them grow!" I thanked him for his good advice and reassured him that I was not going to pull out any of the plants. I said, "I was just trying to clean it, so it could get some sun easier." I thought it was great that Turner does hear us when we talk about our plants, how they grow, and how important they are. He continued to watch me carefully, almost as if he was definitely making sure that I would not pull it out.

Preschoolers may come to school having heard about the perils of climate change and, as children this age do, they may compress time and believe that the worst is about to happen today or tomorrow. While you cannot ignore reality, you can certainly reassure them that climate change is a slow process, which leaves time for people to find solutions. As always, you also want to Acknowledge and Accept that their fearful feelings are very scary.

Diversity, Equity, and Inclusion

D.E.I. is a big focus in preschool because children can come to the classroom bearing prejudices. Due to their age, they accept beliefs picked up from various environments as givens and don't question them. When schools take the approach of formal teaching about prejudice at group time, or lecture children who make a biased remark, children may feel confused and as though they have done something wrong. The best way to convey the value of difference and equality is by modeling positive responses (Model Kindness), giving children another way to think about others without confrontation.

Gender Fluidity

Preschool children often experiment with gender fluidity, and, by responding positively to the child who opts for a new gender expression, you can help other children understand that everyone has the right to choose how they view themselves, and by extension, how they want to be viewed.

TEACHER: Archie has been coming to school the last couple of weeks with two blankets. One he asks us to tie around him like a dress, and the other he has us tie on his head to be his long flowing hair. He was excited this week when he noticed that he and I were both wearing long skirts. He has been asking us to paint his nails with markers and we do. I tell him I love his skirt or earrings and he seems pleased. He tells us he is a girl, and he doesn't want to be called Archie, only Susan.

In this instance, his classmates followed the teachers' lead and were accepting, but Archie's father was not. Teachers initiated a conference to explain to his parents that their disapproval would be harmful. Archie would conclude that his feelings about his gender were unacceptable and needed to be hidden, with the result that he would, in effect, be forced to live a double life as a three-year-old. Parents may also bring their preference for strict gender distinctions into the classroom, and you may have to educate them not to make disparaging comments when another child's appearance is ambiguous.

TEACHER: In the toddler group, Justin has hair past his shoulders. A toddler's gender is usually only apparent based on hair or clothes, so Justin is easily mistaken for a little girl. He's happy with his long hair, but it can be confusing for the other kids. During his first class, Justin grabbed at a toy that Allie was holding, and she said, "She's taking my toy!" Some of the moms were referring to him as a girl as well. One mom became especially angry. She was irritated that he had a boy's name and girl's hair, and felt it was his mom's fault for not making his gender clearer. I said, so all the moms and children could hear, "Actually he's a boy with long hair and his name is Justin, and people wear their hair however they choose just like what clothes they put on."

When you create a classroom culture that accepts all kinds of differences, children feel comfortable telling you about their feelings of gender.

TEACHER: Tilly was showing me her baby doll. I wondered if it was a boy or a girl. She replied, "It's a girl." Eloise said, "Did you know I am a girl and a boy." I said, "Thanks for telling me. I wonder if you want to tell me more about that." Eloise replied, "I am just like Henry, the man in the grocery store. He's a boy and a girl." Before I could reply, Eloise asked about Tilly's doll, and the conversation moved on.

When you communicate freedom of choice, children get the message that gender identifiers can be perceived and imagined in multiple ways.

TEACHER: I overheard Ayla say, "Kai has a pink dress on!" Scarlett and Frieda looked at him and Frieda said, "I think he likes the pink dress." Scarlett said, "Or the purple dress." Ayla said, "Oh yeah, but I never saw him with one on." The girls went toward the dress-up clothes and grabbed dresses to dress up in. I noticed that they were all with Kai afterwards making wands to be fairy princesses. I told them all how I could see they were all fairies with different styled colored dresses having a great time together.

Rather than correct or confront these children, you can just ask them to tell you more about their understanding of themselves.

TEACHER: On Monday Kinsley came to school with a ponytail in her hair and, as the other children came in, we noticed who else had a ponytail. Lettie said, "Randy and Nathan cannot have ponytails because they are boys." Wanda piped in, "Yes, boys can have ponytails if their hair is long enough." I said, "Yes, Wanda, anyone who wants to wear their hair in a ponytail can, it's up to them."

When you model tolerance toward the bending of gender norms, children may copy you and correct each other when they hear others being rigid.

Racial, Ethnic, Class, and Religious Diversity

There are differences between children's life experiences and circumstances that are best addressed directly. The best way to create respect for cultural difference in the classroom is to make many traditions fun, interesting, and personal. For example, you can include different cultural and religious traditions around holidays and inspire children to teach each other about their special traditions. When preschool children act out or speak their prejudices about class differences – for example, if a child doesn't have the same vacations or toys – you can communicate the value of non-discrimination you want children to adopt by stating the rule that everyone is valued for their unique story, and no two people have the same special things. You can make a game of naming special things that each child values to demonstrate that personal value is not about money. As is so often the case, it is always more effective to demonstrate non-discrimination in play.

> **TEACHER:** The other day Easton, Archer, Edmond, and Devon were making a clubhouse with string taped to a chair. Esther came to the table to use the art materials. Archer said, "There's no girls allowed." The other boys followed suit. I said, "Well, it's OK to have a club, but girls can go anywhere in the classroom, just like you can go anywhere." Archer said, "Ok, but only nine girls!" I said, "We don't exclude anyone because they are girls or boys or for any other reason like skin color. If there are more than nine girls they can all come in. You don't have to play with them, but you can't keep them out." Then Easton said, "And teachers can come in my club too." I said, "Thanks Easton. Teachers are allowed everywhere in the classroom also, and I would love to come to your club."

In an earlier section, we noted that when you are teaching with S.M.A.R.T. principles you would not force children to play together. But this example shows that the issue is different if children are excluding others on the basis of gender or skin color. Here the teacher wasn't telling the boys they had to play with Esther, but rather that they couldn't keep her from entering their space. And if they had refused to play with her because of gender, race, or other characteristics, the teacher would have told them neutrally that that was not a reason to exclude a classmate from their play.

Eventually, children will follow your example and learn to recognize exclusion and reject it. When inclusiveness is always a given in classroom activities, children feel something is not right when, as, in the next example, a group is excluded, even from a song.

> **TEACHER:** Henrietta was thinking about a song called "Girls just want to have fun" and asked me to play it on my phone. I played it and Wendy and Lettie were familiar with the song too. "It's from the Trolls movie!" Lettie exclaimed. After dancing to it, Wendy asked, "What about the boys? They just want to have fun too!" I said, "I wonder how we could sing it differently." Wendy said, "We could sing like this … 'Boys just want to have fun!'" Then Lettie added. "How about, 'Everyone just wants to have fun!'" I replied, "That's right, we all just want to have fun … it feels good to have fun together!"

You want to incorporate different ethnicities, religious beliefs, and cultures into the classroom in ways that underline that there is no one way or right answer, and that all viewpoints are respected. You may frequently hear children asserting their version of religious truth or moral values and this is an opportunity to convey that every child has a right to a different opinion. In your explanation, you are not lecturing the children because you are not telling them *what* to think, but rather emphasizing that they each have the right to their own opinion, regardless of what other children think or believe.

> **TEACHER:** Palmer and Teo were at the water table. Palmer said, "You know, when you die, you're not dead. You go to heaven and then you're with God, and everybody who dies is there and God takes care of you." Teo said, "When you die, you're dead." Palmer said, "No, you don't stay dead, you wake up in heaven." Teo said, "You're dead." I said to Palmer, "Teo thinks you're dead after you die, and you think you go to heaven to be with God after you're dead. It sounds like you have different ideas about it. These are subjects that people have very different views about and there is no way to know the answer for sure. You each have your opinion,

which means your own way of thinking about it, and that makes school interesting!" They went on playing together.

You can also show children that differences can be fun and interesting when children are bilingual or their native language is not English. What better way to be introduced to a foreign language than through a playmate's expertise?

TEACHER: Alberto asked for the toy screwdriver while we were outside, so I handed him the toolbox and he said he was going to do some fixing. I asked him if he would like some help, and he said, yes, that I could be his assistant. I helped him fix the stairs, and then he said it was time to fix his "casita." I asked Alberto what part of the casita needed fixing and he said, "The bathroom and kitchen." While we fixed his casita, Andrew came towards us and asked what we were doing. Alberto responded, "We're fixing the casita." Andrew said, "What's a casita?" Alberto replied, "My casita." Andrew didn't understand, so I said, "It's the Spanish word for 'house.'" Andrew said, "I want to help fix the casita!" Alberto handed him a tool and Andrew told Cassie, "I'm fixing the casita!" Cassie, who was with Esther said, "What's that?" And Esther replied, "It's Spanish for house!" Cassie said, "Oh, I did not know that. I just learned a new word today." Andrew said, "Me too!"

Acceptance of diversity extends to preferences. Some children recognize and accept that other children's likes and dislikes can differ from their own, while others can respond to your Modeling Kindness. Differences of taste can range from food to music to what colors or toys children prefer. There are a lot of opportunities throughout the day to be excited by differences of taste and preferences, and you can bring positive attention each time.

TEACHER: We were creating clay hedgehogs when Lettie said to Elsa, "You're making the smile wrong. Smiles don't look like that." I said, "Why can't Elsa make her hedgehog smile any way she wants to? I see she's working really hard on it. Just like you can make your hedgehog smile any way you want to." Elsa chimed in and said, "Anyway, my hedgehog isn't smiling, it's laughing!"

There are books you can read with children to stimulate discussions of the value of respecting differences, but it is important to choose ones that have a positive message rather than ones that make children feel guilty.

SUMMARY

When you use S.M.A.R.T. principles rather than traditional techniques of classroom management (disapproval, time-outs, lectures, rewards, or restriction of privileges), the classroom culture becomes cooperative and caring. You can respond positively, accept all feelings, understand what is age-appropriate behavior, model but not demand politeness, set as few rules as possible, and be creative in anticipating typical preschool problems having to do with toileting, transitions, manifestations of the all-powerful self, social interactions, sharing, bullying, altercations, hurt feelings, and so on. If you find yourself standing apart in the classroom, partner instead with children in play, which makes them accessible for emotional support and to facilitate cooperation. If you're in the children's conversations, you can also help instill respect of differences and other values into classroom activities by modeling them, not by lecturing. Children thrive on this approach, imitate it, and learn that you are a trusted source of keeping the classroom respectful, happy, calm, and healthy, even when frustrations and conflicts arise.

CHAPTER 3

The Smart Love Teacher

Now that you have learned the S.M.A.R.T. approach to social-emotional learning and classroom management, you can see that being a Smart Love teacher benefits both you and your students by establishing a positive, trusting relationship, eliminating the need for most rules and all negativity, and allowing you to help children acquire a positive and inclusive view of themselves and others. You can also see that adopting the S.M.A.R.T. approach requires new and challenging skills.

Because adopting Smart Love practices entails absorbing a lot of new information and applying it accurately, you need and deserve time for learning and mentoring. For this reason we recommend that teachers using Smart Love guidelines get time every week for studying, discussing, and getting input as needed. The rewarding result of all these efforts are children who trust and look up to you, are happy and engaged learners, and who love their entire school experience.

In a Smart Love preschool, or if you are incorporating S.M.A.R.T. practices, you want to have the space to focus on the needs, feelings, likes, dislikes, and interests of individual children. Your goals have to do with making the classroom fun, exciting, welcoming, positive, accepting, and fertile soil for individual learning. Some of these goals are:

- To inspire children to be eager, curious learners;
- To create a culture of cooperation and helpfulness in the classroom;
- To help individual children recover their equilibrium when upset or angry;
- To be available to hear all feelings of each child;
- To establish good relationships and communication with parents;
- To convey curriculum materials through play only in ways that engage children's interest and enthusiasm;
- To manage children's behavior only with Loving Regulation, that is, only positively;
- To advance social-emotional learning by using S.M.A.R.T.

principles and modeling positive social-emotional responses and understanding;

- To respond knowledgeably and constructively to children's dreams and fantasy play;
- To model positive acceptance of differences of race, class, ethnicity, religion, and gender;
- To apply the Smart Love understanding of child development and expect only age-appropriate behavior;
- To know when to recommend that a child needs professional help and/or parents need parent counseling.

Unfortunately, you may find it difficult to reach these goals if your mandate is to create order in transitions and group activities, insist that children play nicely together, enforce polite responses, teach to the test, show children coping mechanisms for extinguishing upset or angry feelings, use rewards to advance desired behavior, and use various forms of discipline (such as time-outs, restriction of privileges, disapproval, and lectures) to manage behavior. You may be evaluated on whether your classroom is orderly and on how well children learn material as measured by state or national tests. This gives you little space to focus on the feelings of individual children, to develop close and trusting relationships with children, to encourage children to learn at their own pace and from activities they choose, or to allow children to be boisterous and enthusiastic. In addition, there are schools that disapprove of fantasy play and have rules for how all materials are to be handled, which leaves teachers little room for pedagogical creativity.

If you are able to use the Smart Love approach, you will engage and partner with your students. This involvement creates an entirely different atmosphere from when teachers stand apart, instruct, give directions, and only occasionally get down on children's level, for example, to read a book or sit in a circle at group time. Some teachers worry that if they participate in children's play, they will lose their authority or be unable to manage the room. But children love, admire, and learn from teachers who join in activities as a way of modeling cooperation, fostering joy, helping with upset feelings, and introducing interesting ideas.

Distinguishing Between Personal and Caregiving Motives

One of the most important skills a Smart Love teacher learns is to distinguish between what we call "personal" and "caregiving" motives. Your goal is to respond always with your caregiving motives, and to change course when you realize you are responding with personal motives.

Caregiving Motives

Your caregiving motives are motives to respond to your students in ways that are developmentally facilitative. This means that you Stay Positive, Model Kindness, and offer individualized, caring, and developmentally appropriate responses that children will benefit from and appreciate. When you respond with caregiving motives, children feel understood, and the fabric of the relationship with you remains consistently positive.

Using caregiving motives, you can respond with understanding even when children are angry at and rejecting of you. In this way, children are helped to understand that though they feel angry when someone does something they don't like, they can still like that person and that person can still like them.

TEACHER: Omar was making loud siren noises. I said, "Kids are still having snack. Let's go outside – that's where you could play this emergency game loudly." Omar said, "I'm going to scream so loud outside." I said, "Great! That's the place to do it." Omar headed toward his coat but then turned back, still running. I put my hands up to stop him. Omar got upset and kept trying to run past me back into the class. I said, "I am stopping you from running in." Omar started to cry and threw himself onto the couch. I stayed near him and said, "I can see how sad you are." Omar said, "I heard a real siren, and you made me miss seeing it out the window." I said, "I'm sorry you missed it. I can understand feeling upset about that." Omar continued to cry and said he wanted to be with a different teacher. I said, "I'm wondering if you are asking for another teacher because you are feeling angry with me." Omar said,

"Yes." I told him, "It's OK for you to be mad at me. I understand why, and I can still help you. You can still be mad at me while I help you." Omar nodded and eventually let me read him a book.

This teacher remained committed to her caregiving motives as she continued to recognize and accept Omar's upset and angry feelings. Personally, she may have felt irritated at his accusations, but irritation did not spill over into her responses.

Personal Motives

Personal motives are motives that reflect how you are feeling rather than how children are feeling and what they need. All teachers have both sets of motives. The skill is to be aware of both, but only to respond to children with caregiving motives. For example, if a child is taking a long time getting ready to leave school and you have other children to help, your personal motive might be irritation and impatience. But your caregiving motive would be to understand that the child has their reasons to be reluctant to go home, and to think of creative and positive ways to help with the transition. Often this distinction isn't recognized and, in fact, teachers are encouraged to share personal feelings with children. For example, a teacher will say to a child who is taking a long time to get ready, "I am feeling frustrated because you are making it really difficult for me to help other children, and I need you to get ready faster." A lot of harm can be done to children when teachers communicate negative personal motives by saying, "I don't like it when you ..." or "It makes me feel angry when you don't ..." When your approval is conditional, children tend to hide behaviors they know you won't like, to feel ashamed of their inability to live up to expectations, to feel angry at, or alienated from you, and, in some cases, to provoke negative responses in order to get attention.

Choosing Caregiving Motives Over Personal Motives

Personal motives can include irritation, dislike, boredom, exhaustion, and anger. However, as long as you respond with caregiving motives and communicate understanding, helpfulness, and acceptance of feelings, the existence of contradictory personal motives will not cause children to feel hurt or alienated. Nonetheless, distinguishing personal and caregiving motives on the fly in the classroom is one of the hardest skills to learn. When a child is creating a distraction or being resistant, it can be difficult not to express irritation or impatience. Yet when you choose caregiving motives, you engender a positive, growth-promoting relationship with your students. One way to facilitate making the correct choice is to ask yourself, "What does this child need from me right now in the way of kindness and understanding." That focus, rather than thinking about how you are feeling, can allow you to respond in a caregiving rather than personal way.

Personal motives include feeling irritated if a project you worked hard to set up doesn't spark children's interest. Caregiving motives would include the recognition that rather than try to force children to involve themselves in a project that doesn't engage them in order to make your life simpler, you need to start over and create a project that has more appeal.

In the next example, a child was rude and rejecting of the teacher. The teacher's personal feelings were that she didn't like being talked to that way, but rather than focus on that reaction, she followed her caregiving motives and helped the child understand why she was angry.

> **TEACHER:** I had to clean up the modeling clay before I could read to Camilla, and I asked if Camilla would like to help. She said no, she wanted me to read right then. I said, "I know it's hard to wait, and I will read to you, but I have to do this first and if you help me, it will go faster." Camilla said, "I don't like you anymore!" I said, "I hear that, but there is a difference between not liking what I'm doing and not liking me. I don't think it's that you don't like me. I think it's that you don't like what I'm doing, but I know you like me." Camilla scowled but waited for me to clean up and then sat in my lap while I read a book.

You can see what a gift the teacher gave Camilla by putting her caregiving motives over her personal motives. She showed Camilla that she could express anger at her for not doing what she wanted, have those feelings understood, and continue to feel the relationship was positive and undamaged, so that she wanted to sit in the teacher's lap and hear a story.

Caregiving motives include remaining positive when children exclude you from a discussion they are having. Personal motives would be to act as though your feelings were hurt and to tell the child she wasn't being "nice." When you respond with caregiving motives to children's rejection, children learn that they have a choice about who they want to relate to at a given moment, and that you will neither ignore that choice nor feel hurt by it.

> **TEACHER:** Neddy was sharing a bad dream in which there were two Neddys. I began to tell Neddy that dreams are stories we tell ourselves for a reason. Before I could go on, Neddy said, "I wasn't talking to you. I was only talking to Lainey." I said, "I'm glad you let me know. It sounds like you'd like to talk only with Lainey right now, and that's fine. I'm here if you change your mind."

As in the next example, if you make the not-uncommon mistake of responding with personal motives, you can realize your error from the way the child responds and switch to caregiving motives.

> **TEACHER:** While creating rainbows with paste and tissue paper, Kendra asked if she could mix in modeling clay. I responded, "Well if we mix them together and can't get the tissue paper out of the clay, we might have to throw it away and we wouldn't have enough for the week." Kendra said, "Well, what if I save some of my clay? That way I wouldn't have to throw it all away if it gets stuck." When Kendra said this I realized I could always make more clay. But I was happy that Kendra had figured that out on her own. I told her I had been wrong and that there was no problem with what she wanted to do because I could always make more modeling clay. I asked, "Do you want to show me what you're making? She showed me the balls of clay wrapped in tissue paper and pasted shut like little packages.

The teacher was thinking of conserving supplies rather than facilitating Kendra's project, but was alerted to that personal motive by Kendra's sensible compromise.

Caregiving motives entail allowing children their own process of learning and not trying to control how much they learn when. Personal motives tell us to want students to advance academically as a group, and to learn what you want to teach when you want to teach it. Caregiving motives mean you want to follow each child's process and enrich their learning based on what makes them feel joy in the learning experience.

S.M.A.R.T. Responses Keep Students Close

You will find that when you use Loving Regulation to manage your students' behavior and S.M.A.R.T. principles to help with their feelings, the children continue to feel connected to you. You will feel much more positive about your work than if you are cast in an authoritarian role. And when children recognize the difference between the way you as a Smart Love teacher respond to them and typical adult responses, they will feel able to share confidences. Equally important, they will know and appreciate how they deserve to be treated.

TEACHER: A group was digging for worms when Skylar and Poppy both grabbed the bin of shovels. Skylar screamed at Poppy, "That's my job! I'm passing out shovels. You're not my friend!" As Skylar raised her arm to throw a shovel, I picked her up and brought her to a bench. Skylar said, "Fine, I'm going home, and Poppy is still not my friend!" I said, "It's OK to have upset feelings because it looked like you really wanted to pass out the shovels, and I also know how much you like to play with Poppy. It felt hard because you both had the same idea at the same time, and she didn't know you wanted to pass out the shovels, and you didn't know she wanted to pass out the shovels. If you go home every time something feels hard, you'll miss all the fun at school like playing with your friends and teachers. Skylar said, "Poppy didn't know because she wasn't thinking my thoughts. I think my thoughts." I said, "That's right!" I asked Sklar if she was ready to talk with Poppy and she said, "Not yet. Let's write down what happened first." We began writing it down, then had fun practicing the letter S in shovels together.

Rather than disapprove of Skylar's impulse to throw the shovel, the teacher spent Time With her and helped her recognize the misunderstanding that had caused the anger. When Skylar felt her feelings Acknowledged and Accepted rather than criticized, her relationship with the teacher was preserved and she was able to be reflective and move on.

SUMMARY

Getting the Support You Need

Teaching children of any age has its challenges, but their immaturity and impulsiveness make two-to-six-year-olds especially difficult. As a preschool teacher, you need mentoring and support if you are to feel confident and competent and enjoy your work without burning out. Unfortunately, many teachers are thrown into their classrooms with management techniques that ignore their natural impulse to connect with kids. Often this means you are expected to teach to the test, and are required to keep children orderly at all times, making you feel like policing and power struggles are just part of everyday experience. The consequence is that your students are unhappy a lot of the time, and you have no good way to forge a close, trusting relationship with them. It is vital if you are learning new skills and putting them into practice that you have the time and support you need to discuss them and ask questions. If your school does not have a culture that allows for this, you might put together a group of other dedicated and interested teachers and staff.

CHAPTER 4

Play-Based Learning That Is
Truly Play-Based

Whether you come from an academically oriented preschool or a play-based one, incorporating aspects of the Smart Love approach of *playful learning* into your curriculum will enhance your students' curiosity and love of learning and make your job easier and more enjoyable. True playful learning builds entirely on children's interests and enthusiasm. By the end of the year, your children will have met and often exceeded academic benchmarks, but through ways that come naturally, and not with worksheets, drilling, testing, formal learning of any kind, or directed play. Parents report with delight that Smart Love students go on to later grades as competent, eager learners.

Academic/Skills-Based Preschools

Academically focused preschools can be identified by how you approach student choice and activity. If you are in one of these preschools, you find that you are expected to direct and manage the students for most of the day, except for designated "recess." In these classrooms, you lead children in a structured way, often based on a prescribed curriculum, and then guide children through a curriculum. There is often an emphasis on teaching the academic skills that children will encounter in elementary school. Usually, much classroom time is devoted to formal learning of letters and sounds, shapes and colors, telling time, and so on.

There is increasing recognition that this approach is not optimal for twos through fives because these ages are not developmentally ready for formal instruction and tend to become bored, dislike school, and develop unpleasant associations to learning.[12] However, many governmental and private funding sources continue to evaluate and fund schools on the basis of test scores, which can make it hard for these schools to become play-based. And the problem with assigning scores to preschoolers is that at this age children's skills are dynamic and changing. Therefore, numbers don't reflect children's progress, and labeling them is ephemeral and counterproductive.

Play-Based Preschools

Play-based programs are now widely considered to be higher quality early childhood education. A curriculum based on play is developmentally more appropriate and reflects the importance of play to a child's intellectual, social, emotional, and physical development.[13] However, "play-based" can have many iterations, from lack of any structure to more structured/directed play classrooms. You may have experienced one of the many schools that call themselves "play-based" that have a combination of free play and "directed play."[14] While many educators refer to "Developmentally Appropriate Practice," in our view you are still too often required to direct learning and focus on meeting "core" standards. You can also be expected to put children in groups and move them from learning center to learning center. We find that this is not true playful learning because it is too often rule-driven and doesn't emerge spontaneously from children's interests. In many of these classrooms, when you must instruct children how to use things in order for them to play, children's creativity is dampened and the process of tinkering (figuring things out themselves) is truncated because you are where they turn for answers. This model discourages exploration and flexibility in both your and your students' experience, encourages hierarchal thinking, and undermines the children's curiosity and their ability to know when they need help and when they don't, all which are crucial characteristics of resilient, diverse learners.

Learning Playfully

High-quality play is the key ingredient to learning inside a Smart Love classroom, or to using Smart Love strategies in whatever environment you find yourself. *For us, "play" is defined as activities that are chosen solely out of interest and for enjoyment.* Certainly, content mastery follows, but it is not the focus. It is not *when* children learn to read or add and subtract that matters, it is whether they love these activities and want to do more of them. Shifts in emphasis of this sort allow your teaching practice to preserve curiosity, love of learning, and enjoyment of others as a primary goal.

Additionally, in a Smart Love classroom there are no required worksheets, and no times when children need to sit and learn content. You will learn to participate in and use children's spontaneous play to foster their learning potential by identifying and introducing cognitive concepts to the play. As a result, children will experience learning as joyful rather than laborious, and as something that they want to do more of. Also, because you put no restrictions on expression and children can choose whom they want to interact with in play, children are free to be their true selves and to bring those whole selves to learning.

There are also preschools in which you are expected to manage materials so they can be played with in one preferred way. Using Smart Love approaches to teaching and classrooms, you encourage creative and imaginative use of materials – a truck can be a hat! You will want to choose materials that are familiar and experience-near, open-ended, and flexible, and which appeal to the children on a variety of intellectual levels. You can enthusiastically endorse children's imaginative reworking of materials and applaud when they think of many ways to arrange them. When you provide open-ended interesting materials and activities, you can successfully build on children's expressed enjoyment to introduce academic content.

> **TEACHER:** Today after the children painted with colored ice cubes, I filled a bin with warm water and asked if they would like to place the ice cubes in the water. I said, "I wonder what will happen to ice after you place it in warm water." Crane shouted, "It's melting and changing color." The children named all the colors they saw before the water turned muddy brown!

Notice how the teacher made sure to ask the children if they wanted to place the ice cubes in water. If they had said no, she would have come up with an activity that interested them. Children can use or change the purpose of any materials in the classroom to suit their creativity and interest. In other words, there is no insistence that things be done a certain way, even the "correct" way, so there is always space for individual input and creativity.

In the next example, a child wanted a song sung "correctly" and the teacher was clear that there is always room for personal variety!

TEACHER: A group of children was singing "Herman the Worm." Manny sang, "Herman ate one grape." Luka said, "No he ate two grapes." Manny said, "No Luka, it's one grape." I said, "Manny, it sounds like Luka is making up his own version of the song." Manny said, "That's not OK." I said, "It sounds like you really like the song the way it is played, so you can sing it that way and Luka can sing it his way. Or we can make up our own song together." Manny said, "Let's make our own song." As I continued singing the song, I asked the children how much food Herman ate, so they all had a chance to add their own numbers to the song. The children had so much fun, and we did a lot of counting!

You can enhance children's creativity and enthusiasm by encouraging them to add their unique approach to any activity from washing hands to playing with toys. This happy experience is not possible when activities are broken down into steps children must follow and materials that must be used "correctly."

TEACHER: Alona had the idea of tracing the robot puzzle. I thought it was interesting how she picked out certain pieces of the robot puzzle to make her own robot. She had many ideas of how to make the robot look different. After she traced the pieces, she decided what details her robots were going to have. Jonah and Winona saw what we were doing and were very interested. After asking if they could join, they each made their own unique robot. The conversation was about shapes, patterns, numbers, and parts of bodies!

You can find ways to build on what children are interested in as a gateway to learning.

TEACHER: Paxton wanted to fill a wheelbarrow with snow. I wondered how many scoops of snow would fill the wheelbarrow. He said it should be 20. I asked who should be the scooper and who should be the counter. Paxton let me know that I should scoop and he would count. When we got to 10, I asked how many more scoops we needed. "Ten more. It needs 20," he replied. "Keep scooping." Paxton counted 20 scoops and said, "It's ready!" I said, "What's the next step?" "Decorations, we're making a snow cake," he replied.

You can see what a difference it would make if Paxton were asked to learn that 10 plus 10 is 20 rather that have that knowledge arise naturally within play he initiated. When you partner with your students in play, you gain the opportunity to teach academic skills children have an appetite to know.

Assessment Under the Radar

At this age formal assessment is notoriously unreliable, both as to future achievement and also as a way to identify where a child is at a particular moment. Moreover, when children know they are being assessed, they begin to focus on their performance and on how teachers evaluate them rather than being inspired by their own curiosity and desire to learn. It follows that in a Smart Love classroom there is no formal testing because it interferes with the true objectives of preschool, which are to enhance children's curiosity, confidence, and love of learning. Testing confronts children with what they don't know, invites invidious comparisons with other children, and suggests that teachers have a predetermined idea of where they should be academically rather than applauding where they are. Also, children's willingness to show what they know varies from day to day and hour to hour depending on how they feel emotionally and physically, so test scores at this age are notoriously inaccurate and non-predictive. Assigning a number to children's knowledge is not only questionable, but also gives the wrong message that children's knowledge is static rather than dynamic and variable. Moreover, when testing is used as a yardstick of preschool success, the curriculum revolves around teaching to the test, and non-academic subjects like art, music, and drama tend to be curtailed. Many schools ask children to demonstrate academic competence ("How much is 2 plus 2?" "What is the first letter in your name?"), and many give the kindergarten readiness test, which confronts children with what they don't know about reading, math, social skills, science, and so on.[15]

In a Smart Love classroom, all benchmarks in reading, math, science, and other subjects are reached in play and evaluated under the radar without focusing children's attention on achievement. Rather than asking children to show you what they know, you want to give your students the opportunity and choice to tell you what inspires them. Parents, influenced by a culture that can get bound up in comparing children, often come to you with their anxieties about testing and assessment. When talking to parents, you want to emphasize the progress a child is making – i.e., when your child first came she was having trouble recognizing her written name, and now she knows it. This kind of progress reporting will help parents recognize what their child is learning in concrete and individualized ways.

> **TEACHER:** Joshua's parents were concerned when they enrolled their child in the Smart Love Preschool that he would struggle with learning colors, numbers, and letters if all he did was play. After Joshua had been in the preschool for only two months, his parents remarked how amazing it was that he knew all of his classmates' names, was already interested in beginning letter sounds and the letters of his name, had tried new foods during lunch, counted and told them how many toy cars were in the classroom, and had begun autonomously to choose to do many of the optional projects. They also noticed he seemed happier overall and was even getting along better with his sibling.

It can take a leap of faith to trust that children will assimilate the necessary skills from interest and enthusiasm in play, but it turns out that this is exactly how children learn best.

Group Projects

Much of your training or teaching experience may have been about introducing concepts and skills to children who have been gathered together in groups. Typically, this can be frustrating and difficult because children this age often resist the assumption that they want to learn the same thing together at one time, and they can be wiggly and inattentive. In Smart Love pedagogy, you would design group projects in what's called the "magic basket" that involves a range of activities, including science experiments and creative arts and games that children find intrinsically appealing. There is no requirement that children participate, which distinguishes these projects from directed learning. Rather, in designing these, you put the effort into making the magic basket projects attractive to as many children as possible.

In the next example, a teacher got children interested in geography and writing by connecting the activity to their experiences. There was no pressure to participate, and the children worked together because the project interested them.

> **TEACHER:** I got children interested in our map of the Great Lakes region by asking if anyone wanted to write the names of states or lakes. We discussed the places and where people had been – Michigan, Lake Michigan, Wisconsin, Indiana, etc. – and I thought this could be a good incentive for the kids to label. Gerry wanted to write, and he said he's been to upstate New York to visit family, so he wanted to label New York. He wrote it out very carefully, copying the printed name, and wanted to write more. He had also been to Michigan, so he did that next. I asked if he wanted to write Illinois, which is the state we all live in, and he said yes. I told him these were some very long state names and he seemed proud. Elsa was also interested in writing. When I would tell them the names, different kids would say things about each state – Larry's dad had been to New York, George's dad was born in Minnesota, Allie had been to Indiana, Erica's mom had been to Canada. I wasn't sure how this activity would go over, but the children all worked on it together and enjoyed it.

In your classroom, children can start their day wondering what the magic basket activity will be. Here a group forms around a fun activity identifying and matching colors.

TEACHER: I was playing a guessing game with Emory and Amanda with the colorful gummy bears. Emory set up the game, and Amanda and I took turns picking a cup to see if we got the same color as the toy gummy. After this, Emory had us match the bears by using the pattern pieces. We noticed after we went through them that there weren't any purple circles to make a pattern as a bear. Amanda decided that it would be a fun idea to make our own pattern board so we got paper, scissors, and markers. Each child had their own ideas on making their pattern.

Older children often ask if they can create a magic basket project for the group, which is another way for children to lead and be sensitive to other children's interests. When you model leadership in positive ways that children emulate, children develop leadership skills that promote genuine community and harmony.

TEACHER: We were playing school outside, and Kate wanted to be the teacher. She stood up but didn't know how to start so I asked, "What are we doing today, teacher?" And she responded with a big smile, "Today for magic basket we are going to do an experiment with ice and paint and water and then we're going to mix it." She kept talking as the teacher and the others were excited and joined in.

Traditionally, if children are restive or uninterested in a project they may be disapproved of and made to focus or isolate. Sometimes it happens that you put a lot of effort into developing projects you think children will like, but if children aren't interested, rather than pressure them to stick with the project, you Stay Positive, go back to the drawing board and come up with something else.

TEACHER: Our magic basket project was to use beads in patterns to make necklaces. Leo started the project but almost immediately became diverted and began throwing beads. I showed him how to slide them, but he lost interest in that approach. So I brought the tea set over and showed Leo that we could fill different cups with beads and pour them into other cups. He was more interested and kept bringing different size cups and bowls over to pour his beads in. He came up with a system where he would pour beads into my dish, and I would pour beads into another dish, and he would keep going with the cycle. I showed him how we could sweep up the beads if they missed the bowl or cup and fell out onto the floor. I knew that Leo loved to transfer objects, so it was a positive way to redirect him from the original project so he would enjoy the beads in his own way.

Sometimes when children reject a project, you may conclude that they don't realize they would like it, and you can gently and in an unpressured way try to involve them.

TEACHER: We set up a magic basket activity of printed sheets of snowflakes and mittens for the children to decorate. Leona and Oscar had begun the activity when I noticed Emilio observing. He often doesn't want to do art activities and prefers to play (which is fine), but I asked him if he would like to try. He said, "No," but kept observing. I said, "I can show you how to make a circle stamp." I demonstrated and he came closer. I asked him what color I should do next, and if he would like to try, and he said, "Yes." He made a few tries with the dot marker and was excited to see that the stamp was a circle and that he had made it himself.

You can always be on the lookout for ways to inject learning into group projects children have spontaneously created and are showing interest in. In the next example, the teacher was able to turn a project with a slightly negative cast into a fun learning opportunity.

TEACHER: While the children were playing in the block area, Tristen took the lead on one of his ideas for construction. He led

Waylan, Easton, and Mike in wrapping a gourd with tape. He explained that they would hang the gourd by the countertop, so if someone came to play under the countertop, they would bang their head! He laughed. The kids had a lot of fun wrapping the tape around the gourd. I got them interested in learning about the attributes of their gourd. We wondered about the weight, the width, and whether it could stay there for a long time. At the beginning of their construction, it seemed as though it would not turn into constructive play, but after the project got underway, the original purpose turned fun and positive.

The teacher never told the boys that it wasn't nice to set up a trap for others to bang their heads on, but rather used Loving Regulation to divert the play into something constructive and educational.

Sometimes group projects may continue for days or weeks, but the duration and the content of the teaching should always depend on children's continued interest and creative expansion of the basic idea.

TEACHER: We were preparing to open another classroom. Furniture deliveries meant that lots of big boxes had been accumulating. Last week we brought the children to the new classroom so they could have a look at the boxes. We asked them what they thought we should do with all the boxes. Some suggestions were to make a rocket ship, a pirate ship, a house, a house with a hiding place, a train, a robot, a ninja, a lion, and a zebra. After recording these wonderful ideas, we asked what they thought they needed in order to create their house, rocket ship, etc. Kids suggested things like paint, doors, windows, scissors, tape. The next day we prepared the things they had suggested and worked with them to carry out their plans. Kids drew doors and windows for us to cut out. They worked to complete these projects in small groups over a few weeks. We remained available to guide, organize, and add a framework to the kids' creativity, excitement and interest. We allotted weeks for this project to allow children the chance to think about their ideas. They could decide, "I thought one window was enough yesterday, but now I see I need a door so people can get inside the robot I am creating." Kids were also anxious to share their skills and ideas with each other: "Here, I'll draw gears in your rocket ship like the ones on my train. How many do you want?" "Seven. OK, let's count 1, 2, 3 … and then one more, OK, 8."

You will work hard to facilitate children's industry, but you don't want to take over and tell them what to do. Unobtrusive guidance of this kind can take patience, and if group dynamics begin to deteriorate you can use any of your S.M.A.R.T. practices to help resolve things in a positive way, being sure to acknowledge feelings and go from there.

No Scaffolding/No Limits on Help

In preschool education, "scaffolding" means removing help when children demonstrate competence. It is a nearly universal approach to learning. The problem with scaffolding is that it teaches children that learning a skill leads to a form of deprivation and it overlooks their normal emotional needs for periodic involvement with teachers in the form of help.

As a teacher practicing the Smart Love approach, you would not use scaffolding. Just as you saw in the section in which children asked for help with personal issues such as washing their hands, in this section you will see that the same positive helpful response applies when children ask for help with projects and other forms of academic learning. Children learn that they never have to feel ashamed for wanting help, even when they are aware that if forced they might be able to do the thing themselves. Offering help without restrictions energizes children and makes them confident and independent learners who are motivated to help others. It does not lead to dependence and incapacity as some fear. You will discover that when you Model Kindness and offer help with an activity without qualifications (you never say, "I think you could do that yourself"), children build on that assistance to go forward happily learning.

> **TEACHER:** Frieda has been working on the water animal puzzle. She uses the picture of the puzzle as a guide. When she is stuck and getting frustrated, she will ask for help. Usually, it's just a question of moving the piece to fit in the spot, something I know she can do. I always say, "Sure," and show her how to fit the piece into the puzzle and then ask her if she'd like to try. She will try, and smiles happily as she gets the piece to fit and says, "I did it!" She has been working on the same puzzle since last week.

Sometimes children who have had high standards imposed on them ask for help with a project because they are afraid they won't be able to get something right. While you never refuse to help, you can also take a moment to help children reframe their thinking about success and failure. That is, without telling children that they can do it themselves, you may help them understand that they actually want to try, but that they hesitate because they are afraid their effort won't be good enough to meet the expectations they have been exposed to.

> **TEACHER:** Lionel wanted to make an airplane out of construction paper but asked me to do it for him. I said, "Maybe you are worried that it won't come out just perfectly?" Lionel replied, "Yes, that's what I'm worried about." I said, "How great that you could realize that, but, you know, at school, any way you try it is always OK." Lionel began cutting and stopped and said it wasn't right. I talked with him about what he wanted it to look like and what was bothering him. I said, "School is a place to try things, and you can try to make a plan lots of times and that's OK. You can try it again if you don't like how it goes the first time." Lionel took this to heart and was able to make a plane he was happy with.

One instance in which you don't want to offer help is when children are struggling with a problem that has arisen in their project but yet they remain engaged and interested. To help a struggling but trying child get the right answer gives the message that the right answer is more important than an unsuccessful but sustained effort. You can step in and offer help when children are at an impasse, however. This teaches the important lesson that asking for help is just a component of learning and emphasizes the comforting nature of the relationship with you.

> **TEACHER:** I was doing rainbow pompom art with Jordyn and Pat but the glue on Jordyn's Q-tip was sticking to everything. She started to feel upset. We had a good conversation about how frustrating it feels when something like that happens. We talked about how we could make it feel better. The conclusion was that we could use teamwork. I helped keep the pompoms in place while Jordyn put the glue on. The girls finished their pompom art feeling happy and excited to take it home.

You can also volunteer to help when a child is getting increasingly upset or angry doing a project, which is an indication that your assistance is needed.

> **TEACHER:** Thomas was trying to cut with a pair of scissors that weren't working for him. I saw him becoming visibly upset and suggested that he try another pair, but he wouldn't hear of it and continued to work angrily with the ones he had. I said, "It's good to want to do things by yourself, but if you are getting unhappy it's great to ask for help. Sometimes it can be hard to ask when you want to make it work yourself, but with help we can get it done together." He accepted another pair of scissors and kept working.

Whether to offer help is one of those crucial decisions you have to make every day. The rule of thumb is this:

- Offer help every time you are asked.
- Don't offer help if a child is struggling but positively engaged.
- Offer help unasked if a child is clearly struggling and unhappy and frustrated.

Praise for Effort, Not Success

In keeping with the principle that learning should be fun, interesting, creative, and never pressured, you want to avoid incentives such as praise or rewards for accomplishments (gold star, child of the day), because the emphasis should always be on effort rather than results. Incentives are coercive and also devalue the activity being rewarded. Otherwise, why would they be necessary? When praise or rewards are given for the right answer, children become afraid they will fail and lose the positive response. Instead, you want to praise a good effort whether it is correct or not. Unfortunately, even when they commend effort along the way, many preschools continue to praise children for correct answers or offer some kind of incentives.

Sometimes you are presented with errors that do need to be addressed, and so when children make a mistake, you want to find ways to encourage and support them diplomatically without any direct confrontation about their error.

> **TEACHER:** Pedro wanted to write "Rescue Plane" on his plane. I helped him sound it out. He was waiting for me to say whether the letters were accurate. They weren't, but he was employing inventive spelling which is a wonderful phase in developing literacy. I said, "Oh yeah, that's right! It is a "q" sound (for res-cue). Let's do it together." Pedro became anxious about getting it right. I said, "You are making great guesses. Let's look at the way it's spelled on our toy rescue truck." Pedro looked pleased when I said he was doing a great job at figuring out letter sounds.

The goal is to inspire children to keep trying and thinking, and not cause them to feel inadequate by giving or withholding praise or incentives. This approach builds persistence without any fear of failure – trying is learning – and children will continue to persist as long as they are focused on effort rather than success. In the next example the teacher got the child to rethink her answer without ever correcting her.

> **TEACHER:** Today Kali brought up that 200 plus 200 was 400. She said, "And 300 plus 300 is 600!" I responded, "Oh, I see, 300

plus 300 equals 600." She said, "Mhmm, it's easy. You just add the hundreds." I said, "Ahhh. If 300 plus 300 is 600, I wonder what 400 plus 400 is." Kali said, "That's 800." I said, "Wow, 800! That's a big number. Hmmm, I wonder what 800 plus 800 would be." Kali said, "Uhhh hold on, give me a second." She began counting with her fingers. She announced, "15!" I responded, "Oh, 15, OK, let's see." I pulled out my hands and began to count up to eight, then another eight more numbers until I got to 16 and Kali said, "16!" She said, "So 800 plus 800 is 1600!" Her eyes widened and she said, "That's a huge number!"

It can be hard to resist giving students the correct answer when they make a mistake, but your correction can make them feel inadequate and as though they need to look to you for answers. If, as in the above example, you can find a way to help them correct themselves, they will both learn and also maintain their enthusiasm and self-confidence.

Learning Timetables

In contrast to the traditional program of trying to bring an entire class along the same learning curve, the Smart Love emphasis is always on allowing each child to have their own process of learning. Concerns with group achievement are usually about meeting artificial standards for success or to please sources of external funding. In reality, children this age vary widely in the pace of their development, and this has little or nothing to do with their future academic success. You will want to encourage each child's progress, regardless of how that relates to the rest of the class.

TEACHER: Elena went up to a box Austin was working on and scribbled on the top of it. Austin said, "Hey, what did you do that for?" Elena answered, "I was just writing your name so that everyone would know it's yours." Austin said, "That's not how my name looks!" I said, "That's how Elena writes your name. I think she's trying to help. Would you like to show her how you write your name?" Austin said, "Yeah." The two stood close together and

> Austin wrote his name correctly. Elena exclaimed, "Hey, you have an 'N' in your name like me!" Austin agreed, "Yeah!"

Many children enter preschool convinced that they have to perform, comply, cooperate, and behave well in order to be liked. You want to make every effort to Model Kindness and show children the same care and support regardless of their state of mind, success at a project, level of achievement, or social graces. This is another reason not to use incentives (gold stars, special privileges, crowns), which convey the message that you like children better when they perform well.

It is a lifelong gift to show children that they can be loved just for themselves. The following is an example of the progress made by a child who, when he first started, was convinced he had to do well in order to be cared about.

> **TEACHER:** I was building with magnetic tiles and using the Lego people with Quincy. He completed what he was building and said, "Look!" I said, "Wow, Quincy, you worked so hard on your building. Are those rooms for all your people?" He said, "Yeah … do you like it when I build?" I responded, "Do you like to build with the magnetic tiles, Quincy?" He replied, "Yeah, do you like me when I build?" I responded, "Quincy, I like you no matter what you do!" He said, "You'll like me no matter what?" I assured him by saying firmly, "Quincy, I will always like you no matter what, and everyone else should too." He hugged me and wanted to keep building.

When children correct other children for mistakes, you can step in to protect the other child's right to their own process, but without shaming or criticizing the child doing the correcting.

> **TEACHER:** Lou and Colter were rhyming together. Lou started rhyming cat, hat, bat and Colter started rhyming with lightning, blightning, hightning (mostly made-up words after lightning). Lou said, "Colter, that's just making a pattern not rhyming." Colter

replied, "I know how to rhyme. I rhyme all the time." This made all three of us laugh because his last sentence rhymed. I said, "You are really rhyming, Colter! And Lou, you're right, that was a pattern of the words Colter was using to rhyme, since they all ended with the "ing" sound. But it was a pattern and rhyming so it was a rhyming pattern! Patterns can be made of all kinds of different things, for example, made-up words that start with "T.""

One advantage of having mixed ages in the morning session is that children accept that others have different levels of skills and understanding, and they can both teach and learn.

Subject Areas

One of the reasons for the inappropriate preschool focus on structured academic learning is the belief that children will not learn enough through play. Even play-based schools have absorbed this misconception and mix free play with directed play. Directed play is not true play because although play materials are involved, children are told what to do with them and are expected to comply. The Smart Love approach of learning playfully builds entirely on children's interests. The key is that you participate in the play and introduce learning content where appropriate, but children never feel pressured or forced.

Writing

Writing is usually taught from the board or from worksheets. Children are asked to copy letters, but these have no meaning for them as they can't do anything with them or get anything out of them. As a result, many children hate writing exercises and have no desire to pursue writing in their free time. If you follow Smart Love practices, your students learn writing in order to facilitate their play, and use it to communicate in new and interesting ways. From the beginning they see writing as augmenting play, and not as taking away from the enjoyment they could be having elsewhere.

TEACHER: Cecelia brought over the play birthday cake and told me it was my birthday. I made a wish and blew out the candles.

Cecelia wanted me to cut out a piece and pick which topping I would like. Tom asked if he could have a piece, too. Cecelia said, of course. Then they decided to have a party and make invitations! With a little help from me, they both wrote invitations.

You will find that children love making lists because they facilitate interactions with other children. In the process they also practice writing skills, but most importantly they experience this new expertise as chosen rather than imposed.

TEACHER: Amber helped with a snack list to give everyone a check mark when they had their snack. Amber was very engaged making sure who had already gotten snack and who still needed it. This was also a fun way for Heidi and Amber to connect because Heidi noticed Amber's list and decided that she wanted to make a list of everyone's favorite colors. She wrote down her classmates and some of her family on the list.

While the teacher started the list, Amber became excited to help write it. If writing the list had been a requirement, she wouldn't have been so enthusiastic, and Heidi wouldn't have voluntarily joined in to make her own.

Reading

Reading is another subject that is often taught in worksheets or very simple (and boring) readers. Too often, children get little pleasure from this instruction and then don't think to read for fun. Moreover, whereas children used to learn to read in first grade, now preschoolers are expected to show "reading readiness" and kindergarten students to show "reading skills." Children are not developing any faster than they were in the past, they are simply being inappropriately pressured. Some kindergarten students are able to learn to read, but others aren't. The ones that don't read enter first grade and are put in remedial classes, which gives them the completely wrong sense that they are inadequate, when all they need is the time to learn that students had available in prior times.

When you avoid formal worksheets and universal instruction, you can individualize how you help children with reading. Some children respond well to phonics, others to seeing letters and words and some to a mixture of both. Most important is that your students want to read because they perceive that words convey something important to them. For this reason, you will usually start with children's own names and those of their classmates.

TEACHER: Jerry was looking at the name tags we use during snack. He went through each one and was able to correctly identify them. He was even able to recognize who was missing a name tag. He found his own name first and picked out Andrew's and even said Andrew's first and last name when he found it. He continued to correctly name each one as he picked it up.

You can play reading games with sticky notes. You can write a clue or instruction ("Look up at the sky!") and put it first on your shirt. Then the children pick the one they want and "read it" by putting the messages on their own shirts. Children love these playful games and are eager to read the words because they are connected to active play. Many schools give children lists of words to memorize, which takes all the fun out of reading. Using your own ingenuity and creativity with language will be what inspires your students the most.

Math

Like writing, arithmetic is usually presented in worksheets and, similarly, the problem is that children see no connection with anything they care about. Many children's games and interests involve counting, adding, subtraction, multiplying, and dividing – and all you have to do is look for opportunities to be positive and facilitative. If you do this in engaging ways, children can easily do mental math involving quantities and symbols.

TEACHER: Susan was sharing the birth story of her new cousin. When she began the names of her cousin's older sisters, I put my fingers up to count and said, "Wait, I think they added a new family member to their family, I wonder how many kids are in the family now." Susan gave each finger a name assigning the biggest finger to the oldest girl's name and the pinky finger to the baby. She counted my four fingers and said there are four kids in that family. Susan told me to put up three fingers on my other hand for another family of cousins, again assigning fingers to names. I said, "There are four kids in one family and three kids in the other family, I wonder how many kids that makes all together." Susan counted my seven fingers and exclaimed, "Four and three is seven cousins all together!"

Children constantly invent fun ways to learn and use counting, and you can build on their enthusiasm. When you partner with children in play, you never have to quiz them to demonstrate their mathematical skills, but instead you can initiate counting and see how they respond.

> **TEACHER:** Rhett said he was "marinating" something with modeling clay. I asked him how long it took to marinate, and he said five minutes. He asked me to start a timer for five minutes. After about two minutes, he came back to check. We looked at the timer and I said, "If we set it for five minutes and two minutes are gone, I wonder how many minutes are left?" He held out five fingers and we took two away. "Three!" We both observed the timer together as the time got smaller and smaller. He was so fascinated with watching the numbers change from three, two, one, and then a number disappeared when it got into the seconds. We talked about how a minute has 60 seconds, and now the seconds were counting down. I let him know that when the timer gets down to zero it will make a sound to let him know that the marinade is ready.

You will find many opportunities to inject adding and subtracting into children's play.

> **TEACHER:** Jeri said she wanted to make up her own game with hoops. I wondered how many hoops she would need for her game. She said six. As I handed her the hoops I counted, "One, two, three, wait how many do you need?" Jeri said, "Six," I said, "So I wonder how many more we need, since we have three right here." Jeri counted, "One, two, three hoops" then, using her fingers counted "Four, five, six. We need three more hoops. I just added three plus three." "You sure did, how did that feel?" "It felt fun!" exclaimed Jeri.

You can build fun into counting by turning it into a game.

TEACHER: Lonnie asked me to play a number game. I said, "I wonder what game you would like to play." He said, "You have to guess what number I'm thinking of." I said, "Sure! That sounds like fun!" Lonnie said, "OK, guess!" I guessed a random number and he said, "No, that's not it!" After two more guesses I said, "Hmmm, I wonder if you can give me a hint?" He responded, "It's in between one and ten and rhymes with tree!" I guessed three, and he said, "That's right!" I asked if it was my turn and he said yes. I said, "I'm thinking of a number in between one and ten that rhymes with freight." Lonnie and Roger shouted, "Eight!" We continued to play this game and Adam jumped in as well. We found words that rhyme with all the numbers between one and fifteen.

When you count for fun with younger children, they will often join in.

TEACHER: I joined two-year old Robin in the sandbox, and together we made cupcakes. I put my cupcake in the oven and counted to 20 while my cupcake baked. I said to Robin, "I wonder if you would like to count with me, and we counted together. After my cupcake was baked, she placed her cupcake in the oven and asked me if I would count with her again.

Multifaceted learning concepts like comparison and measuring are always most robust and assimilated when they arise out of spontaneous play rather than from directed play or lessons.

TEACHER: Diego was playing with the animals by himself. I said, "Wow I see so many animals over here." Diego responded, "Yeah I'm collecting all of the cats." I said, "I see. We have some lions and some tigers ..." and he said, "and some cheetahs and leopards." Then he took out a lizard and said, "This one has a long tail!" and pulled the tail so it could extend. I said, "Ooh that is really long! I wonder if it's longer than the lion's tail." He held it next to the lion's tail and compared the two. He said, "Yeah, it's a lot longer than the lion's tail. It's as long as the lion." He pulled out an elephant and put the lizard next to it to compare. He said, "It's longer than the elephant's tail too. It's longer than its trunk." I said, "Wow, yeah, I can see that." He pulled out a giraffe and said, "Let's see if it's longer than the giraffe's neck." I said, "Yeah let's find out." We got the tape measure and compared the two.

Allowing room for the natural curiosity of a child to introduce a lesson about comparing is just one of the many opportunities that flow from play. This is another example of the advantage of partnering with children in play rather than standing apart.

Colors

Preschool children need to learn their colors, but there is no reason to make them study or to test them.

> **TEACHER:** Two-year old Lennie saw the purple flowers planted outside and was pointing at them. I said, "Wow! I see the flowers, Lennie. I wonder what color they are," and he said, "Purple!" I wondered if we could spy any other purple plants in the backyard. He got up and ran to another pot of purple flowers and continued to run to all the purple flowers in the backyard. After this we did the same with the yellow flowers.

Colors are best learned in discovery games as they appear in the real world.

The Arts

Artistic efforts enhance creativity, build relationships, and give children a different kind of enjoyment. Drawing is also good preparation for writing. If given the opportunity, children love to make up stories, draw, read books, and put on plays. Putting on a play isn't just about writing it, but also learning to count seats, tickets, make signs, etc. Ideas flow and expand as the "production" unfolds, often based on experiences the children bring. It is truly unfortunate that due to the inappropriate emphasis on academic objectives in preschool and kindergarten, the arts curriculum in many schools has been curtailed. Often children have no opportunity to pursue drama, dancing, or singing. In a Smart Love inspired preschool, we encourage you to bring all of the arts into your classroom day. Bringing instruments out is a simple way to engage kids in the physical and emotional power of music, and one favorite activity is to build a stage and perform various kinds of shows.

> **TEACHER:** Joy was playing with our class instruments and asked if I could help build stage for a show. Making a stage for children to sing and dance on is something we do often, so I was trying to think of ways to expand on this project. After we set the stage, I asked Joy if there was anything else she wanted for her show and she said, "We need a place for the audience!" We set up chairs all around the stage and a couple of children got excited and began to sit around her. I asked her if it was going to be a musical show since she was playing the instruments, and she said yes, so we put the piano on the stage. She said she wanted to play the instruments, but she also wanted a singer and a dancer. We asked some of the other children if they would like to sing or dance on Joy's stage. While most of the children wanted to sit in the chairs as the audience, Esther let Joy know that she would like to be the dancer. Together they performed for their audience of me, another teacher, and three other children. I let Joy know that I recognized how hard she worked on her show and how much we all enjoyed it.

You can let children develop their confidence in the classroom with artistic projects, but you can also encourage the students to bring artistic interests from home.

> **TEACHER:** Wanda mentioned to me that she was taking a violin class and said she would love to show me what she knows. I said, "What a great idea!" And today she brought her violin and was

eager to play it for me and the other children. She gave us a lesson on what each string was called and how they sound.

Art projects emphasize children's creativity – i.e., no paint by numbers. Even when you have a project in mind, you can let the children know that whatever materials are introduced can be explored and manipulated in any way.

Science

The STEM[16] emphasis in the upper grades has made its way down to preschool and kindergarten. Children are formally introduced to STEM topics and sometimes even tested on them. However, as the long-term goal is to introduce children to STEM in ways that will ignite their interest and imagination, you can do much more for them by bringing science and technology in through the medium of play. For example, children love watching balls roll, which gives you many opportunities to introduce concepts of gravity and acceleration.

> **TEACHER:** Today Stef asked me to make a ball out of modeling clay so he could watch it go down all the ramps. We made a ball, and I asked him what he thought would happen if we made a smaller ball. He was so excited to see how much faster it went than the larger one. We spoke about how things that are lighter move faster than heavier ones because there is less resistance!

It was Stef's idea to make the ball go down the ramps. The teacher just built on his interest to introduce the concept of resistance.

Learning about biology is embraced when it arises from children's interests rather than formal instruction. Children love making books about animals and learning about them.

> **TEACHER:** The children have been interested in the difference between African and Asian elephants. We had a lot of fun making elephant books, and so much conversation came up. We found

that elephants like to eat grass, fruits, and they even like bananas. Someone asked if elephants have noses. Another child said that they have a long trunk as a nose, and Lettie said, "Yea! It's like the elephants have a really long straw attached to their bodies!"

While you can try to interest children in the facts of biology by introducing ideas like the difference between African and Asian elephants, the important thing is that your project ignite their enthusiasm as it did in this example. You always want to have another idea at the ready if the first one doesn't light a spark.

Research

In any of the subject areas, you can always find ways to introduce the concept of looking things up or finding out more. Research is most enthusiastically embraced when children are not assigned to look things up but rather encouraged to follow what interests them. You can inspire children to want to know more by asking about something integral to the play. This applies even to the youngest ones.

TEACHER: Two-year-olds Leo and Maia were playing magnetic sticks and balls. Leo let me know that one of them needed a repair by saying "broken" and pointing at the magnetic handle. Maia also noticed that it needed a repair, so I grabbed some tape to see if we could fix it and still use it. I said, "Hmmm … I wonder if the magnet will still work inside with the tape over it." We found out that it would still stick to things. Maia searched for things in the classroom that were magnetic. Leo found that both cymbals would stick onto the magnetic handle.

As in this example, play is the best pathway to research because it stimulates children's curiosity and can lead to genuine motivation for investigation.

SUMMARY

Playful learning is different in a Smart Love-inspired teaching practice because it builds entirely on each child's interests. There are no formal worksheets, testing, learning centers for children to rotate through in groups, rewards, or directed play that is solely determined by teachers. You will find that the atmosphere of your whole classroom becomes more relaxed and joyous, and yet your children continue to learn writing, reading, and subject areas. Because you join children in play and use that opportunity to introduce the learning content in a fun way that children enjoy and amplify, you feel much greater connection with them. Children get help when requested and you prioritize their effort over immediate right answers. When you suggest a project and children don't seem interested, you know to simply offer another idea. Using these simple viewpoints in your practice, you preserve and enhance creativity, curiosity, and enthusiasm.

CHAPTER 5

Responding Knowledgeably and Helpfully to Dreams and Fantasy Play

Children's imaginative life is hugely important to their everyday experience of themselves and others and is readily accessible to you through dreams and fantasy play. As a teacher, you have an opportunity to show children how to connect their dreams and fantasy play to underlying concerns and wishes. You can also help your students know themselves more accurately, thoroughly, and realistically. One obvious difference between dreams and fantasy play is that dreams have already occurred, and are therefore circumscribed, whereas fantasy play is ongoing and interactive.

Fantasy Play

Fantasy play is a favored activity in preschool, but typically fantasy play is ignored as "just kids playing." The result is that teachers lose the opportunity to help children understand the important communications being expressed. Play is not only about having fun, but is also a coded message of what is on children's minds or just below the surface. When you understand and respond accurately to these communications, you aid children in the understanding of their minds, and also the value of turning to relationships for help with their feelings.

Helping Children Understand Their Fantasy Play

In general, the social-emotional benefits of fantasy play are that when you help children understand why they are acting out a particular scenario, you allow them to get in touch with feelings that are affecting them, but that they would otherwise be unaware of. Children can feel sad, angry, upset, frightened, jealous, or anxious, but they rarely know why. It is an exceptional child under 10 who can say, "I'm really out of sorts this morning because my parents are paying too much attention to my little sister." Making sense of the feelings being expressed in fantasy play through the relationship with a caring teacher empowers children and also prevents them from feeling helpless and victimized when feelings are unpleasant.

In order to make sense of fantasy play, it helps to know what is going on in a child's life outside of school, which is why partnerships with parents are important. In the following example, a child was driven to play dead to avoid the upset of moving, and he needed help from a teacher to arrive at a more realistic and constructive solution. The teacher would not have been able to help the child make sense of his behavior if his parents hadn't told her about the move. Dramatic fantasy play, such as playing dead, is almost always a communication of painful feelings children can't talk about easily, and the play gives you the opportunity to connect the play with upsetting real-life events.

> **TEACHER:** Carter was playing with Maya and Owen. After a few minutes, Maya came to me very upset and told me that Carter was dead. I went up to the loft and Carter was lying down with his eyes closed. Maya asked me if he was OK, and Owen said, "He's dead. A bad guy did it." Owen seemed uncomfortable with the game, and Maya was clearly anxious as well. I told them that the game was a little too scary, and invited them to cook something with me in the house. Maya and Owen happily accepted and went down to the house, but Carter continued to play dead. I came back and asked him if he was feeling sad about something. He did not answer but opened his eyes. I said, "Carter, we know you are moving and maybe that's why you are pretending to be dead, so you don't have to move?" Carter insisted, "I am not moving. I don't want to move, and I want to stay in school!" I said, "I hear that! But I bet we can find a way to be in touch when you move, and unfortunately pretending to be dead won't stop the move, but talking about it with teachers will help you feel better."

It can be challenging to decode children's messages in fantasy play. Even when you know the stimulus behind the play, you may need help seeing the connection.

> **TEACHER:** Maeve likes to play dead a lot. I had a conversation with her last week where she shared with me that her Grandpa had died and that he was very old. She told me that she saw him

in Florida once, and that he just "walked away." She shared with me that he was 100 years old and was in heaven. What should I say to her about her wish to play dead?

DR. PIEPER: Maeve plays dead because it makes her feel close to her grandpa, that is, she feels that she is like him. You could let Maeve know that there are other ways to feel close to him besides pretending she is dead. You could talk with her about keeping people alive in our minds by remembering them. Try to shift the play from her acting dead to talking about what it was like when Maeve was with Grandpa, and what types of things they did together.

Perhaps the most important precept in responding to children's fantasy play is not to puncture the veil of play. That is, you do not want to respond as if a child's playful actions were occurring on the level of social reality. Insisting on polite speech cuts off the flow of communication and robs you of the chance to understand what is on a child's mind. When the distinction between play and appropriate forms of social relating is not adhered to, children are often told that rude or angry expressions in play are unacceptable.

TEACHER: Holly had a lion puppet and Andy had a giraffe. Holly's lion said to Andy's giraffe, "You are really, really bad, and you can't stay with the other animals." I didn't comment on the rudeness to the giraffe, but said, "What did the giraffe do?" Holly said, "It peed in its bed." Andy as giraffe said, "I did not!" Holly replied, "Yes you did, and now you are in big trouble!" I said, "If the giraffe had done that it wouldn't have been her fault. That happens sometimes to children and it's nothing to punish them for." Holly said, "Well, my parents get mad at me!" I said, "Maybe we can talk to them and explain that it's nothing to be upset with you for." Holly said, "OK."

The point is that preschoolers are generally unable to walk up to you and say they are upset because their parents got angry at them for wetting the bed, but this upset can emerge in fantasy play if they are allowed to express any and all feelings.

Connecting to Children's Worries and Self-Doubt

Because fantasy play is so often a form of communicating feelings that are worrying children, without puncturing the fantasy you may gently and diplomatically ask children if there is a connection between the play and current concerns.

> TEACHER: The preschoolers were writing their names on sticky notes to play a game. Christie said, "I'm not Christie anymore. I have a different name." I said, "Wait a minute. I love to play with Christie. I wonder if you want to change your name because you're still learning to write the letters, and it feels hard to write your name?" Joy piped in, "When I was four, I didn't know how to write my name, too!" Christie said, "I changed my mind. I do want to be Christie."

When the teacher sensitively connected Christie's wish to pretend that she had a different name with her embarrassment at not knowing how to write hers, Christie immediately went back to being herself and allowed the teacher to help. This example illustrates the advantage of knowing every child well. Even when you do, the meaning of fantasy play can be obscure, and it may take several attempts to connect it to the stresses in children's lives.

> TEACHER: During nap, Aspen said, "OK, I am going to tell a bedtime story for everyone." She told a story whose characters were based on them. Lydia asked if she could add to the story. Aspen agreed. Lydia added animal noises. Aspen said, "Pretend there's a stuffed animal that your person wants but can't get." I've noticed that during her dramatic play, there is often someone who wants something they can't get. Should I ask her if she wants something she can't get?

> DIRECTOR PEREZ: When you have a close moment with Aspen, do connect the dots for her about the theme of not getting what

you want. Ask her if there was something she wanted but feels she can't have? And tell her you know it's hard to really want something and not be able to have it. Then connect it to her graduating from the Preschool to go to kindergarten and that maybe she feels she would like to stay and can't. In other words, that's something she wants and can't have. Then remind her that she can always come back to visit, or she could come for summer camp, and that we will find ways to stay connected.

As Director Perez suggests, when you are trying to understand what your students are communicating through their fantasy play it is helpful to look for themes – as in this example, the theme of not getting what you want – and then try to connect those themes to events in a child's life. If you had asked Aspen what she wanted and couldn't have, she would have been unlikely to come up with "to stay in preschool," but if you had made that connection for her, she would have been likely to see it and accept it.

Making Sense of Anger in Fantasy Play

Children's fantasy play often involves fears of being chased by monsters and "bad guys." Monsters and bad guys almost always represent the projection of angry feelings children are uncomfortable owning. You can help them distinguish angry feelings from actions, which will allow them to be less terrorized by monsters, own all of their feelings, and become more of a whole person.

> **TEACHER:** Emery was talking about bad guys and telling a story about them chasing her. I could tell others were not liking the story, and I suggested that the story sounded scary. Emery laughed and said, "I love bad guys." I said people weren't truly bad, but were just feeling sad, angry, or upset inside and needed help. She replied, "I've never seen a real bad guy because they live on different planets. Which planet do all the bad guys live on?" I said, "Sometimes children take their angry feelings and put them outside into bad guys and monsters because they don't think the

angry feelings are OK. But all feelings are OK, including angry feelings, and feelings can't hurt anyone and you can let teachers know if you are feeling angry." Emery didn't say anything, but I noticed her talk about bad guys was considerably lessened and she moved on to other activities.

Children may incorporate anger into their fantasy play as the result of a loss they experienced with a teacher and, in that case, the teacher can Acknowledge and Accept their distress and connect it to their angry feelings. It takes training and experience to understand the connection between anger expressed in fantasy and an experience with you that is bothering them. If you aren't certain, and you have a mentor available, you can ask them to help you understand the underlying meaning of the angry play. If not, it can be helpful to think back on your interactions with a child and identify where they might have felt a disappointment that took on the meaning of rejection. As in the next example, it is always helpful to know about stresses at home because these can also lurk behind the anger being expressed in fantasy play.

TEACHER: Austin sat down next to me and said, "I want to sit by you." I said, "Sure, Austin." Shortly afterward, Shelly was starting to grab another child's lunch box, and I told Austin I would be right back. A few minutes later, Austin picked up his lunch and moved it to the table where I was helping Shelly. He said, "I want to sit here." I said, "I know, I was sitting with you and I'm sorry I didn't come back right away. There is a chair here if you want to sit at this table." He said, "OK." Then he said, "Angry birds." I said, "What are angry birds?" He said, "They shoot at piggies because the piggies take their eggs." I said, "Do you think the angry birds could ask if they could have their eggs back?" He said, "No, the piggies don't understand. They just keep taking them." I said, "Shelly took me from sitting with you so maybe that made you angry like the angry birds?" He nodded. "And also maybe you are thinking about when Brody and Melanie (twin siblings) take your toys or something you have, and that makes you feel angry?" He nodded his head yes and said that Brody and Melanie were his babies. I said, "It's not OK that someone takes your toys from you. If they do that, go to Mommy or Daddy and tell them you don't like it when they take your toys, and I'm so glad you are letting me know how you feel." He looked happier and stayed sitting next to me.

When children are angry because of a classmate's incivility, they may pretend to be an aggressive animal because they are uncomfortable expressing or acknowledging their own hurt and anger, and you can gently help them untangle their feelings.

TEACHER: As soon as Liz walked in the door, Donald greeted her, saying, "I don't like you, Liz." Liz came over to me a few minutes later pouncing, growling, and crawling around like a tiger. I said, "Good morning, Liz!" and she snarled at me. Donald said, "No, stop!" when Liz got close to him and snarled. I told Liz that I saw her being a tiger really close to Donald, and that the tiger seemed angry, and it looked like he didn't like that very much. He said, "Yeah, Liz, I don't like that." I asked him if it made him scared and he nodded. I told Liz that if she wanted to be a tiger, she needed to do it in a place where she wasn't going to get in the faces of other children. She said, "I'm not Liz, I'm a tiger." I said, "I've noticed that when someone says something hurtful to you like Donald did this morning, you respond by becoming an angry tiger. It's fine to be a tiger, but maybe when you are feeling hurt and angry with another child, it might feel better to come and talk about it with a teacher, and if the teacher knows she could talk to Donald about how he hurt your feelings." Liz said as Liz, "OK. And I don't like Donald!"

When conflicts occur, it is good to keep them in mind because, as in the above example, reactions to them often surface later in play. Because she had noticed and remembered Donald's negative greeting to Liz, the teacher was able to connect it to Liz's wish to be an angry tiger. As a result, the teacher was able to help Liz feel that she, as herself, could own those angry feelings and tell the teacher about them.

Reworking Painful Experiences in Fantasy Play

Sometimes children use fantasy play to re-create situations from home that make them unhappy, and you can find ways to get them to talk about them – again diplomatically. Frequently this play has to do with discipline at home, such as being sent to their rooms. Some children like to put others, mostly teachers, in "jail" and pretend to lock them up. Then they let whoever is in jail escape so that they can run and chase them, catch them, and put them back in jail. You never want to agree that you were bad and deserve jail, but by talking about the distress you would feel if you were in fact jailed, you can help children connect with the stressful experiences that are being worked out in their play.

> TEACHER: When some of the children were trying to get me to go to jail, I wasn't sure what upsetting experience lay behind this game so, while staying in character, I made an open-ended remark, saying, "It's not fun to be locked up. I want to be with you. I don't want to be by myself. What did I do that was bad?" One of the children said, "You were rude and talked back." I asked if the boys ever talked in ways adults didn't like and if so, what happened. The children immediately said they were given time-outs at home, and that they hated being sent to their rooms. I said, "It sounds like when you get a time-out it feels like being put in jail." Both children agreed. I said, "We don't do that here and maybe we could talk to your parents about not doing it at home. Would you like that?" One child said, "Yes." The other, "No."

Without realizing it, by putting other children and the teacher in jail, the two boys were identifying with their parents and using isolation to control others. When the teacher talked about how she felt in jail, the children were able to connect the fantasy play with their discomfort during time-outs. They progressed from identifying with their punishers to staying in touch with their own feelings.

The above example illustrates the reason time-outs, which are used in some form in many preschools, are not benign, which is the way they are often presented. When teachers give time-outs when they don't like children's behavior, the lesson to children is to isolate yourself when you are upset rather than seek help in a caring relationship. Moreover, as adults, they may be unsympathetic with people in their lives who are unhappy or have differences of opinion. On the other hand, when you manage problematic behaviors with Loving Regulation and Time With, that is, firmly but in a way that preserves the relationship, children will grow up to know that differences of opinion don't have to lead to acrimony and alienation but can be resolved with love and kindness.

Helping Children Understand the Unreal in Fantasy Play

Children who are not used to imaginative play may often conclude it is simply inaccurate and try to correct it. In this case you may have to step in and defend the value of pretending.

> **TEACHER:** At lunchtime, Iris was swallowing and telling everyone the food had disappeared by magic. Maya insisted it was not magic, that Iris had just swallowed it. Iris insisted that she had not swallowed it, and they both got upset. I quietly told Maya that Iris was pretending her food had disappeared, that sometimes it was fun to pretend. This did not mollify Maya, who continued telling Iris that she was "lying." I reiterated that pretending was using your imagination, not "lying." A similar scene took place the next day. Maya insisted that Iris was "tricking" her. I said that pretending was just for fun, and not meant to be taken as real. I asked Maya if there was something she would like to pretend about and she thought about it but didn't say anything.

Unfortunately, Maya has gotten the message that any departure from reality is bad. This is the kind of misconception that inhibits the fun of pretending and that you need to gently correct. Some children who take fantasy play literally can be frightened by it. In that case, you do need to pierce the veil of play and help them understand that pretending is not real and can be fun.

TEACHER: The kids made star wands with special powers using various art materials. Autumn's power turned people into objects or animals. She said to me, "Magic, magic, you are now a shoe!" Quinn overheard this and ran to get his wand. He quickly turned to me and said, "Magic, magic you are now a teacher again." Autumn went back and changed me into a horse. Then Quinn said, "Zap! Now you are a person again." I said, "Quinn it sounds like you are worried that Autumn's wand really has magic powers to change me, but this is just a pretend game, and I will always be here to play with. But you can pretend to change me back from my pretend change." Quinn looked relieved and waved his wand again and said, "Magic, magic, you are always my teacher."

DR. PIEPER: Since this child is obviously unused to fantasy play, once this game is over, it would be a good idea to do very benign pretending with him as a way of initiating him into enjoying fantasy play. For example, you could pretend to be an airplane and fly around and ask him if he would like to fly with you.

A surprising number of children believe pretend powers, as in magic wands, are real. This is related to the belief that some feelings are dangerous or unacceptable. So when we help children understand that pretend magic is just for fun, we also advance their understanding that feelings don't have real world consequences.

Other Benefits of Fantasy Play

It sparks curiosity

Sometimes fantasy play is stimulated by classroom observations and learning. Rather than direct children's attention back to the learning task, if you go along with the imaginative discussion, children's imagination will be piqued and they will want to know more about the topic.

TEACHER: Looking at the butterfly chrysalis, the children wondered what was going on inside. Ellie asked if they are dreaming. I said, "Hmmm, I wonder?" This led to a conversation about whether animals dream or not. I said, "I wonder if animals dream like we do." Some of the children shared some dreams they had in the past, and they liked to guess what they thought the butterflies might be dreaming about.

In some schools the question about butterflies' dreams would have been seen as a digression from learning about the butterfly life cycle and curtailed, but this type of playful fantasy stretches children's minds in other important ways and also keeps them interested in learning about the subject matter.

It reveals misconceptions

Often children reveal important misconceptions in fantasy play, which gives you the opportunity to correct mistaken beliefs while staying within the play. Correcting misconceptions is different from the principle of not puncturing the veil of play in that the misconception is not fundamental to the frame of the play and children take the revision matter-of-factly and go on playing.

> **TEACHER:** Gail was pretending to be a mommy to a couple of babies. Gail said, "I just had these babies!" I said, "Oh you did? They are very cute." Gail said, "Yeah! They were in my tummy and then the nurse cut my vagina open and took the babies out." I said, "Well, I see that there are two of them. Are they twins?" Gail said, "No, I think the girl is a little bit bigger. See this is the girl (points to the doll's vagina) and this is the boy (pulls up the blanket and points to the boy doll's penis)." I said, "You know, babies grow in mommy's uterus, not her tummy, and they can either move down into the vagina and be born from there or, if they have trouble coming out, the doctor will cut open the uterus, take the baby out, and sew up the uterus again." Gail said, "Oh." I went on to ask questions about the names of her babies, and if we should get them bottles and other baby things.

You see how you can make slight corrections without interrupting the flow of the fantasy play because the issue wasn't part of the frame of the story. As in this example, children take the new facts in stride and go on playing.

It advances social-emotional learning

Imaginative play can strengthen social skills and problem-solving when you make sensitive interventions. For example, when play starts to devolve into conflict, you want to Stay Positive and solve the problem in a fun way within the story rather than use negative responses like sanctions or disapproval that feel imposed from outside.

> **TEACHER:** Riker and Andrew announced that only firemen were

allowed on the firetruck. Jonathan wanted a turn but he said he was Spiderman. Riker said Spiderman was not allowed. In response, Andrew said, "I say Spiderman can come on the firetruck." Riker didn't know how to respond to this announcement, so he sat there. After a moment he said, "I made the firetruck so I can say, 'No Spiderman is allowed.'" At this point I stepped in because the situation seemed to be deteriorating. I observed that since both boys had made the firetruck, they should both have a say. Andrew said, "Yeah and I am saying Jonathan is allowed." In the meantime, Jonathan had climbed on the fire truck. Riker said, "Well, Jonathan, how about if instead of being Spiderman you are the fire dog?" Andrew said, "Yeah, Jonathan, can you be the fire dog?" Jonathan began barking in agreement and remained on the firetruck. I said, "You guys did a wonderful job of working this out. Everyone compromised here!"

The teacher stepped in just in time to avoid a meltdown and made a minimal but strategic input that put the children on track to work the problem out among themselves without tearing the fabric of the fantasy play. She never lectured them about social obligations to include others, but simply facilitated their ability to work out the solution themselves within the story line they were creating.

It allows antisocial expression

With some exceptions, you can allow antisocial fantasy play that could never be acted on in the real world. For example, children with younger siblings often like to "eat" and "dismember" dolls. Children learn the important lesson that angry feelings are not the same as real acts, so children do not need to feel that these feelings are shameful and need to be sanitized. Even when you can't connect aggressive play with a child's specific issues and feelings, you want to Stay Positive and avoid disapproval or lectures so as to preserve their freedom to express antisocial feelings in play. Unfortunately, when adults fail to make the distinction between feelings and actions, they tell children that this game isn't "nice," and children have to hide feelings rather than own them.

TEACHER: Norm is cooking babies and seems happy about it. He has been enlisting followers to cook the babies, who also think it's hilarious. He announced, "Come on guys, let's cook some babies!" Wanda wanted in on that. She loves babies and brings her own special doll to school. However, I saw her laughing and spanking the babies with a spatula. I asked why she was spanking them, and she said, "Because they were bad." I said, "Why are they bad? You know maybe they just have unhappy feelings inside, and we can help them with that." With that, Norm said, "No, they're just bad." Vicki gave the babies another spank. This morphed into other cooking and play.

Sometimes children who have absorbed the principle that play is for fun and that they can move on to something else if they aren't happy, may decide that the antisocial fantasy that is being enacted doesn't appeal to them. This is a crucial aspect of social-emotional learning – namely, that if you are part of a friends group whose play is not making you happy, you can find a more enjoyable activity without giving up on the friendships.

TEACHER: Norm, Lea, and Lottie were cooking the babies. Mariana said, "Hey guys, don't cook my baby, OK?" They all said, "OK." But then they started to take things nearby to "burn," and she said, "Hey, they're burning everything." I let them know that they were upsetting Mariana, but also emphasized to her that they were just pretending. She put her baby down and said, "I'm leaving. I don't want to play this anymore. You guys can burn everything." I talked to her and said we could play with her baby elsewhere, but she said, "That's OK. I want to play something else." I said, "It's great when you can decide something isn't fun and you choose something that will make you happy!"

When children act out angry feelings toward dolls or play animals, it is important to avoid the mistake of anthropomorphizing the object of their anger. To do that is to contradict the message that feelings are not actions and so all feelings can be welcomed. For example, if a child hits her doll, you would never say, "Ow, poor doll," or anything about the doll's feelings. Rather you want to stay with the child's feelings: "I can see you are feeling angry at the doll – would you like to talk about it? Can I help?"

> **TEACHER:** We have noticed that when Damian holds his bear, which he clearly loves, sometimes he will throw it or mistreat it. At dismissal he threw it down the stairs. Then he said, "Oh, no, Bear." He looked like he was going to cry. So I picked it up and gave it to him, saying, "Oh, here he is." He threw it again. Then he said, "I want my Bear. Bear!" I picked it up and said, "We know you love Bear, but it seems like sometimes you are angry at him and want him to go away and sometimes you want to love him. When you threw him, you were angry, but now you miss him so much. Maybe next time you feel angry, and you want him to go away, put him somewhere where you can get him again."

If the teacher had focused on Bear's feelings ("Bear is sad" or "You hurt his feelings"), this would have had the counterproductive result of making Damian feel that angry feelings are in fact harmful and should not be acknowledged or expressed.

Limits to Antisocial Fantasy Play

There are exceptions to the principle that you should go along with children's fantasy play even when it is antisocial. These generally fall into the categories of children asking you to be negative toward them or of children frightening other children. Even when you put limits on play, you want to Stay Positive and make clear that there is a reason and that the play can simply be revised or redirected.

Teachers Refuse to Be Negative Toward Children in Play

When children ask you to pretend that you dislike them or are angry at them, you can ask why they feel those responses would be appropriate, but you never want to actually act out those negative feelings. For example, children may request that your superhero figure "kill" their superhero, that your puppet tell their puppet that they are stupid, or that you hate them, that your doll tell their doll that you don't want to play with them, or that you act like a monster and scare them.

Children who want you to enact angry or rejecting behaviors through play are feeling badly about themselves and concluding that they are deserving of punishment. Rather than agreeing with them, you have a wonderful opportunity to help them. You can speak through your play persona and say something like, "I would never hurt you – why do you think I should?" Often children have their play puppet or animal respond that they deserve a negative response because they are "bad." You can tell children that they do not need to feel guilty about angry feelings, that feelings are not the same as actions because they don't have consequences, and that everyone feels angry sometimes. If children say their puppet has done something "wrong," you can explain that everyone occasionally makes mistakes or breaks rules, and that telling you and finding a way to correct the mistake is much better than looking to be punished.

TEACHER: Felicity is generally a very happy and creative four-year-old. While playing in the doll house she told me to be the mom and asked me to be mad at her. Playing the mom, I said I would never be angry at her but asked why she thought I should be. She said, "Because I'm still sleeping in my crib, and I don't want to sleep in the bed." She said, "When the new baby comes the baby will be sleeping in my crib." I asked how she felt about that, and she said she didn't care. "Maybe that's why you still want to sleep in the crib while you can?" Then she asked me to continue to play as the mom. I played but voiced the mom in a positive way. For example, when the girl doll was found sleeping in the crib in the middle of the night, I said, "Maybe you're not sleeping in your bed because you don't want the baby to sleep in your crib, and that's totally understandable." Felicity kept up this pretend game until she was satisfied that the teacher/mom was not going to be upset with the girl doll and then she moved on to other activities.

When you don't go along with children's wishes that you be angry with them, but instead show children that there are perfectly normal feelings underneath the "bad" behavior, children have a chance to rethink their critical judgments about their behavior and themselves. The above example showed a teacher responding in a healing way to the fantasy play.

When Fantasy Play Frightens or Hurts Others

Another exception to the principle that antisocial feelings are allowable in fantasy play is when children are too aggressive and frighten other children. When you step in to defuse the content of the play, you give children the important message that play is only for fun.

> **TEACHER:** Two boys were having a great time playing Superman and Batman until they decided to see who was more powerful and began shoving each other. I stepped in and said, "I can see you are playing superheroes, but you need to pretend to fight, not actually fight because someone could get hurt. Anyway, Batman and Superman are usually on the same side. Do you think they could work together?" At this point the boys climbed into the loft and peered down on the "city" pointing out people in trouble who needed their superpowers.

Rather than lecture the boys about the virtues of being nice to each other and not shoving, which would have felt critical to them, the teacher preserved the fantasy play and successfully appealed to Batman's and Superman's positive social motives. When overly aggressive fantasy play occurs, you can use Loving Regulation to help children reframe and rethink aggression and turn it into cooperation.

When children are frightened by others' fantasy play, you can step in and offer alternatives to the scary behavior. Toy guns are not allowed in our Smart Love preschool, but children often use pretend guns in their play. There are schools that prohibit children from using fingers or blocks as play guns. The problem is that children will play with pretend guns anyway outside of school where there is no supervision. Our belief is that by allowing children to play with invented guns in school, we give them a chance to learn from teachers not to scare other children and to reflect on the anger behind the gun play.

TEACHER: Sometimes Bentley uses a wooden tree block as a gun. He pretends to shoot people and makes gun noises. Dakota looked afraid. I said, "You are scaring Dakota, so if you want to pretend it's a gun, you can do that, but you can't point it at other children. I'm not saying pretending is wrong or that you can't express anger, but it has to be expressed without scaring anyone or directing it at other children." Bentley pointed the "gun" in another direction and then asked me if my mother was dead. I said, "I know your grandmother died recently. Maybe you are feeling sad or angry and thinking about people dying?" Bentley nodded.

Because the teacher used Loving Regulation and allowed Bentley to continue to express anger while preventing him from scaring Dakota, he felt sufficient trust to mention the death of someone close to him, which was what was upsetting him and making him angry enough to feel like shooting someone.

Teachers are sometimes unclear about what to do when children are frightening themselves and others and often don't know what is driving the scary scenario. Director Perez offers suggestions for exploring the genesis of the play.

TEACHER: Karen and Susie like to bond over their shared love for Halloween. Susie will say "I just love scary things and blood," and Karen will say, "Me too! Nothing scares me. I love creepy and scary!" I know Susie had dreams that really scared her during the Halloween season. Sometimes, the girls will talk about their stuffed animals dying. Karen told Susie, "Pretend your stuffed animal had to go to the hospital, and I did everything I could, but it died." Susie went along with it but then said, "This is making me sad. I don't want to play this game anymore. Let's do something else." Karen immediately agreed. I am wondering what I should say to them in these situations, especially when I hear them talk about scary things?

DIRECTOR PEREZ: Ask Susie what scary things she "loves." If she tells you, then you can ask why they are so scary. You could also say, "There is a part of you that feels like you want to be scared, but that doesn't feel fun and it can feel hard or scary later." Perhaps these feelings have to do with feeling scared about something currently in their lives. You can talk about blood, as it's actually not scary. How it helps to bring oxygen to all of our body and keeps us healthy, etc. You could do more research on this with them. Since this conversation turned to dying, it may be the source of the scary feelings. Let's get to the source – did someone die, is she worried someone will die, did a pet die, is someone sick? I know Karen's cat died some time ago and maybe she is using this opportunity to talk more about it or connecting it with ongoing upset. "I wonder if you're thinking about your cat and wish it were still here? It is sad when your pet dies."

As in this example, you may not always know what is driving the scary feelings being expressed in fantasy play. As Director Perez suggests, in that case you can ask about relevant life events, suggest that being so scared isn't fun, and offer reassuring factual corrections to any frightening concerns. The important thing is to show children that you take the fright being expressed in play seriously and would like to help them understand it.

Dreams

Many teachers are unsure how to respond when children tell them their dreams, but like fantasy play, dreams are communications that children can be helped to make sense of. The important message to offer about dreams is that children wrote them themselves for a reason and that you can help them think of the reason. Once dreams are turned into puzzles children can solve, children feel empowered and dreams lose their potency.

Bad Dreams

When children have bad dreams, they are frightened not only by the bad dream, which seems utterly real to them, but also by the conviction that they are at the mercy of these dreams. This helpless feeling can make children afraid of bedtime, with the result that they miss out on needed sleep.

Unfortunately, when children tell adults their bad dreams, the usual advice they receive is that the dream isn't "real." This doesn't help the preschooler, because dreams are much more real to children than to adults. When adults try to convince them otherwise, children feel misunderstood or, worse, ashamed, and they remain fearful despite adults' reassurances. That monster may not be under the bed now, but it could come back, and it was certainly there before because the child "saw" it.

Rather than dismiss children's bad dreams as unreal, you can help children figure out why they dreamed them. Children come to understand that bad dreams are an attempt to deal with lingering emotional upsets. When a child shares a bad dream, the best way to help is to explain, "Dreams are stories we tell ourselves for a reason. We just have to understand the reason."[17] When children go from being frightened of their bad dreams to trying to figure out why they created them, they become the agent of the dream rather than the victim.

Interpreting Children's Dreams

Interpreting children's dreams is not terribly difficult when you know what is going on in a child's life, because children's dreams are usually fairly transparent. Typically, any experience that makes children sad, angry, or worried can cause bad dreams. Examples are everyday stresses such as sibling rivalry, the flu, a spat with a friend, starting or ending a school year, or disagreements with parents. Certainly, the dreams may be caused by more traumatic occurrences, such as parental divorce, a grave illness in the family, the death of a pet, or social or environmental disasters.

When you ask children if their bad dream might be caused by something that is bothering them, children over three can often identify a relevant worry or upset.

TEACHER: Lottie said she had a scary dream and she was still scared. I said, "Can you tell me about it?" She said that a giant snake was trying to crawl into her bed and eat her and she couldn't get away and she called for her parents and they didn't come. I said, "That sounds really scary!" She said, "Yes!" I said, "You remember from the Mommy, Daddy, I Had a Bad Dream! book that there is some reason you told yourself that dream. Did anything happen recently that upset you?" She said, "Yes, I found a worm on the sidewalk that wasn't moving, and I tried to save it by putting it in the grass, but it still didn't move, and my mom said it was dead." I said, "That sounds really hard. Maybe you felt like you should have been able to help the worm and it came back in your dream and was angry?" She nodded and said sadly, "I didn't want it to be dead, and I wanted to help it." I said, "That makes a lot of sense that you felt badly and that you made up that dream!" She agreed and went off to play with her friends.

As in this example, because children love a puzzle and prefer to feel in charge rather than terrorized, they often enthusiastically engage in the process of connecting their bad dreams to recent events.

Good Dreams

Like bad dreams, good dreams can be used to help children get in touch with their feelings. Frequently children have good dreams in which their all-powerful selves make them feel indomitable. Children may fly, wipe out legions of bad guys, have unlimited access to a candy store, or chase off a lion.

As with bad dreams, your goal is not to tell children that their dreams aren't real and couldn't happen. You can share in children's enjoyment of good dreams while at the same time helping them understand that good dreams, too, are usually responses to something that might have happened in their lives.

TEACHER: Ariel went on a birthday trip to an amusement park and was thrilled to be tall enough to go on some rides. The next morning, he couldn't wait to tell his parents about his wonderful dream. He was Batman's assistant and flew all over Gotham helping Batman catch bad guys. His parents commented that sounded like a lot of fun and how it must have seemed like flying to him when he got to go on the more "grown-up" rides the day before. The little boy saw the connection and nodded enthusiastically.

You can see that when you know children and their lived experience well you will not find it difficult to understand and make sense of their dreams in a way that they will find enormously beneficial.

SUMMARY

This chapter illustrates ways in which you can decode and respond helpfully to children's fantasy play and dreams. By showing children that there is another dimension to their imaginative life besides the surface story, you enrich children's experience of their own and others' minds. You can also help children recognize, make sense of, and defuse feelings that are troubling them. As they become increasingly able to solve the puzzle of their feelings, children become more in charge of their own minds. Equally important, by responding constructively and warmly to dreams and fantasy play, you establish the superiority of turning to caring relationships for help and comfort in times of distress.

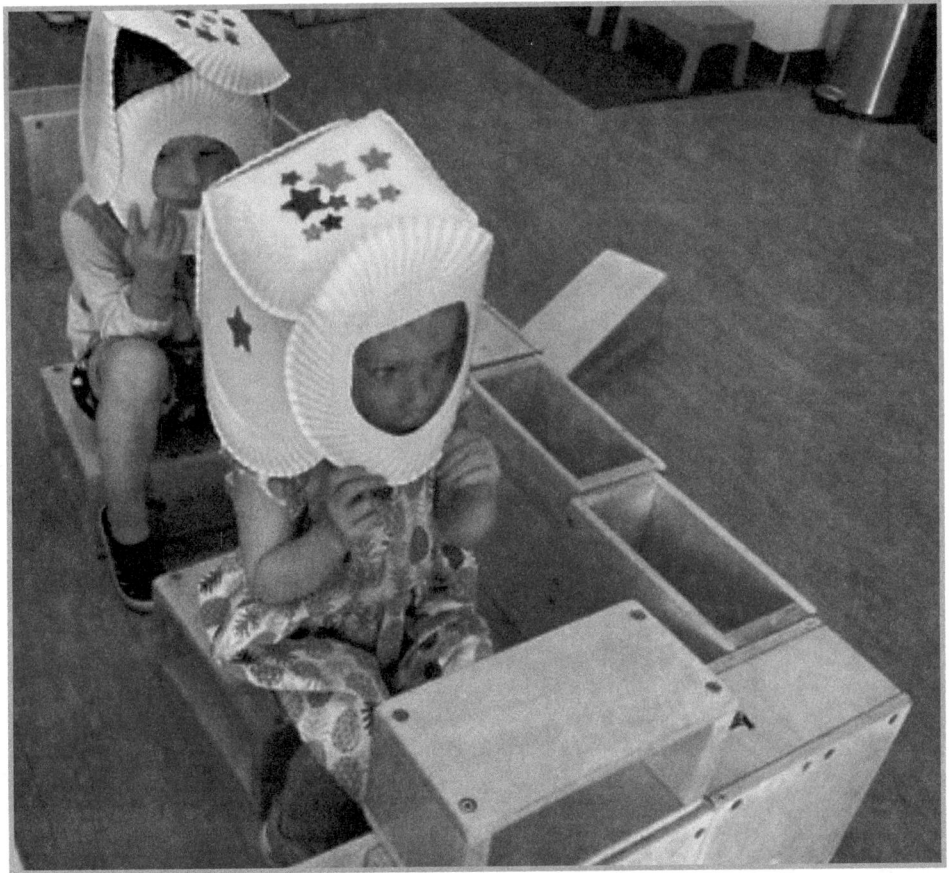

CHAPTER 6

Responding to Concerning Emotional Issues in the Classroom

There are some children whose reactions and behaviors go beyond what is developmentally appropriate and who could use some psychological help. This is one reason having clinical consultation available in your preschool is so important. Smart Love insights into child development will help you distinguish normal, age-appropriate unhappiness, anger, and upset from behavior that won't resolve with maturity and that requires professional help. One advantage of a Smart Love preschool is that its expectations of preschoolers are age-appropriate. Preschoolers are not expected to share, to wait patiently, to sit quietly in groups, to learn subjects through worksheets and mandated exercises, or to be silent during transitions. Many preschoolers who are diagnosed with mental illness and, even, expelled from preschools would perform within a normal range if they weren't burdened by age-inappropriate requirements. For example, children who have an age-appropriate difficulty conforming to rules about sitting quietly, doing worksheets, and waiting, often receive a diagnosis of hyperactivity when what they really need is a more suitable classroom culture.

Children who are at times stressed, upset, unhappy, resistant, anxious, or angry are helped to recover when teachers understand what is developmentally appropriate and respond with Loving Regulation and the other S.M.A.R.T. principles. Teachers are partners in play rather than observers or authority figures, which makes them immediately available to hear and respond to children's developmental needs. As a result, children turn to teachers to recover their equilibrium when they lose it in class, and few have such persistent dysphoria that they are in need of professional help. Still, there are instances of children whose chronic unhappiness means that they could benefit from child therapy. Here are some characteristics that would help you identify those children.

Overreactions to Frustration

There are children who cannot relinquish a disappointment, and these children spend much of their time feeling miserable. The child in the next example was chronically unable to recover when he couldn't immediately have what he wanted. He would become obsessed with the desired object and even with a teacher's help and undivided attention could not move on while waiting for the thing to become available. Teachers did try to connect his obsessive behavior to his life experiences, but no suggestions about connections with family or school issues made a difference.

TEACHER: Today Lionel and another teacher were at the sand table. There were two ladles for scooping sand, a bigger and a smaller one. Timmy walked up just as Lionel took the big one. Timmy said, "Oh, I wanted that big ladle." I said, "Well, it looks like Lionel is playing with it, but look here's another." Timmy insisted, "I don't want this one. I want that one! That one's bigger." I replied, "I know it's hard to wait. Maybe you can use it when Lionel is done." Lionel chimed in, "Timmy, you can use it when I'm done." Timmy said, "I don't want it when he's done. I want it now." He began to cry. I said, "I can tell you're sad about not being able to play with the ladle right now." I picked up a pot. "What about this? It's even bigger than the ladle Lionel has." Timmy said, "No, I don't want that one. It's too big." I tried to help by getting a measuring cup off the table that was relatively the same size as the ladle. "Look! This one is pretty close to the ladle." Timmy said, "No, that's too small." I said, "I've noticed that when there's something that you want and you can't have, it's really hard to wait. How can we help you with that? I can see it's hard to have fun with other things when you want something you can't have at the moment. Is there something you can think of that you would enjoy doing while you wait?" I picked up the next two sizes of cups and involved him in comparing the measuring cups to the ladles. That seemed to help calm him. I found one scooper that was the right size, and he was able to fill his pan with that and played with it. But I could see he would not take his eyes off Lionel's ladle. About five minutes later, Lionel dropped the ladle and went into the other room. Timmy immediately grabbed it. This is how Timmy makes himself unhappy. He focuses on one thing that he can't have and can't get over it.

At this age, it is normal for children to react unhappily at not getting what they want when they want it, but, once their feelings are Acknowledged and Accepted, children are usually able to accept your help to find something fun to do. Timmy's inability to move on in spite of the teacher's understanding and caring attempts to help him is a sign that staying with his unhappy feelings is more important to him than letting them go. Children who are chronically unable to let go of angry or unhappy feelings might benefit from professional consultation.

Aversive Reactions to Pleasure

Children who need psychological help often have aversive reactions to pleasure, that is, in addition to wanting to have fun, they demonstrate reactive needs to make themselves unhappy. We call this an "Addiction to Unhappiness." The understanding of aversive reactions to pleasure is unique to the Smart Love approach, and because they go unrecognized or misunderstood, children who react to various kinds of pleasure by creating unhappiness are often labeled unstable, antisocial, ADHD, on the spectrum, and so forth. Aversive reactions to pleasure are one source of teacher dissatisfaction because children who have been making progress socially and academically suddenly and, seemingly mysteriously, backslide. Teachers conclude either that these children are not teachable or that as teachers they are not teaching correctly. Neither is true of course. In reality, aversive reactions to pleasure characterize all psychopathology and may be as mild as a child who spills the paint they are having fun painting with, or as severe as a child who hits another child after an enjoyable time playing.

The addiction to unhappiness begins when young children routinely experience uncomforted unhappiness: for example, they are left to cry themselves to sleep, their behavior is managed with disciplinary measures rather than Loving Regulation, more is expected of them than is age-appropriate, parents have debilitating health problems or major job stress, or parents are prevented by environmental or social deprivations from being physically or emotionally available. Because young children love their parents and think they are perfect, they then assume that unhappiness is what they are supposed to feel, and they develop needs for it. In this way, unhappiness becomes misidentified as happiness[18], which is why psychopathology can be so resistant to change and, in more severe cases, require professional help.[19]

When you understand and recognize aversive reactions to pleasure, you can help children anticipate that they may cause themselves some form of discomfort in reaction to having fun or feeling close to others. Most important, you will Stay Positive and not be confused or irritated by children's seemingly paradoxical behavior, and you will know what to do and say to help. With gentle comments, you can reveal to children that they can be driven to feel unhappy after they have been enjoying themselves.

> **TEACHER:** A group of children was playing together in the house and having pretend meals. Suddenly, out of the blue, Seth pushed all the plates and food onto the floor. The other children yelled at him, and he got upset. I asked him what was wrong, but he just shook his head and looked at the floor. I said, "Gee, I noticed you were having such a good time and did something to stop it. Maybe we can work on making those good times last longer."

The teacher didn't comment on the aggressive act, but, because she recognized his aversive reaction to pleasure, she tried to help Seth see that his aggression was in response to the fun he had been having. Other children might throw plates and pretend food on the floor, but this would normally be in response to some sort of identifiable frustration, hurt feelings, or anger at another child or children. In Samuel's case his aggression was unprovoked with no obvious cause except the fact that he had been having a good time. Also, this example was only one of many instances of his reacting negatively to enjoying himself. So this is the understanding the teacher tried to impart.

Aversive reactions to pleasure often seem to come out of nowhere, but when you understand what is driving these reactions, you can help a child make sense of them. Without this understanding, children's behavior can seem entirely incomprehensible.

> **TEACHER:** Joey and Skip were building a structure together. They were mutually helpful, laughing, and having a great time. Joey sat with Skip at snack time, and they were still giggling and talking about their toys and the tower they had made. Before he went outside, Joey

told me he was going to have Skip over to his house. But as soon as we got outside, Joey was fixated on the idea that Skip was going to hurt him or hit him. I reminded Joey that they had just had a great time together. Then, he said, "I hate Skip and he isn't my friend." I said, "Maybe there is a part of you that felt uncomfortable about having such a great time with Skip and in reaction you are feeling you don't want to play with him anymore. Maybe I can help you reconnect with him." He said, "Maybe in a little while."

Children who need psychological help can have aversive reactions to the care and affection they get from teachers, and they may express these responses in behaviors teachers must regulate.

TEACHER: Marty wants to have positive experiences with teachers but then reacts by seeking negative attention from them. He can be playing nicely with a teacher and suddenly will throw something or do something else that needs regulating. Teachers help him understand this dynamic. "Gee, we were playing for a while and having fun and now it seems like you are feeling like you need me to come and stop you from doing this." Over time, this behavior decreased. Recently Marty was able to play much longer with a teacher without making himself unhappy.

When you consistently help children understand that they create discomfort for themselves in reaction to enjoying closeness in a relationship or just having a lot of fun, children become able to go for longer periods without resorting to aversive reactions.

Self-Hatred

One definite sign that children need psychological evaluation is when they are relentlessly negative about themselves.

TEACHER: Eric and Colter were playing the Lunch Box Game, which requires that there be space between them. Eren got up and sat in the middle of their game, which made them upset. I said, "Eren, do you want to play their game too?" He said, "No, I don't want to play their game. I want to mess it up so they can't play." I said, "It sounds like you might have some unhappy feelings inside right now. Did something happen that made you upset?" He said, "No, I'm just a bad kid. I do bad things cause I'm a bad, bad kid." I said, "Eren you are a great kid. No matter what you do, we know that you are a fantastic kid, and nothing can change that. I'm sorry you feel that way, but even when you're having a tough time, you're still a great kid." "No, I'm a bad kid. I'm evil inside. It starts at the bottom and it goes up, up, up, and when it gets to my head, I turn evil and I can never be good again." I replied, "It sounds like you're talking about when you're feeling upset and you can't control it. That can be pretty scary. It's so great that you can tell me about it. Maybe that can help you feel better." He responded, "I don't want to feel better. I want to feel bad. I like to feel bad. And evil. I didn't like feeling good, so I changed to evil and I'll never change back to good."

This teacher tried to help Eren with his negative feelings about himself, but she also realized that they were extreme and that professional help was called for. In this case, Director Perez contacted his parents and they agreed to consult a therapist.

Asking a Child to Leave Preschool

Research indicates that three- and four-year-olds are expelled from preschool at a rate higher than children in grades K-12.[20] As a teacher using Smart Love strategies, you would make every effort to help children who are struggling emotionally. You would use age-appropriate expectations, manage behavior with S.M.A.R.T. strategies, welcome all feelings, and model kindness and caring – and most children who are struggling would absorb the compassionate and cooperative classroom culture and become happier and better regulated. Yet sometimes there is a child who cannot control his aggressiveness and has become hazardous to other children. In this case you would work with your preschool to recommend child therapy and parent counseling. In contrast to the finality of being expelled from other schools, the child and his parents could be told that he/she would be welcome back. You can explain to other children that the child is not alone or "bad," and that his parents and all the teachers still love him and he will be back when he feels better.

SUMMARY

While children at this age are frequently upset, angry, sad, or frustrated, they are more often engaged, interested, enthusiastic, sociable, and cooperative. Children that need professional help spend more time unhappy than their peers. They also have aversive reactions to pleasure, which means they cannot play happily for long with teachers or other children without disrupting the fun. They often express a degree of negativity about themselves that is more than a passing insecurity. And they may be unable to recover when things do not go as they wish. When you understand that these children are suffering from an addiction to unhappiness and are not being willful, attention seeking, or just plain naughty, you can respond with caregiving motives rather than with personal feelings of anger or irritation. With child therapy, even the most unhappy and difficult children can usually remain in the classroom, and they do improve and become much happier and able to enjoy uninterrupted relationships.

CHAPTER 7

Helping Children and Parents With Issues From Home

All children come to preschool with issues, emotions, problems, and relationship stresses from home. This is one reason why it is important that parents feel included and valued as part of the preschool community. Too often the message to parents is that only the children matter, and parents are there just for drop off and pick up. One aspect of a happy preschool that is often overlooked is maintaining positive relationships and good lines of communication with parents. When parents feel respected as partners, and you show them the same acceptance of all feelings and concerns you show their children, parents relate to you as a trusted confidant. This is good for both children and parents. In our preschool, parents share concerns about parenting and get help from teachers and Director Perez. And children benefit when parents communicate issues from home that impact them at school.

Partnering With Parents

At arrival time, there is always a teacher in the vestibule to greet parents and children, and parents feel free to ask the teacher for parenting advice, and also to share stressors at home that children may import into the classroom and need help with. Moreover, if teachers see a child's behavior deteriorating for more than a few days (the child is more aggressive, more tearful), they will reach out to parents to ask if there is something they should know about at home. In many schools, parents see teachers only at parent-teacher conferences where parents are likely to get negative information about their child.

Introducing Parents to S.M.A.R.T. Principles

When the parenting style at home is different from the Smart Love approach, you can help parents by starting with the S.M.A.R.T. acronym: Stay Positive, Model Kindness, Acknowledge and Accept Feelings, Loving Regulation, and Time With.

TEACHER: Eleanor and Alaina were getting ready to go in the hallway when Eleanor started to snap her fingers in front of Alaina's face. I let Eleanor know that I could not let her do that, and that nobody should do that in front of her face either. Eleanor said, "Well, my dad snaps his fingers in my face and my mom's." I said, "If someone wants to do anything near your body, especially if it's not going to feel good, they should always ask you first and you can say no ... it's your body."

At the parent-teacher conference the teacher related to Eleanor's father that what he thought was a game felt unpleasant to Eleanor, and that she was making her classmates angry by doing the same thing to them. Her dad was surprised that something so seemingly innocuous to him was having this effect, and he agreed to stop. In general, parents often don't realize the extent to which physical forms of teasing, such as tickling, can feel like aggression to children.

Helping Parents With Uncertainty Around Parenting

When you make the effort to create partnerships with parents, they will feel comfortable sharing painful feelings about their relationship with their children. Part of the education of a Smart Love teacher is learning how to give parents guidance. Most important is to listen to how parents are feeling (Acknowledge and Accept) and help them transform their doubts and uncertainties into a positive view of their children's puzzling behavior. You will find many opportunities to impart the Smart Love understanding of child development, which will reassure parents that in almost every instance behavior they worry about is normal.

TEACHER: Colson's dad stopped by the building to pick up mittens Colson had left at school. When he came in, he mentioned that his wife was out of town for work a lot and he was a stay-at-home dad. He said it had been a very hard week and added, "It just feels like Colson loves his mom more than me." I find parents saying things like this to me and would like more guidance on what to say to them that's aligned with Smart Love. I can easily navigate the responses to the children, but the parents are more difficult for me.

DR. PIEPER: Colson is probably more excited to see the parent who isn't around as much, and he is comfortable taking Dad "for granted." You can explain to Dad that being "taken for granted" is a really good thing because it means his children have an inner security about his love and availability.

In many schools parents would not feel comfortable sharing their insecurities with teachers out of fear of being judged. But when you make the effort to Model Kindness and create positive partnerships with parents, they will trust you with their questions. When you help them see things in a more constructive and developmentally appropriate way, you facilitate their enjoyment of parenting and of course this will benefit your students as well.

You can look for opportunities to help parents understand and adopt the Smart Love principles. You will find that you often need to gently correct parents who try to impose expectations on their children about what they should be doing in preschool. It is frequently hard for parents, who have a lot of say over what children do at home, to let teachers make the rules in preschool. You can tactfully explain that in preschool children are free to choose their activities.

TEACHER: At pickup time, Leslie's dad asked, "Did Leslie make something for her mommy at school today?" I said, "I don't know if she made something for her mom, but we were doing beading and she made a necklace." Dad said, "Oh, I was just wondering because I told her to make something for her mom. Her birthday is Thursday." I said, "Here at the preschool, we don't force children to do specific things. My suggestion would be, if you want her to make something, why not sit down with her at home and make something with her."

Parents may take you aside to ask about behaviors that are concerning them at home, which gives you an opportunity to educate parents on how to parent with S.M.A.R.T. strategies. One of the most common corrections you will make with parents is explaining what are developmentally appropriate expectations. Helping parents relax and enjoy children as they are is a gift you can give parents.

> **TEACHER:** After toddler class, Edward's mother asked me if I had heard Edward talk about a person named Apple. She believed that Edward had an imaginary friend named Apple, and that at home he had said, "Apple made a big mess." I thanked her for telling me, and I said I would be listening to see if Edward talked about Apple in class. I added that imaginary friends are common and sometimes are the result of demands that are too much for this age. When children feel they can't live up to expectations, they often invent an imaginary friend who either makes mistakes instead of the child or is perfect when the child isn't. I suggested that maybe she and Edward's father should think about whether they are expecting too much from him. I said we would be happy to talk with them about what is reasonable to expect from toddlers.

Working with and educating parents is an important and usually neglected part of a preschool teacher's job. Many of the behaviors you see your students struggle with in class can be ameliorated if you take the time to explain to parents how to apply S.M.A.R.T. principles at home rather than the traditional expectations and discipline they have been using. Teachers should always have time built into their schedules for counseling parents when appropriate.

When Children Act Out Discipline From Home, Talk to Parents About S.M.A.R.T.

Children often mimic harsh parenting styles by "disciplining" teachers. Children make very clear that forced isolation, as in time-outs, is very traumatic and painful for them. You can help them with these feelings in the classroom, but also you can use these interactions to show parents the true impact on children of regulation they mistakenly think of as benign.

> **TEACHER:** Teagan was throwing things in the classroom and generally having trouble regulating himself. Using Loving Regulation

and Time With, I told him we were going to take a break in the office together. Teagan was seated in the armchair, and I was kneeling next to him. I asked him if he would like to read a book and he replied, "Yes." I took the book he handed me and began to open it. Teagan said, "No, you aren't listening to me! When you don't listen, you are naughty!" I said, "I'm listening, Teagan. What is it that you would like me to do?" He replied, "You're naughty so you have to go sit over there until I count!" I looked at him and said, "Is this what happens at home?" He stated, "Yes, now go over to the wall!" I said, "Well, at preschool we don't have naughty teachers or kids, and we don't have to stand against walls. If children have a hard time with something, we help them with their feelings, and if children need a break, we just come to the office together." I sat on the arm next to him in the chair. He looked relieved. "Were you upset because I was reading on the ground?" He said, "Yes, that's where you should sit." I said, "OK, I will, and you can always tell me where you would want me to sit when we read together."

We set up a meeting with Teagan's parents to talk about the problem with using words like "naughty" and imposing time-outs, and we explained the advantages of Loving Regulation and suggested they use that approach instead. When children get the hurtful message at home that they are "naughty," they often share these painful feelings with you because they know you will help them feel better rather than agree with their parents. This communication also creates an opportunity for you to talk to parents about switching to Loving Regulation. For example, you may often hear children say they are "bad" for making mistakes, which gives you a chance to reframe this view and also to talk to parents about better responses.

TEACHER: Gail was playing in the kitchen and broke a bowl. I was moving kids away and sweeping, and Gail continuously apologized. I told her I wasn't mad at her and that sometimes dishes break and then we just clean up. She continued to explain that it was an accident, and she was sorry for being bad. I told her she was not bad, and that I would never get angry at her when an accident happens at school. "I wonder why you feel you are bad when you make a mistake and drop something. Are you thinking about how you feel when you have an accident at home?" "Yes," she said. I said, "Well, we will explain to your parents that mistakes don't make you bad."

You may find that children will criticize their expression of emotions based on how their upset feelings are responded to at home. This gives you a chance to advance their social-emotional learning by correcting their negative labeling of feelings and then talk to parents about adopting the S.M.A.R.T. approach to discovering the feelings behind behaviors.

TEACHER: Today Ron told me his leg was hurting and then suddenly asked, "Am I being whiny?" I said, "No, you are letting me know something is hurting. Does someone say you are whiny?" He said, "When I go to the doctor and get poked it hurts, and they say, 'Stop being whiny.'" I said, "I am sorry that happened. You can let your mom and dad know it is OK to share how you feel. Maybe you can ask your mom or dad to hold your hand before and after the poke?" He said, "So I am not whiny?" I said, "Absolutely not, and thank you for sharing how you feel with me."

Because he knew his teacher would listen without judging him, Ron had enough trust to share his shame about being "whiny" and to get reassurance that he was having a normal reaction to going to the doctor. When the teacher told his parents that she was worried about Ron's critical labeling of his feelings, his parents considered her advice and agreed that they would be more understanding in the future when he was upset or afraid.

Reframing a Parent's Negative Speech

When parents of preschoolers say things to you or other parents in front of their child or to another child at pickup or dismissal that contradict the Smart Love approach, you need to step in and ask them to be more positive. You can remind parents that when adults talk about children in front of them – they are essentially telling them what to think about themselves. If it's positive, great. If it's negative, the children will accept and start to incorporate these messages into their self-image. As a result, you can ask parents not to make negative statements in front of their child or other children.

> **TEACHER:** Yesterday at dismissal Wyatt's mom was there to pick him up. I took Joshua, Shelly and Matt into the yard to play. Joshua yelled to Wyatt to come over to say goodbye, and Wyatt naturally ran away from his mom to say goodbye. Wyatt's mom followed the kids, walking at least 100 feet out of her way, and called over to Joshua. Joshua came close to the gate to see what the mom wanted, and she called Joshua "a mischievous little boy." I did my best to redirect Joshua back over to me, so we could quickly get inside. I said to Joshua, "That wasn't right what Wyatt's mother said to you. You are not mischievous. You are a wonderful boy and are friendly and curious and that's terrific, and we will talk to Wyatt's mother about not saying things like that to you." I asked Wyatt's mother to wait, and I said, "Please never say negative things to other children. You said to Joshua that he is mischievous, which is not the Smart Love approach. The way we talk with the children is to preserve their emotional well-being and we would ask that you not say anything negative."

This example illustrates that S.M.A.R.T. guidelines apply everywhere at school, including pickup and drop off, and that you can make sure that parents adhere to them, even though they may follow different rules at home.

Educating Parents in Toddler Classes

In toddler parent-and-child classes, parents frequently respond in ways philosophically different from Smart Love. You want to try to show the difference diplomatically, but clearly, so the children can absorb the information. You can make clear that you are not telling parents what to do at home (although you hope they will adopt S.M.A.R.T. strategies), but that at school they need to follow the Smart Love philosophy.

Because refusing to share is age-appropriate for toddlers, it's important to have many duplicate toys. You can simply redirect children who want another's toy. Parents often have a difficult time watching their toddlers refuse to share, but this presents an opportunity to help them understand age-appropriate expectations.

Parents of toddlers often impose expectations about the correct use of toys, which is counter to the Smart Love emphasis on effort rather than success.

TEACHER: Nineteen-month-old Gemma is in the Toddler Exploration class, where parents are required. She played with her mom throughout the morning. Her mother continuously told Gemma which colored ring to put on the dowel so the rings would be in the correct order. When Gemma placed one ring out of order, her mother told her "That's not the purple one." Gemma was about to put another color which was out of order, but she stopped and took off the previous ring to put the purple one on as her mother had suggested.

DIRECTOR PEREZ: "As long as she is trying, that's great. We ask that you let her try without concern about her getting it right. Our experience has shown that when we interfere with the joy of trying, whether the effort is correct or not, it inhibits curiosity and initiative to further explore. Over time, with an abundance of experience and positive feedback, Gemma will successfully learn to do it. I know you want to tell her how to do things correctly, but it's called Toddler Explorations because here we want them to explore. Sometimes they will make mistakes, but that's all part of the learning process and we want them to feel that is a normal part of trying. When your child is here, we ask that you do it in this way."

The toddler classes are also an opportunity to help parents understand that if toddlers can't get positive attention, they will often seek negative attention.

In order for this dysfunctional pattern not to become habitual, parents need to seek out more opportunities to enjoy positive interactions with their children.

TEACHER: In Toddler Explorations class, Lincoln (2.5 years) seemed to be seeking out conflicts by throwing things across the room, taking things from other children, attempting to climb completely into the water table, and dumping water. I stuck with him and his mother and used Loving Regulation to ensure that he could still have fun. He seemed to accept most of my suggestions to regulate his behavior. For instance, when he wanted to dump water all over the craft table, he allowed me to steer him toward a water bin instead, or when I told him that I couldn't let him climb into the water table because it wasn't safe but that he could play with the toys in the water table, he accepted that cheerfully as well. However, his mother seemed very exasperated and embarrassed by his behavior. She kept on yelling, "Lincoln!" at him, and saying, "I don't know what's gotten into him today." Actually, this is not unusual behavior for Lincoln. I said, "I think he's definitely trying to get a negative response from you. When you spend a lot of time talking to the other mothers, he gets you to pay negative attention since he can't get positive attention. I suggest you try to make as many positive responses as you can. Also, the problem with saying negative things about him is that it becomes a self-fulfilling prophecy in that children want to become what they hear parents say about them."

This is one advantage of partnering with parents. You establish a positive relationship in which you can refocus and reframe their parenting choices to better help both them and their children. Parents tell us that teacher input about parenting has helped them enjoy and feel more confident in their parenting.

Helping Children With Stress and Worries From Home

Much of the social-emotional learning that takes place at school occurs when children share worries and problems from home with you. When you Acknowledge and Accept all feelings, you give children an outlet for communicating and getting help with their concerns. Whenever you are able to show children the connection between their unhappiness and their home experiences, their dysphoria will start to make sense to them. Facilitating this understanding is so much better than presenting children with coping mechanisms, which only drives their unhappiness underground. Moreover, you can make suggestions to parents about how to help children with what is bothering them.

Wrong Messages

Children frequently bring warnings from home that are worrying them, and this gives you the opportunity to correct them. For example, children are often cautioned that bad things will happen if they don't do what they are told.

TEACHER: Jim said, "Did you know potatoes grow out of your ears if you don't wash them. Uncle Edward told me that." I let him know potatoes grow in soil and need water and sunshine to grow. They do not grow out of ears. I pulled the diagram of how a potato plant grows off the green house and showed him. Jim said, "I think you need to tell my Uncle Edward about this. Do you have his number?" I said, "I don't have Uncle Edward's number, but we can write this down together for you to take home so you can explain to him all about how potatoes really grow."

Going to sleep is another topic children often are made to worry about.

TEACHER: Steph brought a book about a pigeon who didn't want to go to bed and said, "You know if you stay up late, you'll get sick, right?" I said, "What do you mean you'll get sick?" She said, "If you stay up late, you could get sick and even die." I said, "No, Steph, you won't get sick or die from staying up late. But if you think that, it could be scary if you don't feel like sleeping at bedtime. If you stay up late all that will happen is you may be tired the next day, and that makes it harder to have fun and play." Steph said, "And you could get sick, right?" I said, "Your body does need to rest to be healthy, but usually if you don't have a good rest on one day you can get good rest the next day. I wonder if it's hard to go to sleep when you want to stay up and play or be with Mom and Dad and your sisters. That's normal, but it won't make you sick. You can take a nap or sleep more the next night." Steph nodded and looked relieved.

At the parent-teacher conference the teacher explained to Steph's parents that inventing dire consequences in order to get Steph to go to sleep was actually making it harder for her to sleep because it was frightening her. The teacher suggested they just tell her she would naturally get the sleep her body needed.

Parents sometimes confuse children by anthropomorphizing inanimate objects to get children to do what they want.

TEACHER: The other day Maver's mom came in with him at arrival and when he said he didn't want her to leave, she said, "The car is missing me. Can you hear it asking for me to come back?" I wasn't sure what to say regarding the car comment and was hoping you could advise. In general his mother is always very anxious, talking rather quickly, and telling Maver she has to go now when she comes inside with him at arrival. I'm not always sure how to handle these situations.

DR. PIEPER: Say to Maver, "That's a funny joke because the car can't really miss you because it's not alive. If you are upset when your mom has to go, you don't have to hide those feelings and the teachers want to hear about them and will help you get set up at school."

Children often share misconceptions they attribute to parents but that are more likely coming from their own worries.

TEACHER: Karlie asked me if I brush my teeth. I replied, "Yes, I do. I brush them before I go to sleep at night and when I wake up in the morning." Karlie said, "I don't brush my teeth. My mom said you can get coronavirus from toothpaste." I told Karlie that sounds scary, but you can't get the coronavirus from toothpaste." She asked, "What's in toothpaste?" I said, "That's a great question, let's look it up." Karlie and I discovered that toothpaste has water and baking soda in it to clean our teeth.

DIRECTOR PEREZ: That was a good response, but also she invented this worry because she is scared about the coronavirus. It might have been a good idea to talk with her about it and say that wearing masks as we do in school is the best way to keep from getting it, and that most children her age are OK even if they happen to get it.

As Director Perez suggests, outlandish consequences, such as getting coronavirus from toothpaste, usually arise from worries that are plaguing a child. It can be tempting simply to reassure the child with a factual correction, but it is better to take a moment and try to get at the underlying concerns.

Interruptions in Family Relationships

Children often worry about their family's well-being when they are at school, especially when someone in the family is ill. You want to acknowledge children's fears before suggesting a fun activity so that they know you are listening carefully and taking their fears seriously.

> **TEACHER:** Barb was playing in the tunnel. I said, "We are having snack now. Would you like some?" Barb answered, "No." I said, "I would be happy to come with you to get snack." Barb replied, "I am sleeping in the tunnel." I said, "I see you made a cozy place. Are you tired?" No answer. Barb continued to talk from the tunnel and disrupt the group. I said, "You can come lay down in the office if you are tired." Barb said, "No. Mom is dead." I said, "Mom is dead?" Barb said, "Yes, my mommy is dying." I said, "That's a really scary thought. We can call or email her if you want to check. I'm glad to know what you are thinking about. I know your mom is sick sometimes and that feels scary and you really worry." Barb said, "Mom isn't dead, and my dad and sister are OK too." I said, "I can see you are thinking about your whole family right now." Barb replied, "Yeah, I'm going to stay here forever." I said, "Sounds like things are scary right now at home and maybe that's why you want to stay here. Would you like me to read you a book?" Barb said, "Yes." We read for a while and then she said, "I want snack."

It would have been hard for the teacher to understand Barb's withdrawal if she hadn't known about her mother's illnesses, which again emphasizes how important it is to have good communication with families. The teacher called Barb's parents and suggested that when her mom wasn't feeling well she make sure to reassure Barb and remind her how much fun they will have together after school. It is always a good idea to tell parents to share stressful events at home with teachers, particularly the illness of a close family member.

Another stress from home happens when a close relative moves away. Children can feel devastated, and these feelings often get expressed indirectly in school. In the next example, the teacher didn't understand the child's odd behavior because she wasn't aware that a relative was moving.

TEACHER: Pat is a sweet, loving kid who plays well with others and is verbal with both kids and teachers. Lately I have noticed that any change in the classroom has been a challenge. The other day, chairs were missing from the kitchen because some children were using them in the library. He stood in the kitchen, frozen, looking upset but not crying. When I asked what was wrong, he just replied, "There are no chairs." I let him know that other kids had them in the library, but we could get some from another room. There have been other incidents where things have changed, and he has just had a lost or forlorn look. How can I make disappointments less painful? Is there something else that can be said to him to ease changes that may occur?

DIRECTOR PEREZ: His grandmother is moving to Norway, and so that big change is making these other small changes feel much harder. Tell him you know changes in the classroom feel harder because he has a big change at home with his grandmother moving. And call his parents and tell them we see how sensitive he is to changes, and we think it's related to his grandmother leaving. They really need to promise him that they will video chat with her on a regular schedule. And his grandmother should give him a present when she leaves, something he can hang on to.

When you know about the stresses children are experiencing, you can put two and two together and Acknowledge and Accept their feelings. If a separation is involved, it is always a good idea to suggest to parents that they help by arranging ongoing contact between the child and the person leaving.

Scary Events

When scary things happen outside of school – an accident, crime, sudden natural disasters, family arguments – children may deny feeling upset. When parents make sure to tell you what has happened, you can gently help children unpack their denial and get more in touch with the traumatic experience.

> **TEACHER:** Walt came in late on Wednesday. His mom, who had obvious bruises, said, "I just wanted to mention that Walt and I got into a bad accident this weekend. This is the first time he's gotten in a car since then, and he was afraid to do it at first." She mentioned that the impact was strong enough for the air bags to come out. I told her how sorry I was to hear that. She said she was letting me know in case he mentioned anything. I thanked her for telling me, and said we would definitely listen for anything related and help him in whatever way we could. When I closed the door, Walt had some kind of car in his hand. He kept saying, "Crash!" and making crashing and exploding sounds. I said, "Walt, your mom told me that you got into a car accident. I bet that was scary for you." He said, "Yes. Crash then the air bags come out." I patted his back and said, "Sounds really upsetting!" He made some more crashing sounds and said, "I wasn't scared. I'm gonna turn into a firefighter and crush the airbags and make the smoke go away." I said, "I can hear that you wish you could change it so it didn't happen." I was kneeling next to him. He didn't say any more about it, but he kept playing with the car without crashing it. Other children walked up and he started playing with them.

When children tell you about scary events and worry that they will happen again, you can listen to their feelings and help them think of solutions.

> **TEACHER:** While we were playing, Ana said that she went to the beach with her mom, dad, and uncle. When she went into the water, the waves pulled her in and it was scary. I said, "Oh, yes, that can be surprising if they pull you and you didn't want that to happen." She told me that it was her mom's fault because she was not holding her hand strongly enough. I said, "I'm sorry that happened, Maybe the next time you go into the water you can let Mom know that you want her to hold your hand tighter."

Because the teacher was playing with Ana rather than simply observing her play, Ana had the space and opportunity to share her traumatic experience. She was obviously reluctant to express her upset with her mother directly, so she turned to the teacher, who then gave her suggestions about how to communicate her fears to her mother.

Siblings

Sibling rivalry can be expressed in seemingly irrational and angry behavior in the classroom. It is always helpful to know which children have siblings and whether they are older or younger, because then you can often connect children's distress to their feelings about their brothers and sisters.

> **TEACHER:** Bette and Letty wanted to measure each other's height. When Bette didn't get to be measured first, she said, "Then nobody gets to be measured!" and blocked the door. I asked Letty to get a clipboard and marker to record the measurements, which gave Bette and me some space to talk. I acknowledged that she wanted to go first, and how hard it can feel when you're not first … like when you have a big sister. Bette let me know that her sister Mary has a computer to do her schoolwork on, and that she likes to type on it when Mary is not home. I told Bette I had an idea of something that she could type on here at school. I brought in the label maker and Bette was thrilled to type and print her first and last name. "Mary's computer doesn't print stickers with words."

While this was going on, Letty was measured first, and then it was Bette's turn.

Rather than lecturing about taking turns, the teacher used Loving Regulation to defuse the conflict and then connected Bette's sensitivity about being first to her relationship with her sister. As a result, Bette accepted being measured second while remaining positively involved with the teacher.

A related home stress that it can be important to know about is pregnancy. Children have many types of reactions when their mother is pregnant, and they can be quite strong and confusing when you don't know the cause. Some children want to stay at school and avoid being confronted with the upsetting reality. Loving Regulation means you focus not on the behavior, but on the feelings that are causing it.

> **TEACHER:** Lately, Lon has been running from teachers at dismissal. He will shout things like, "Stop following me!" or "Go away!" or he will laugh and act like it's a game. Many times a teacher has to pick him up and carry him to his cubby. He gets upset when this happens and hits, but then he gets very sad and cries. We know his mom is pregnant and doesn't feel well a lot of the time. I said, "Your mom mentioned to us that she doesn't feel well sometimes. We know that you have so much fun here. Maybe that makes it hard for you to leave. We're glad you like it here so much and we look forward to seeing you tomorrow."

You want to focus on children who have new siblings, because the existence of the new arrival can radically change their behavior. You can help them understand why they are suddenly so fragile. When children react negatively to new siblings, it is always a good idea to suggest to parents that they spend special alone time with them. This extra attention has proven to be immensely helpful.

> **TEACHER:** Tony had always run into school in the morning happy to be there. But suddenly he was reluctant to come and was tearful

for the first few minutes. We knew he had a new baby brother. I said, "It must be really hard to leave home when you have a new baby brother. Before when you went to school your parents weren't taking care of a brother, and so maybe now with the change it's hard. Why don't we talk to your mom and see if she could spend some special time just with you before school?" Tony nodded emphatically and brightened and went to join the other children.

Siblings' birthdays are another big and stressful event in preschoolers' lives and can explain much upset that you can help with when you know about them.

TEACHER: Bonnie was having a hard time putting her shoes on to go home. I said, "I wonder if it's feeling hard to go because it's Beatta's birthday?" Bonnie nodded and began to cry. She said, "There's balloons and presents for Beatta and she doesn't share." I said, "That can feel hard because I know you like presents and balloons, too. Sometimes it feels so hard to have both a big sister and a little sister. I wonder what could help you feel better." Bonnie said, "If today was August 21st and my birthday!" I said, "That would feel better! Let's find August 21st on the calendar." We found the day and circled it. Looking at February we saw Bonnie's 4½ birthday celebration marked on the calendar. "Beatta didn't get to have her birthday at school with cookies," Bonnie said. I said, "No she didn't. That was something special just for you." Knowing how much Bonnie likes to cross off the days on the calendar, I tore off the month of February for her to take home. Bonnie was able to put on her shoes and go home taking a little of piece of school with her. I also called Bonnie's mom and told her Bonnie was having a hard time and wondered if she could have something to open on her sister's birthday. Her mom agreed.

How creative of the teacher to give Bonnie a piece of the calendar. She didn't focus on Bonnie's reluctance to put her shoes on but went right to the issue of her sister's birthday. Also, because she had forged a good relationship with Bonnie's mom, the teacher was able to call her and arrange for Bonnie to get a present, too.

Another home stress that affects school behavior is younger siblings grabbing toys. This is why it's good to keep in mind the ages of siblings, so that you can be understanding of the problem and also help children think of solutions.

TEACHER: Addie told me the picnic she was planning was a secret and no babies were invited. I said, "Wait, Addie. You have a sister, Ivy, and she's a baby." Addie said, "I didn't know you knew I had a baby sister." I said, "Addie, can I tell you something?" she nodded, "Sometimes it can feel hard to be a big sister." Addie said, "Yes, and sometimes she takes my toys when I'm playing." "She takes your toys? That can feel hard. They're your toys and you're playing with them." "Yeah, and she has her own baby toys." I said, "Well, Addie, when Ivy takes your toys you should let a grownup know, and they can help with that because nobody should ever take the toys you're playing with. Maybe there's a place at home just for you where you can play with your toys." Addie thought maybe downstairs would be good and said she would check with her mom.

As the year goes on, children will increasingly come to view you as their advocate and admit that they want help with sibling problems at home.

TEACHER: Lexi said, "So Jordan are you going to kill my little brother for me? I need you to get rid of him." Jordan replied, "Yeah, I can make that happen just like that." He snapped his fingers. I said, "Lexi did your brother do something that makes you want him to go away?" Lexi said, "Yeah, he takes me away from my family." I asked, "Does he play with mommy and daddy when you are trying to? Does he take you away in that way?" Jordan said, "No, he takes her away to the wild. Don't worry, Lexi, you will like the wild, there are tigers." Lexi corrected, "No, we need to get rid of my brother." I said, "You want him to go away because he takes you away from your mommy and daddy." Lexi said, "Yeah." I replied, "Thanks for sharing that, Lexi. We can think about other ways for you to get more time with your parents besides getting rid of your brother. Would you like me to talk to them about more special time for you?" Lexi said, "Yes, OK."

If the teacher had reacted disapprovingly to Lexi's request to have her brother killed, Lexi would never have shared her feelings of being left out and her wish for teachers to help.

Bilingual Issues

You may have children in your class who come as foreign language speakers. Occasionally a parent has to remain in the classroom for a while to translate, but if children aren't pressured, they usually pick up enough English quickly. Sometimes, though, parents express ambivalence about their children speaking English because they worry that children will abandon their native language. This can create conflicts for preschoolers.

TEACHER: In Toddler Transitions, Lena is making great strides speaking in English in the classroom. Her parents have felt strongly about speaking to her entirely in Spanish while she is at home, but within the past few months they have been more open to including some English. She usually starts off speaking entirely in Spanish, and as the class progresses, she uses more English. Toward the end of class the other day, Lena appeared very uncomfortable while speaking with us in complete English sentences. I said, "I notice you are telling this story in English, and that's just fine, but I'm wondering if you are worried about how your parents would feel if they could hear you. But school is a place where you can speak in either English or Spanish depending on how you feel at the moment, and your parents know you will speak English here." Lena smiled and continued to speak in English.

As in other areas, you consistently convey that school can be very different from home in having more freedom and fewer restrictions.

Parents' Absences

You want to encourage parents to tell you about "normal" absences that they may not think will have much effect on their children, like work schedules or traveling. Because they often downplay the stress to their children caused by what seem to them like everyday events, it can be difficult for parents to see the impact.

> **TEACHER:** Rowan pulled one of the heart stickers off his valentine and said, "You're going out of town." Then he kicked some of the toys that were lying around. I said to Rowan, "I wonder what going out of town means …" He looked at me and said, "Like if my dad's going on a trip." I wondered how it feels for him when his dad goes out of town. He said, "It's great!" I responded, "You know, Rowan, sometimes you might feel upset when he leaves, and you might miss him." He said, "No, I do not." I said, "Well, if you do it would be entirely understandable because you love your dad and want him around. It's important to know that if you do have angry feelings about dad leaving, your angry feelings won't hurt you or your mom or dad." I asked whether he is able to talk to his dad while he is gone. Rowan said he does talk with his dad on the phone. I offered to talk to his parents about his having more contact when his dad is gone, and he nodded appreciatively.

Because his parents weren't recognizing how much he missed his dad when he went out of town, Rowan communicated his feelings during the course of doing an activity. This shows the value of the close relationship teachers establish with each child when they partner with them in play.

Parent-Teacher Conferences

In all communications with parents, especially parent-teacher conferences, you want to offer support, understanding and a partnership that will ensure that parents feel included. Frequently, parents leave conferences upset and worried because they hear negative things about their children, and teachers indicate that it's the parents' responsibility to fix the problems at home. You want to give parents the positive view of their child that you and the other teachers share. Often this is more optimistic than the parents' own view and is a good corrective. Any struggles the child has can be described with understanding. For example, "He has trouble with transitions to the outside, but that's just because he's having so much fun in the classroom. We have to be very creative to help him realize there is a lot of fun to be had in the back yard."

Helping Parents Feel Positively About Their Child's Progress

You want to explain to parents why a Smart Love preschool doesn't use rating scales, testing, and evaluation forms. They are static – that is, they are a snapshot of a child at a given moment. You can explain that if you look at your students over a period of three months, their growth is obvious, and reducing them to a number is at best misleading, and at worst undermines future success. The assessment of progress is dynamic and follows a trajectory of optimal growth.

For instance, the focus isn't on rating children on a specific competence. Children aren't evaluated on whether they can zip up their coats, write the alphabet, or color inside the lines. Rather the focus is on the progress a child is making: "When your child first came, she didn't want to try writing, but now she loves putting her name on her drawings, and she likes making lists of who is present and who is absent."

You want to invite parents to bring both their child's joys and challenging behaviors to the conferences. Sometimes parents ask for negative feedback about their child, which is an opportunity to give parents a positive perspective on their child's progress, strategies to support their child at home that have been successful at school, and to explain that children develop in different areas at different speeds.

The parent-teacher conference can also be used to emphasize to parents that when you are told about significant events at home, you can help with reactions at school.

TEACHER: Over the last few weeks, we have noticed that Cooper is talking about bad guys and guns as well as having a harder time separating from his mom in the mornings. When we told his mom about this, she realized that she should have told us about the man who approached them while they were out playing. She said the man held up what appeared to be a gun and threatened her and the kids. She was pretty certain that Cooper had not heard or seen the interaction between her and the man, but when she got home he observed her being upset while talking about the incident with his dad. She told us that she was very emotional, and that Cooper would still at times bring up the "bad guy" to them. It is apparent that Cooper is still upset about what he heard his mom telling his dad. He still talks about guns and bad guys every day at school. We emphasized to his mom how helpful it would have been to know about this event when it happened, and that it is always easy to underestimate how much children understand about events. After Cooper's mom told us what had happened, I was able to address it in class when he brought it up again. I said, "I understand someone threatened your mom with a gun. I can see you're still upset. Do you want to talk about it?" He told us how scared he was and said he worried about his mom when he was at school.

Parents frequently don't realize that children understand and are affected by unpleasant events that parents think have gone unnoticed. If you see unusual behavior at school, it is always a good idea to ask parents if anything noteworthy has occurred at home.

Connecting Behavior at School to Pressures at Home

Parent teacher conferences are also an opportunity to let parents know about reactions you are seeing at school to pressures at home. Then you can talk to parents about the long-term value of letting children develop at their own pace.

TEACHER: Kindergartener Greyson and I were playing with Legos. He asked me which of the Legos were longer. I told him that was a good question and asked if he could help me figure it out. He told me to guess, and I pointed at the shorter one. He said, "No. wrong answer. Try again, and get the right answer." I asked Greyson if he ever had to get the right answer at home. He said, "Yes, when I do my homework on the computer." I said, "I wonder how you feel about doing homework?" Greyson said, "I don't like it!" Then he scowled and pointed to his scowl and said, "This is how I feel when I do homework." I said, "It sounds like it's too much. How often do you do homework?" He said, "I have to do it a lot on the computer." Greyson is very cognitive and knows a lot about the body, outer space, and how things are built, but it's clear that a lot of this knowledge comes from parental pressure. At the parent conference, Greyson's dad spoke extensively about how hard Greyson worked the night before to figure out a math problem. I explained that Greyson had made it very clear that he is not interested in doing "homework," and at his age, it seems like too much to ask. I suggested to his parents that they take the pressure off because in the long run this "homework" will not make him a better student in that it is causing him to dislike learning.

In the following example, a child was so pressured at home that he felt the only way he could do what he wanted was to eliminate all adults.

TEACHER: I was sitting with Frank, and he said, "I want to kill all the teachers!" I asked him why, and he told me that if we weren't in the classroom, he could say bad words and do all the things he's not supposed to do. I told him that teachers are there to play, read, teach new things, and to keep everyone safe. He just shook his head at me and that was the end of the conversation.

DR. PIEPER: That's a tough one. Your answer was OK, but I might have had more of a discussion with him. "What is it you'd like to do? I'm glad you could tell me that. You can do anything here that doesn't hurt yourself or the school including saying what you call bad words." Let's try to draw him out more. The real problem is that dad has strong feelings about "bad" words and Frank is feeling that pressure. It's classic. The more you prohibit something, the more it will happen. The teacher should set up a conference with his parents and explain that dad needs to take the pressure off as Frank is getting angrier.

This teacher's temptation might have been to worry about Frank's wish to kill the teachers, especially in light of current school shootings, but by remaining neutral and asking why, she allowed Frank to express his frustration that adults were unduly pressuring him. His childish solution was that they should disappear so he could do what he wanted. The better solution, which the teacher was going to pursue, would be to have his parents take the pressure off him and allow him to enjoy his relationship with them and other adults.

Suggesting That Psychotherapy Is Indicated

Sometimes at parent-teacher conferences you may communicate to parents that their child is struggling enough with emotional issues that they might want to consider psychotherapy.

TEACHER: One child only wanted to be with the teachers. He didn't want his name ever called or sung as we do at snack time. We tried not to go along with his wish not to be recognized, but to say things like, "The fun boy sitting between x and y." But also he seemed to come to school unhappy. I felt we needed to reach out to his parents for a conference. His parents said they wanted him to be emotionally secure but were worried because he didn't seem to be. I agreed and said that he feels very insecure and doesn't want his name called, and it's hard for him to play with other kids and to participate in group activities. I said we had learned the value of early intervention and the benefit of child therapy. I suggested this would really help him be more secure and feel better about himself and be more confident. I told his parents that when children get psychotherapy, they become much happier and get along with other children much better in the classroom and find being at school so much more enjoyable. The parents said they would like him to start.

When it is appropriate to suggest to parents that their child might benefit from child therapy, it is important not to dwell too much on the struggles the child is having, but rather to describe in detail the benefits the child will derive – especially how much happier they will be and that they will have more free energy for learning and socializing. This way the parents will be more likely to feel they will be doing something positive for their child rather than something they may feel is shameful or embarrassing.

SUMMARY

In a Smart Love Preschool, parents receive the same helpful and caring responses as students. Moreover, parents are viewed as partners in the care of children at school. When you establish warm and respectful relationships with parents, parents do not hesitate to communicate difficulties or stresses at home, and they are eager for help with parenting questions. When children bring difficulties from home to share with you, you not only help children with their feelings, but in many cases return to parents with suggestions about how to make home life more pleasant and constructive. Parent-teacher conferences are made informative and positive. Occasionally you may convey that a child would benefit from professional help or that parents might be helped by parent counseling. The goal is that parents leave every interaction with you feeling positive and energized about their parenting.

CHAPTER 8

Questions and Answers
About Common Preschool
Issues

I t is asking a lot of teachers to always respond with caregiving rather than personal motives, to understand what is developmentally appropriate and facilitative, and to apply that knowledge in the classroom. Teachers need and deserve access to knowledgeable, positive, mentoring. Most of our teachers say that in their previous schools they were just given a class to teach and had little or no chance to ask questions and get answers. So, below are examples in which teachers from the Smart Love Preschool had questions or submitted interactions that were answered or commented on by Dr. Pieper or Director Perez.

Helping Teachers Distinguish Personal and Caregiving Motives

Irritation is a personal motive.

TEACHER: Clara and Elsa were drawing with chalk, and I announced that the lunch "train" was boarding. Clara said, "No it's not," and they kept drawing. I said, "It is boarding! Come on, let's go." Then they both said, "No, it's not, I don't see anyone boarding." This time I came closer to them and crouched down to speak to them, and I said, "Yes, the other students are getting their things and I don't want to repeat myself every time. It's time to go." This was probably not the right thing to say, but they had done a similar thing to me earlier when it was time to go outside, where they basically said, "No it's not time for that," and kept playing. How should I handle this in the future?

DR. PIEPER: Saying you don't want to repeat yourself is an expression of irritation, which is a personal motive. The more caregiving response, which will enhance your relationship and give the children a better model, is that you can acknowledge that you can see they are having fun drawing and that it is hard to go in.

Then try to attract them in – "We really have to go in" – "What ideas do you have to make it more fun" – "What can we look forward to in there?" Along those lines, ask them if they would like to bring the chalk inside to continue to create their drawings on large butcher paper on the floor.

Needing to show children you are good at things is a personal motive.

TEACHER: Freida asked me to draw her a giraffe with chalk. I said, "One thing I am not good at is drawing, but I'll try." I googled the one-by-one steps to draw a giraffe. I said, "OK, I got it. I will try my best." Ralph and Hester cheered me on. When I was done, I said, "We did it, and thank you for helping and cheering me on." Then we did a happy dance. They are tremendously kind. Freida was happy with her giraffe. They all colored it together!

DR. PIEPER: I know you felt good that the children were so positive and helpful, but needing to draw well is a personal motive. The caregiving motive would be to model being comfortable with the fact that drawing is not one of your best skills, but that you are learning and will try anyway, and if they want to help, that would be great. Again, we always want to get across that effort, not success is what counts.

Wanting children to use normal voices is a personal motive.

TEACHER: Noelle was asking for more water in her watering can. She was asking in almost a screaming voice and doing something strange to her voice, basically being very silly. I told her I can't understand her when she talks like that and if she can ask in a normal voice, then I can help her. Andy asked me for more water, so I gave some to her. I said, "Thank you for asking!" Then Noelle also asked normally and I filled up her watering can as well. Almost the same thing happened later when she asked for something else. I said very slowly, "Noelle, I can't understand you when you're asking like that. Can you ask in a normal voice, so I know what you mean?" Then she asked in a normal voice.

DR. PIEPER: This is a personal motive to want Noelle to talk normally. Children know you can hear them perfectly well and that when you say you can't, the message is that you don't like the way they are talking. The caregiving motive is to understand that she is expressing some unhappy feelings, and the way to respond, as always, is to show her those can come into your relationship. So it would be better not to comment on the tone, but rather just to give her the help she is asking for. My guess is that she has had some bad experiences asking for help, and so she is disguising the request by making it "silly."

Finding the Time Required for S.M.A.R.T. Practices in a Full Classroom

TEACHER: I like the S.M.A.R.T. idea of Time With, but what happens when we are shorthanded in the classroom and other children need our attention or there is more than one conflagration at once. How do we give individual children the attention they need when there are only two or three of us for an entire class?

DIRECTOR PEREZ: There may well be moments when it is not possible to respond optimally to children who are struggling. In that case the important thing is to Stay Positive and Model Kindness and tell the children who have to wait that you are sorry you can't get to them right away but that you will not forget and you will come back to them. Then you can focus on the behaviors that most need Loving Regulation. The important thing is to Model Kindness in the midst of chaos, and to make sure that when there is space you return to the children who had to wait and give them your full attention. However, when you set up the classroom so children are able to follow their own interests rather than having programmatic learning imposed on them, you will find that normally most children will be enjoyably occupied so that moments when you have to triage will be relatively rare. Certainly there will be times when you need to focus on individual children, but much of the time you will have a group around you pursuing common interests, which frees up other teachers to step in when needed elsewhere.

Questions About Loving Regulation

Inappropriate behavior

TEACHER: Morley and Allie like to build and then smash sandcastles. While they were doing that, Morley got close to me and he had his tongue out. I said, "Oh, Morley, what are you doing?" He said he was trying to lick my hair. I said, "I can't let you do that." He responded that he was going to lick the sand. I said, "I can't let you lick the sand either. It's not for eating. We can lick food like ice cream and Popsicles." Then we discussed what some of his favorite foods are and how we can lick those, but that licking sand isn't safe. Do you have suggestions? I felt I was being too negative, but also I had to stop him.

DR. PIEPER: He went to licking the sand because he felt rebuffed about wanting to lick you. There is a more positive approach you could have taken by thinking of his wanting to lick you as his desire to be close to you. Using Loving Regulation, you could say, "I can't let you lick my hair, but you are right, some animals do lick people they like, for example dogs do that. People have other ways of being affectionate like giving a hug or saying, 'I like you.'

Do you have a dog at home that likes to lick you, or do you know any dogs that do? If you want to be close to me you can sit on my lap or sit next to me while you play."

When children ask for something that is your personal property

TEACHER: Yesterday I was playing magnetic tiles with Clementine, and she asked if she could wear my ring, and I said, "No, this is just for me." Clementine said, "But I want to wear it." I said, "I know, but this is special to me and it's only for me. Maybe we could make a ring that you can have. Clementine said, "But I want that one." I said, "I understand, but this is just for me to wear." Clementine thought about it and said, "Maybe I can ask my mom and dad to get me a ring like that one." I said, "Yes, maybe, you can tell them that when you get home from school today!" She eventually accepted the "No," but was having a hard time with it.

DIRECTOR PEREZ: It might have been better to say, "I can see how much you like my ring, but this is a ring that was given to me as a special gift, so I keep it on my finger." You could add, "I wonder if you have any rings at home and, if not, maybe you could ask mom and dad if they could get you a ring. Since you like this one so much, I can take a picture and you can show them. Maybe we could make a drawing of this one and I can cut it out and you can wear it if you like." You don't need to worry about being protective about your possessions, and it would be better to focus on Clementine's desire to be like you. She wants to wear the ring to be close to you. So be positive, i.e., "I'm glad you like my ring. I can't take it off, but let's see if we can't make one for you that will look similar."

When to set limits

TEACHER: Helen was playing the drum very loudly. Some of the other children stated it was too loud for them and were covering their ears. I told Helen, "It sounds like this drum might be too loud for some of the other kids. I wonder if you could play it a little softer." She immediately got upset and started screaming. I asked her if she would want to play it loudly in another room and she said yes. I took her and the drum into the other room, and then she wanted to read a book. After reading the book she played the drum really loudly, and then she was ready to go back into the classroom. I was wondering if this was all right to do or if I should have tried to find another way for her to play the drum or another instrument in the classroom.

DR. PIEPER: Actually, if the drum is in the classroom, there should be no limits. We should either remove it or let it be banged on. Also, there are drum mufflers. It doesn't make sense to make something available and then restrict it when it is being used correctly.

When children take other children's toys home

TEACHER: We have a little boy, Carl, in our class, who has been putting other children's toys in his backpack. This has been going on for a while now. He is experiencing stress at home with a grandfather who is ill, so we have cut him a little slack and had him return the toy to the child he took it from (which he is very opposed to doing – I often have to help him). He has started to make some close buddies, and I don't want him to be ostracized because of this tendency. Would it be appropriate to explain to him that if he keeps putting other children's toys in his bag, we will have to hold on to his bag until he goes home? Please advise. Thank you!

DR. PIEPER: Routinely look through his backpack before he goes home, because it's not good for him to have the experience of taking other kids' toys. You can say, "Because sometimes things end up in your backpack, I need to look. We know this is a really hard time and your grandfather is sick, and it feels comforting to take things home. But you need to take the takeaway toys, not other children's toys." Loving Regulation means solving the problem in a way that doesn't confront the child and cause shame and upset, and also shows understanding of the unhappiness that causes him to need others' toys.

Issues Around Socializing

Encourage socializing but also welcome solitary play

TEACHER: During extended day, I noticed that Amy didn't want to play with Nona and Helen. I asked her a few times if she wanted to come play with them, but she said no and that she was playing her own game. I think she is feeling nervous because normally Nona would initiate the play with her, but now Nona isn't doing that. She did look over a few times at the girls but always said no to playing. I'm not sure if I should help her initiate that play with Nona or not?

DR. PIEPER: Better not to focus so much on getting her to play with others. If she is playing happily by herself, let's not give her the message that that's not OK.

Children are not responsible for understanding and helping other children

TEACHER: Donald is new in our two-year-old classroom and understands a great amount but is not verbal with others. A couple of times he has snatched a toy he wanted that another child was playing with, knocked over a train another child was using, and so on. We have been explaining to the other children that he is new and has never been to preschool before.

DR. PIEPER: We really don't want to make other kids his caregiver or teacher. We shouldn't be saying, "Because he's new you can't have feelings about his destructive behavior," or that "You need to treat him differently." When kids are having a hard time, we can tell other children that they are having a bad day, but not in any way that makes the other children his caregivers or implies that they shouldn't have feelings about what's going on. We can be clear that the teachers will deal with it and it's not other children's responsibility to manage it.

Culture and language differences

It can be challenging to integrate children who come to preschool speaking another language.

TEACHER: Cyrus, who is Iranian, is the youngest child in the class. He doesn't speak much English but understands enough to get by. We actively name things that he points to. He really wants to play with Juliette, who just recently bonded with Ed. At first the pair were not receptive to him joining their group. Juliette was not so nice, telling Cyrus to beat it. She didn't want him following her. I explained to her that she doesn't have to play with him, but she can't hurt his feelings by the way she tells him. I also tried to help her understand that he may seem different to her from the other children because he doesn't speak a lot of English and doesn't always know how to express himself, but that isn't a reason to hurt his feelings. He wasn't trying to agitate her by following her, he just wanted to play. She understood that but said that she just wanted it to be Ed and her for right now. She did proceed to speak more kindly to Cyrus, explaining that perhaps they can run together outside later, or she would sit next to him at snack. "But right now, I just want to play with Ed, OK?" I don't know if Cyrus understood this. He looked at me for guidance and I motioned and spoke. I reiterated what Juliette said and told him I would play with him. We were just about to do something together, or try to find someone else to play with, when Juliette came back over. Evidently, after further consultation with Ed, they decided Cyrus could play. He smiled and went to get a firefighter costume on, like them. Juliette ended up giving Cyrus her firefighter hat, but he wanted a jacket. It seemed like they were content to let him be on the outskirts of their play, but not necessarily an equal partner. This went on all morning. Do you have any other suggestions as to how we can make Cyrus feel included and help him break into these social situations? Please advise.

DR. PIEPER: That was a good distinction you made between not having to play with him and not hurting his feelings. When you pointed out that his language issues made him seem different, it seemed to register with Juliette that she might enjoy him. In terms of the class as a whole, as long as he is comfortable with being in the spotlight, it might be good to feature him at snack time and talk about Iran and the Iranian language. Show where Iran is on a map. Have the other kids ask him to say certain words in Iranian, etc. Perhaps his parents could send some clothes or food that would represent his culture. This could help make him a bit of a "star" in the classroom. Also, perhaps a parent or caregiver could spend time in the classroom translating. It would be great for everyone to say the Iranian words along with the same words in English to support Cyrus feeling included, as well as meeting his needs.

When Children Are Out of Sorts

Mixed feelings and sharing sadness

TEACHER: Daisy asked if she could sit in my lap and tell me about her grandma and I said sure! She told me that it was the end of her grandma's life and she's gone now and not coming back and she turned into dirt. She said all of this pretty quickly, and so I said, "Oh, yes, that happens to people." I asked her if she wanted to share a memory of her grandma, and she said no. She asked me if I was sad, and I asked if she was sad. She said she was. I asked if she wanted to talk about her feelings and she said no, she wanted to play baby and then she told Kandy she (Daisy) is a baby and she can't talk yet.

DR. PIEPER: When she asks if you are sad, you could say, "Yes, because you are sad." Also, you could say, "When you pretend to be a baby who can't talk, I understand that you don't want to talk more about grandma right now, but I'm here for you if you do feel more like talking."

When children share worries

TEACHER: Angela brought me the snowflake with her picture on it, and said, "I wanted to give you this. In case I'm not here anymore you can have something to remember me." I took the snowflake and told her, "Thank you, that's a thoughtful way to be able to remember you. And I can make something for you to be able to remember me if I'm not here anymore." We made artwork together and she grabbed an envelope and put my artwork inside and put it in her backpack. She put her artwork in an envelope and handed it to me and said to put it in my backpack.

DR. PIEPER: You don't want to scare her by suggesting you might not be here, especially since she's obviously worried about separations. Rather, try to explore why she is concerned that she might not be there, i.e., are her parents talking about moving, changing schools, etc.

When a child is upset because others don't see things the same way

TEACHER: Elsa asked if she could have an icepack for her finger because Vincent stepped on it on purpose. I said, "Oh, I'm sorry to hear that, and it's still hurting?" She said yes. Vincent almost immediately chimed in and said it wasn't on purpose, it was an accident. Gary also chimed in and told me that Vincent wouldn't do that to Elsa. Both of those comments were upsetting to her, but Gary's more so. She started to cry and stayed close to me. I asked if she wanted to tell me more about it. She said Vincent was trying to sit in a teacher's lap, and he saw her finger and stepped on it. Vincent said he was trying to sit in the teacher's lap, but he didn't see Elsa's finger. I said, "Sometimes we have different impressions of something that happened." But Elsa was upset the whole day really. I asked her if anything else happened in preschool she wanted to tell me about. She said no, she just wanted to go home and not stay at school so long. She wanted to be with her mom.

DR. PIEPER: You might have suggested to Elsa that she was upset not just because her finger hurt but also because Vincent and Gary didn't agree with her that it was on purpose. Then you could add that friends don't always see the same things the same way. And when friends see things differently than you do, it doesn't mean friends don't like you or that they aren't good friends. You might even think about showing her that an image can look like two different things at the same time. Then you could show her the picture that can look like a duck or a rabbit.

When children tell teachers to f*** off

TEACHER: Orson came in looking angry and growling loudly. I said that he looked like he was feeling angry, to which he agreed emphatically. I told him it was great that he was letting me know, and asked where he was when he became angry: at home or in school. He told me it was in the car. I said, "That's great that you're telling me. What happened that made you so angry." Then he told me to f*** off and went into the other room. (He's been saying this word a lot lately.) When I checked on him a couple of minutes later, he seemed to be doing fine, but obviously there was still some amount of anger. I was unsure of how to respond to that outburst. What would you suggest? I also am curious about how to handle cursing in general in the classroom. We have not been making any kind of an issue about it up to this point, but now the crowd of preschoolers is starting to repeat Orson's new favorite four-letter word. After another teacher read a book about bears today, I walked over and heard a chorus of "f**kin' bear, f**kin' bear!" from Orson and three other boys. We worry that this might get repeated at home and concern some parents. Please advise.

DR. PIEPER: We have to decide – either we are going to allow that word in school or not. I would suggest that we say to the children, "There is no such thing as a bad word. F*** is just a word. There are words you can always say and words you can only say in certain places. There are plenty of places where you can say this word, but not in school. If you feel you really need to say it, you can go to the office and say it there. In this example, when Orson says, "F*** off," you can also say, "What I understand from what you said to me is that something happened in the car that made you angry and you don't want to talk about it, and that's fine. You can just tell me that without using that word."

When children are upset because they think parents will be angry with them

TEACHER: I've heard Tristen say, "My mom will get mad at me if my clothes are wet from playing with water" or "My mom will get mad if my clothes have glue on them." When his clothes are wet he asks to change them. Recently his shirt was only damp, so I reassured him that it will dry and did not change his clothes. What would you suggest for how to respond to his comment about his mother?

DR. PIEPER: "You can ask Tristen what kinds of things he does that his mother gets angry about, and then respond by suggesting that he probably feels badly when that happens. Let Tristen know that here at school we have a change of clothes for him, and that we would never be mad at him. You can ask him if he would like us to talk to his mom about this."

Answering With the Right Amount of Information

Questions about other children's families

TEACHER: When Katie was on vacation, Foster asked where she was and who she was with. I told him Katie's dad was taking her on vacation. He asked, "What about her mom?" I wasn't sure what to say because Katie's parents are divorced, and I worried that understanding that would be too much information for Foster. I just said, "I'm not sure Foster, maybe we can ask Katie when she comes back." Luckily, he forgot about this, but I have noticed that he is aware that something is different about her parents and I'm not quite sure what to say if he asks again. Whenever Katie says, "I have this at my mom's house and this at my dad's house," Foster seems confused. I am just looking for an accurate response in case the day comes where Foster does ask why Katie's parents live in different houses.

DIRECTOR PEREZ: There is no problem whatsoever letting Foster know that it was just going to be Katie and her dad on the vacation. This happens even when parents aren't divorced. He may have been satisfied with that answer, but if he continued to ask why you could let him know that Katie's parents live in different houses, and she gets to spend time in each house with each of her parents. They don't live in the same house like his parents do. Some parents do and some don't, and some families are like that. But the important thing is that both parents love Katie very much. This is a good opportunity to let children know that there are many types of family configurations.

Questions about body parts

TEACHER: Marcus wet his pants and underwear, so I changed both. While he did not have anything on his lower body, he asked me if it was OK if he touched his body parts. I wasn't entirely sure of how to respond because I know it is appropriate for children to be curious, so I just told him, "Oh, well, I have your underwear right here, so maybe not right now." He said OK and I helped him finish getting dressed.

DIRECTOR PEREZ: Rather than ducking the question, if he asks you if it's OK for him to touch his own body parts, you can let him know that it is his body and of course he can. If he was wondering if it is OK for others to touch his body parts, then to that it's "No."

Questions about death

TEACHER: I was reading a story about a man who falls asleep in the rainforest and various rainforest animals come to talk to him while he is dreaming. About halfway through, George asked if the man was dead, and I explained that he was alive but sleeping. Several of the pages have pictures of the man's face with closed eyes, and so a few pages later he asked me again. I explained that he was sleeping, and George asked, "What does dead mean?" How can I answer this big question in a way that he might understand and that won't be scary?

DR. PIEPER: The main thing is to give an answer without getting into the issue of the afterlife because you don't know what George's family's beliefs are. You can explain that when someone dies, they do not breathe, talk, or wake up anymore. They do not come back to life. It's not like sleeping. Then let him ask questions from there. In general, when kids ask those kinds of questions about death, where babies come from, etc., give short factual answers. Then see what more if anything they want to know.

Adding learning content to children's play

TEACHER: Five children and I created a rain cloud in a jar. We filled the jar with water and added a layer of shaving cream to resemble a cloud. Then I gave them a small bowl with blue watercolor and a dropper. They enjoyed using the dropper to insert the blue water into the "cloud," and they observed how the water inside the jar changed and the blue water drops spread throughout the jar.

DIRECTOR PEREZ: Sounds like fun. You could also reference the clouds in the sky outside and talk more about how they look. Next time we have rain, you could make the same observations. You can enrich the learning by extrapolating from the jar to the real thing.

Helping With Sibling Rivalry

TEACHER: I was reading Mommy Hugs to Tony and he mentioned that he didn't like Mom to be with Bret just with him. And I said, "Is Bret your little brother?" He said, "Yes." I said, "Oh, sometimes it does feel hard when we see our mom and dad spend time with our brothers or sisters." And he said, "Yeah, I like when Mom and Dad are only with me." I told him, "Just because you may see Mom and Dad spending time with Bret doesn't mean they don't like to spend time with you. Mom and Dad can spend time and play with both you and Bret. And they love you very much." And we continued to read the book and he shared that he doesn't like being tickled, but that he likes to give his mom hugs and cuddles.

DR. PIEPER: I know you were trying to reassure him that his parents love him even when they are playing with his brother, but he would experience that as trying to talk him out of his jealous feelings and communicating that he shouldn't or needn't feel that way. Better just leave it that you are glad he is telling you that it is hard when his parents spend time with his brother, and you really get that.

Supporting Children Who Have Toileting Challenges

Recognizing and responding to conflicting feelings about using the toilet

TEACHER: Jayden had two toileting mishaps. The first one I noticed outside, and the second he told me but he was already wet. I walked with him to the bathroom and thanked him for letting me know he had to use the potty, but I added, "It looks like you are wet, so let's go in so we can change into some dry clothes." He said, "OK. I am sorry." I responded, "It's OK. You did nothing wrong, and you don't have to say you're sorry. This can happen and I am here for you." I gathered his clothes, but he started to act like he was going home. I told him, "Jayden, you can always tell me or any of the teachers when you need to use the bathroom, and you can go back to playing when you are done. I know it's hard to stop playing, but it feels better when we are dry at school." I changed him and he said that he felt better dry. During lunch he said, "I have to go now." I said, "OK, go to the potty." He said, "I don't need help." While he was peeing he screamed, "I am going." I said, "I hear it, buddy. Thank you for letting me know." He came and washed his hands and sat back down at the table. A few minutes later he said he had to go again, and he did. This time while washing his hands he started screaming, "I need help, I need help." I asked what happened and he said his mask had covered his eyes. I said, "It sounds like that scared you. Whenever you feel scared or just want to be close to a teacher you can let us know. We are always here." He said, "That was scary," and he held my hand and walked down the stairs. Back at the table he let me know that he feels good to be dry at school.

DIRECTOR PEREZ: This could be his adjusting to school. Try to be more positive about his efforts: "Great you told me you had to use the bathroom." When he is wet and apologizes tell him, "This happens to all children that are learning to use the toilet." Make clearer that we are not pressuring him in any way: "If you would like to wear underwear or a pull-up you can, and if it feels too hard to stop playing to use the toilet, we can put a pull-up on so you can stay dry and then if you like, you can let us know if you have to use the toilet and I can help you." When he says he has to go, ask him, "Would you like to use the toilet?" and if he says yes, then ask if he would like to go himself or would like your help.

DR. PIEPER: You could have responded to his conflict about using the toilet as expressed in his upset about the mask by saying, "I see that part of you wants to and is happy and proud to use the toilet but maybe another part of you doesn't feel ready yet and doesn't want to see that you did it, so you cover your eyes with the mask."

When children wet themselves and don't want to change

TEACHER: Mira was wet but was outside and refused to come in. I told her we should change her clothes because it doesn't feel comfortable to be in wet clothes. She said, "I'm very comfortable!" I responded, "Oh, thanks for telling me, but we still need to change your pants because we can't be wet at school." She had had an accident yesterday, so I asked if we should check her bag for her clothes, and she mentioned that she didn't have any, so I responded, "Oh, well, we have school clothes that you can borrow if there's none in your backpack, but let's check first." Then she said, "I don't believe you!" I asked what she didn't believe me about and she said she didn't believe that there were school clothes. I told her that I could show her when we get to the bathroom, and she said again that she didn't believe me. I responded, "I wonder why you don't believe me," and she didn't answer. Then I said, "I wonder if you didn't believe me because we were playing a lot of pretend games today so maybe you thought I was pretending, too." After that she just kind of looked at me and slid down the slide and didn't say anything else about it. I asked her if she wanted to walk inside or if she wanted me to carry her in, and she said, "Carry." In the bathroom, I showed her the school clothes and we ended up using them because she had shorts in her backpack and she wanted pants. I thought it was strange and interesting that she said that she didn't believe me about the school clothes, and I was wondering how to respond to that.

DR. PIEPER: Perhaps this was just a way of saying she didn't want to stop playing and come in and change. But it would be worth saying, "The teachers here would always let you know if they were pretending. I wonder if outside of school anyone says things to you that don't turn out to be true?"

When children say the toilet smells bad and won't go in

TEACHER: While changing Jerry's pull-up, he started talking about which children go to the bathroom on the toilet. I think he is upset because his two friends recently have become completely potty-trained. I said, "When you're ready you'll go on the toilet, too." He said, "Toilets are stinky, yuck, yuck, yuck!" and I said, "Sometimes when we use the toilet it can smell, but once we're all done and we flush the potty, the smell starts to go away. After this he just kept repeating, "Yuck, yuck, yuck!" I need a bit of guidance on the response once he said the toilet is stinky. I wasn't sure if he genuinely thinks the toilet is stinky, which it can be, or if he is having upset feelings about not using the toilet yet and this is how he's showing it.

DIRECTOR PEREZ: When he says the potty is gross, you could suggest, "Maybe you're thinking the potty is gross because you're not ready to use it and that is just fine. You can decide when you would like to use the toilet at school, Jerry." Yes, this is more about his not being ready to use the toilet and finding a reason – it's stinky. This is what happens when parents make the child use a potty-seat outside of the house because they want them to use the toilet before the child chooses it. Now it will take so much longer because he is conflicted and wants to be in control of something that is holding him back from the joy of feeling competent in this area as well. He'll choose it eventually. With trust in him, encouragement and support of where he is, he'll feel good about it over time. Tell him that some children wear pull-ups and some wear underwear. Keep it there.

DR. PIEPER: Yes, but also add a positive reflection for where he is now." "I know it's hard to think about using the toilet when you think it is so yucky. Is there anything you can think of that would make it less yucky?"

When children make fun of children who are still in diapers

TEACHER: In the bathroom, Danny looked up and saw the diaper shelves. "Kids at school wear diapers?" he asked? I said, "Yep, some kids do." "Oh yeah," he said, "Waylen wears a diaper. I saw it. Waylen is a baby! Diaper! Baby!" I said, "Babies do wear diapers, but some older kids do, too. Waylen's not a baby. He's a kid at school like you." Danny replied, "I don't like Waylen." I said, "Oh, you don't?" I felt I could have helped explore his feelings more, but I wasn't sure how to do so appropriately. When a child speaks badly of another child, how should I respond?

DR. PIEPER: You might say, "Kids do things at different times – we all walk at different times, talk at different times, and use the potty at different times. Everybody gets there. Nobody is going to wear a diaper in high school." Stay very positive.

Understanding Fantasy Play

Explore the wishes that underlie the fantasy play

TEACHER: We were outside and I said, "What are you doing with all these leaves?" Francesca replied, "I'm making a stew so I need to pick even more. Will you help?" I responded, "Sure, I can help!" Francesca found a stick and began to stir. I said, "I wonder what kind of soup we're making." Francesca responded, "It's magic soup," to which I responded, "I wonder if we need any magic words while we stir." Francesca laughed and said," No, no magic words because it's already magic. It's magic soup."

DR. PIEPER: Explore what magic the soup can do in order to get at Francesca's wishes.

How to respond to fantasy play about doing away with siblings

TEACHER: Brian, who has a baby brother, Sten, began to tell a story about a scary ghost. He told his story for about 5 to 7 minutes, which felt quite long, but everyone at the table was listening. He said, "The ghost came in the night and took Sten on the train and put him in a ghost fire." At this point in Brian's story, I said, "That sounds like a very scary story." He said, "The ghost put him under the ghost water and he turned into a ghost, but someone else came and fought the ghost and then he turned into a ghost. Then he spit goldfish at the ghost." That was the end of his story. I wasn't sure what to say, but it seems that he's very upset and conflicted about his baby brother. Is there anything I could have said to Brian? Also, if a kid is telling a scary story and nobody is saying that it's too scary, should I say anything at all? Please advise.

DR. PIEPER: A story is a story. If other children aren't scared, you don't have to stop him from telling it. This one was so improbable anyway that kids wouldn't believe it and would know it's made up. Brian's baby brother disappearing and becoming a ghost is a wish. You could certainly talk to Brian and tell him that all kids sometimes wish younger siblings would disappear, especially because they can be irritating, but that wishing doesn't make it happen. It might help to ask the other children who were listening if they ever had these same feelings.

How to respond to fantasy play that incorporates bad behavior

TEACHER: Ed loves to make things out of tape. He's made masks, a moustache, pouches, and today he made a "smoker." He did this by wrapping the top of his finger in tape and removing the tape. He came up to me and said "Look, I made a smoker!" It looked just like a cigarette holder. I said, "Wow, I've never seen one of those! What's it for?" He put it up to his mouth, puffed like he was smoking a cigarette, and said, "You put it in your mouth and smoke comes out of it." I said, "Well, that's not healthy." He reminded me that it is just a pretend smoker and that real smoke won't come out, but he put it in his pocket and kept it there.

DR. PIEPER: We don't want to tell children they can't have fantasies about negative things. We can use it as an opportunity to talk about smoking. Fantasies are OK; we don't want to make kids feel badly about themselves if they have thoughts about things like smoking. We could ask, "Does anyone in your family smoke? How did you think of the idea to make a smoker?" If they say, "My mom and dad smoke," then you could say, "Maybe you are worrying about them because you know it's not good for you." He may have been bringing this in because he wanted to talk about it and get help, so we don't want to shut him down.

How to respond to fantasy play that incudes "poop" language

TEACHER: Roger and Lionel like to talk about poop and pee and potty a lot. They pretend they are spraying me with something spicy, and I pretend to need water. They think it is very funny. When they do this, they always escalate it and say they are spraying me with spicy poop or spicy pee and I just respond with an "Eww." This response stimulates them further, or sometimes I just say, "You are so silly." I was wondering what you would suggest when responding to potty talk.

DIRECTOR PEREZ: No harm here. Sometimes I just ask questions about it, such as, "What's spicy pee and poop? What does spicy mean? I wonder what that would be like – how would it smell?" Often adults give feedback that implies that this preschool humor is bad in some way. Here at school, we can play this way.

DR. PIEPER: Yes. It fits with the principle of no bad words, no bad feelings, no bad body parts. At this age, fantasy play involving excrement can be fun and exciting and there is no reason to limit it

As in this example:

TEACHER: Jonah said he was making a basket to hold his farts that he was selling. Andy thought it was funny and said he wanted one too. Jonah said, "When I'm finished, I can make one for you." This was very exciting for Andrew, and Jonah did make one for him. Andrew went to Simon to show him. Simon wanted one, too. Jonah made another one for Simon.

How to answer questions about whether fairies, Santa, elves, etc., are real

TEACHER: I was filling a watering can and Sally asked if trolls were real. I said no, and she ran away. I went over to where she was playing, and I asked her why she was asking if trolls were real. She told me that Wanda (who was also right there) told her that a friend had seen a troll. I said, "Oh, that's interesting." Sally asked again if trolls were real and I said, "No, they're made up and they come from the same tradition as fairies." Then the three girls looked straight at me, and all told me very seriously that fairies are real. I said, "Oh! OK." I wasn't sure what to say or how to backtrack, so I asked them to tell me how they know fairies are real. Several shared stories of seeing fairies or having a fairy house, or (like the troll), knowing a friend who saw a fairy. I was confused about how to handle this. My hunch is that I should not have made the connection to fairies. Was it wrong to answer so directly when asked?

DR. PIEPER: It would be better to avoid the generalization to fairies and say something like, "Some people think trolls are real, and some don't, and you can decide for yourselves, and you might decide differently as you get older." If they ask what you think, you can say, "Personally, I don't think so, but again people can have different opinions." This is the same response you want to make to questions of religion, cultural differences, etc.

How to inject learning content into fantasy play

TEACHER: Sally, Justine, and Nan had a creative dramatic play session in which they decided to take a trip on an airplane to a place called "Princess City." They packed suitcases and talked about the food they were going to eat. I made boarding passes, and they were intrigued with how airplanes and airports work. They also set up the airplane with blocks just as we had set it up a few months ago when we did an airplane unit and remembered many other details from that time.

DIRECTOR PEREZ: That's terrific! Some suggestions on furthering the learning. I wonder, once you arrive at Princess City, what will you do there? (I know eating was one of their ideas, so what kind of food?) How far is it? What's the weather like? Does everyone get to go? There is so much rich learning opportunity here. I wonder if either one of them had recently been on a trip or in a plane? You could explore that, too. A plane designer is like an aeronautical engineer, and you could talk about why great big planes can fly. We could find a book about that. What about making paper airplanes and seeing how they fly.

Responding to Children's Dreams

Interpreting dreams

TEACHER: Maurice told me two elaborate stories about a man with a gun in a car. Both times he has come to me randomly to share his story. He says that a man is in his car and driving with his gun pointed at Maurice's house. I've said to him that that sounds very scary and asked him if his mom or dad were there with him. He said no and continued to talk about the scary man with the gun. I know that in the past Maurice has shared "scary" stories with me that turned out to be dreams. This led me to ask him if this guy with the gun was in his dreams. He told me that he wasn't in his dreams. After acknowledging his feelings and assuring him that he is safe, I wonder what more I can say if he brings this up to me again. Please advise.

DR. PIEPER: Children often think bad dreams are real. When they dream about someone wanting to hurt their family, this usually means that they're angry and are scared that their anger will destroy something. Maurice knows that he's going to a new school. You could say, "Sometimes dreams feel so real they don't feel like dreams. But we can try to figure out why you might have that dream. I know you'll be going to new school soon. Maybe you are feeling angry about leaving preschool to go to new school and those angry feelings are coming out in your dream as a scary man with a gun."

Sometimes the stimulus for a dream isn't clear and we just encourage children to share feelings.

TEACHER: Eddie was talking about camping and fireflies. He said he doesn't want to go camping because the ghosts come out at night. I acknowledged that that sounded scary. He said that he also had a bad dream that ghosts tried to get into his body. I referenced the book *Mommy, Daddy, I Had a Bad Dream!*[21] and said that dreams are stories we tell ourselves for a reason. June chimed in and told all she knew about dreams. She said she has that book at home. I brought the book into the classroom the next day for us to look at, but I was wondering if there was anything else I could have said or done to help Eddie. What is the best thing to say if a child asks if ghosts are real?

DR. PIEPER: You can say, "Ghosts are real in our mind, and they can seem very scary, but they are not real in the world." You could add, "Sometimes children dream about ghosts because something is making them scared, angry, or sad. It usually helps to talk about those feelings with the teachers or your mom and dad."

Parents often ask about how to respond to bad dreams.

TEACHER: The mother of Lenny, aged 2½, sent this email: "Last night Lenny woke up at 2 a.m. and he was talking about butterflies and having been bitten or that something bit the butterfly. I think he was trying to tell us about his dream. Lenny saw his first 'real life' butterfly the other day. It was such a thrill for him. Problem is that our cat also saw it and caught it and ate it. I tried to play it off like the kitty was just playing with the butterfly, but maybe Lenny caught on? He kept telling me "butterfly gone" for the next few days and kept asking about it ... and now this dream. I am not sure what to think. Either way, I'd like to read the *Mommy, Daddy, I Had a Bad Dream!* book with him. I'm not sure how to respond.

DR. PIEPER: His mother should tell him, "The cat ate the butterfly. That's what cats do." She needs to make clear to him that she knows it was upsetting to him. It's always better to acknowledge an upsetting situation rather than to say it didn't happen. And children are much more aware of bad events than is usually known.

Evaluating Emotional Problems

School phobias

TEACHER: Melody is a returning student who is very honest about where and with whom she wants to play. There are many occasions when Melody plays by herself. Sometimes she seems happy to play alone, but sometimes she seems sad. The past two days, Melody has played solely by herself, which is different from her usual day. She seems more isolated from the group. Melody was playing in the kitchen when two other children came in. She said, "I just want to play by myself." I said, "You don't have to play with them, but they can play in the kitchen area." I told her if she wanted more space by herself, she could sit by the bookshelf. Melody understood right away and didn't seem upset that other children had come into the kitchen. I think she just wanted all of us to know she wanted to play alone. Melody said, "My mom doesn't want me to play with the other children." I said, "I wonder why she feels that way." Melody said, "Because she doesn't know them." Afterwards, she started to show me all the things she had in a jewelry box she brought from home. I wonder if part of the reason Melody hasn't been playing with other children is a result of separating from her mom in the mornings. It has seemed that her mom has a hard time leaving Melody at school. I'm wondering if Melody struggles to become engaged with others and have fun when her mom feels sad to leave her, and if so, is there anything we can do to help? Please advise.

DR. PIEPER: What is worrisome is the statement that her mom doesn't want her to play with other children. We need to call her mother and say we are trying to help Melody engage with other kids, and could she be careful to be positive about the other kids at drop off. If Melody continues to seem phobic about playing with other children, we should refer her for child therapy.

Aversive Reactions to Pleasure

In the next example a child with emotional problems had an aversive reaction to playing with a friend and turned on her in a mean way.

TEACHER: Miriam really knows how to push Victoria's buttons. The other day after playing happily with Victoria, she told her she was no longer her friend, and she didn't want to play with her anymore. Victoria was immediately upset and started to cry. Jory quickly approached Victoria and asked if he could be her friend. Her sobs turned into a smile, and the two were off playing on the playground and left Miriam by herself. Even though I've never noticed them playing closely before, it didn't matter. Jory wanted to help a sad friend.

DIRECTOR PEREZ: You might have said, "Miriam, I noticed that sometimes you say to others you're not their friend when I know you really have fun playing with them. It sounds like you have some angry feelings about something, but if you say this to other children when you're having fun playing with them or they don't do what you want, they are not going to want to play with you. If you're upset about something, then we can talk about it."

DR. PIEPER: There is quite a contrast here between the child with an addiction to unhappiness that made her hurt her good friend's feelings and Jory, who had absorbed the class culture of caring and stepped in to help.

In the next example, the child had an aversive reaction to the pleasure she felt when her teacher agreed to play with her. The teacher recognized it but wasn't sure what to do.

TEACHER: Abbie asked me to play in the water table with her and of course I agreed. While she was walking in front of me on our way there, she looked over her shoulder to see that I was with her, and then a few steps later she stopped suddenly. I stopped in time to avoid bumping into her, but she collapsed on the floor as if I had bumped her. I said, "Ouch, looks like you fell down," and she said, "Yeah, I'm OK. I'm not hurt." The fall seemed orchestrated, and I wonder if it might have been an aversive reaction. Should I have talked more to Abbie about this fall?

DR. PIEPER: This pretend fall definitely seems like an aversive reaction to your positive response to her. You might say something like, "I notice that sometimes if things are going well or you're enjoying yourself, you make something happen or do something so that you can't have fun. Here I said I would play with you and you made yourself fall down."

Applying S.M.A.R.T. Principles in Schools With Underserved Children

We are often asked how the Smart Love approach would work with preschool and kindergarten children who are underserved, underprivileged, or who have been severely traumatized. These children's needs are voluminous, yet often they are in publicly funded schools that are understaffed and depend for their funding and existence on test results, which means that teachers have little room for individualized attention, innovation, and creativity. When children this age are pressured to make academic progress in order to show "evidence-based" successes, many of them conclude that school and learning are not enjoyable, and they tune out and lose interest.

The most important solution is obviously to offer underprivileged and underserved children the same level of investment, funding, and services as luckier children receive. That will only come with grass roots pressure and powerful lobbying to bring about generous and enlightened legislation. We must educate legislators to understand that the current emphasis on preschool test results is harmful to children, and that funding *high quality* universal preschool education would positively determine the trajectory of children's lives and benefit society.

Given the limitations imposed on so many preschools as a consequence of underfunding and understaffing, *any* application of Smart Love principles will help underserved children. When schools react to these children with increased controls, demands for order, and inappropriate academic and social-emotional expectations, children become ever more unhappy and disinterested in learning. Many are ultimately expelled. However, the more deprived or traumatized children have been, the more important it is to use the Smart Love approach, because it gives children a caring, positive, helpful relationship with their teachers as a model of relating to themselves and others. Loving Regulation, acceptance of all feelings, making help always available, and the other principles of Smart Love will allow underserved children to form close relationships with their teachers and to enjoy learning and each other. When children come to preschool suffering from environmental stressors, the relationship with the teacher can be a real life-preserver. This positive result is possible regardless of the constraints put on schools. The help and understanding available from teachers will also show parents and other involved family members how to make children's home lives more enjoyable and growth-promoting.

SUMMARY

As a preschool teacher there is so much to learn, and much of it requires experience and practice. If you have the opportunity to work with a mentor, you can see the importance of sharing your experiences for feedback. If you don't have a mentor, even a group of like-minded teachers who practice S.M.A.R.T. techniques could come together for some time for reflection and discussion. This could provide a chance to bring your notes into conversation and share ideas. It's important that you are never criticized for mistakes, but rather are provided with helpful suggestions for thinking about and responding to puzzling interactions with children and parents. Without exception, teachers say how rewarding it is to have consistent, ongoing support.

CONCLUSION

We have described the positive effects children, teachers, and parents reap from the Smart Love approach. Most importantly, even if you are in a school that doesn't allow for the implementation of our entire program (i.e., there is no choice about testing and good scores are necessary for your school's survival), adopting any of these ideas will improve the classroom culture, benefit your students, and make your work more enjoyable and successful. Most of the key Smart Love principles can be incorporated into *any* classroom. Examples are:

(1) the advantages for your relationship with your students and for their academic and social-emotional learning of partnering and playing with them on their level;

(2) regardless of other requirements, you can create a positive and caring classroom by responding to your students with the S.M.A.R.T. principles of Stay Positive, Model Kindness, Acknowledge and Accept Feelings, Loving Regulation, and Time With;

(3) while managing behavior when necessary, you can help children get in touch with and understand the feelings that led to it;

(4) as much as possible, you can embed the skills children need to acquire in projects that interest them and spark their curiosity;

(5) you can do your best to respond always with caregiving motives rather than with personal motives;

(6) you can avoid rewards and praise for success and focus on encouraging effort in and of itself;

(7) you can take fantasy play seriously as a communication of importance that you can help children untangle;

(8) you can partner with parents and offer them the same S.M.A.R.T. responses you give to your students; and

(9) generally you can enjoy your students by understanding what is developmentally appropriate behavior and not becoming frustrated when they behave like the children they are.

Appendix

About the Smart Love Preschool

A Brief History

The Natalie G. Heineman Smart Love Preschool (www.smartlovepreschool. org) is entirely informed by Smart Love discoveries about child development and their application in a school setting. To create the most enjoyable and developmentally informed learning experiences, a classroom needs to embrace as many aspects of a child's perspective as can be met in a physical space. From 2010 to 2017, we put these ideas into an existing leased space. In 2017, we had the good fortune to purchase our own building in Logan Square in Chicago, and the pleasure of completely renovating an existing space to create our classrooms. We designed two preschool classrooms for ages three through six and one playschool classroom for ages two and three. We also created spaces for parent education and parent-and-child toddler classes. The Smart Love philosophy contributed to every design choice. Our focus on taking care of staff, parents, and children dictated that our physical space communicate availability, caregiving, and optimal learning as the highest priority.

For example, we appreciate parents as partners in their child's school experience, and we wanted to be sure they knew we were available for them. So we placed the director's office at the front of the building adjacent to a preschool classroom so parents could see the director when they drop off their children and stop in as needed. We also gave a lot of thought to how we could support families whose children weren't quite ready to leave their parent/caregiver. We designed a family space where parents could be with their children, whether children were adjusting to school or having feelings that could best be met by having a parent with them.

To support children's love of, and curiosity about, outdoor learning, we selected a site with a spacious gated front area and extended a parking lot to create a large outdoor garden and greenhouse to keep the fun going while supporting all aspects of play and learning outdoors. These spaces, especially our front yard, also serve as a way for parents to develop a sense of community with one another as they bring their children to and from school.

We carefully chose materials and classroom design to be conducive to children feeling good about coming to school. These choices extend to the design of individual spaces, the dimensions and quantity of the materials/ activities they use, and the amount of open space in each play area, with the goal that every area of the classroom be inviting and available. We made sure to integrate all the learning content (the arts, math, language arts, science, social science, physical development, and health) into every area of the classroom, so that whatever children choose to play will have learning potential that can be naturally integrated. All materials are selectively chosen for open-ended interest, creativity, and learning flexibility. This facilitates and enhances every activity with the power not only to meet a three-year-old's developmental learning needs but also a six-year-old's. The preschool and kindergarten children are together in the morning and the kindergarteners separate from the group in the afternoon. Mixed ages are valuable for all children. The older ones learn by helping the younger ones, and the younger ones look up to and learn from the older ones.

The preschool is part of a non-profit service organization, Smart Love Family Services (www.smartlovefamily.org), which provides mental health services, therapeutic tutoring, community outreach to families of color, free parenting webinars, and parent counseling, among other services. Preschool children and their parents often choose to make use of these offerings. Child psychotherapy, therapeutic tutoring, and parent counseling are located in the same building as the Preschool, which makes access easy. The psychotherapy on site has the same philosophy toward children as the preschool has. Some parents aren't interested, but many are. Teachers say that they are impressed by the positive results being in therapy has on children's ability to feel happier and enjoy school.

Most of our children come from middle class families in the Logan Square area in Chicago (the location of the preschool) and the Board of Directors of Smart Love Family Services is dedicated to raising money for scholarships to the preschool to make it possible for a range of children to attend.

What Children Gain From the Smart Love Approach

Smart Love is transformative of the preschool and kindergarten culture and inspires children to:

- retain and enhance their curiosity,
- love learning,
- learn through play,
- be creative in fantasy play, art, music, drama, and projects,
- cooperate with and show compassion and care for teachers, classmates, and themselves
- regulate themselves without any type of discipline or coercion,
- embrace differences in race, culture, appearance, and language,
- demonstrate unforced, high-level social-emotional learning, and
- move on to the next grades as eager learners who make positive contributions to any classroom culture.

When you uniformly respond positively, helpfully, and in developmentally informed ways, children feel comfortable sharing and owning all their feelings. They come to understand that feelings don't have consequences, and so are not actions and do not have to be ignored, hidden, or rejected. They know that they deserve to be treated well by others, and they treat others well. The social-emotional health they develop results in meaningful friendships, closeness with teachers, enjoyment of shared activities, unforced motives to help others, and a genuine appetite for learning. Also, when you manage all behaviors with Loving Regulation, that is, positively and without disapproval, isolation, or restrictions, children imitate this approach and become able to respond to differences of opinion in the classroom calmly and with an understanding of the other's perspective.

What Teachers Gain From the Smart Love Approach

Teaching in a Smart Love preschool is exciting, fulfilling, and interesting. In our preschool, teachers especially appreciate the mentoring and support they receive in the half day that is set aside for them every Friday for help with classroom questions, curriculum issues, studying Smart Love, and having their own feelings and issues heard and responded to. Director Perez's door is always open to teachers who have urgent questions that won't wait until Friday. And whenever Director Perez feels she could use consultation, Dr. Pieper makes herself available.

At the team meetings every Friday afternoon, teachers share their interactions with individual children, which helps other teachers think about upstreaming issues with those children. The agenda at team meetings also includes discussions about the Smart Love approach to curriculum, how to manage parent-teacher interactions, principles of parent guidance, optimal classroom design (including materials added or removed), and training in the Smart Love model of child development. Director Perez also meets with each teacher individually. At those meetings teachers can talk about any difficulties they are having using the Smart Love approach, questions about responses to specific children, interactions they feel particularly proud of, and so on. For example, when teachers begin to use Loving Regulation, they may have questions or fall back on negative responses they have learned (i.e., disapproval), and they need to be able to get input and ask questions. New teachers often vacillate between being too rigid and too permissive.

Another struggle for new teachers is distinguishing personal and caregiving motives. It is asking a lot of teachers to respond always with caregiving rather than personal motives, which is why mentoring and other supports are so important. Therefore, having time set aside every week for both team and individual meetings is enormously important.

The result of teachers' efforts are warm and rewarding relationships with children who trust and look up to them, are happy and engaged learners, and who love their entire school experience. Smart Love teachers have the space to focus on the needs, feelings, likes, dislikes, and interests of individual children because they are not expected to make children prepare for testing, follow a lot of classroom rules, or behave with the social graces of adults. Teachers find that when they use Loving Regulation to manage behavior, children continue to feel connected to them even when their behavior needs to be regulated. Teachers say that it is intensely rewarding to learn the Smart Love approach because it makes the most sense to them and they can see that it enables them to have close and positive relationships with their children and that their children are happy and eager to learn.

Follow-up With Graduates of the Preschool

Below are selected survey responses from parents describing how well the gains children made at the preschool held up in later grades. The consensus is that as Smart Love students matriculate through their grammar- and middle-school years they possess:

- a stable desire to learn that doesn't depend solely on the appeal of the subject matter;
- the ability to enjoy the process of learning and not just the grade;
- the capacity to stick to the learning goal in the face of difficult subject matter, setbacks, and times of not understanding the material;
- the ability to study in the face of feeling tired or having attractive social options;
- the willingness to ask for help when necessary, yet not constantly seeking help because of general feelings of incompetence;
- social-emotional maturity that enables them to be caring and cooperative, understanding of their own emotions, and able to develop stable and meaningful relationships with classmates and teachers.

Read graduates' stories at https://www.smartlovefamily.org/preschool-wherearetheynow

Additional Resources on the Web

Visit http://www.thehappiestpreschool.org to learn more about:

- Integrating Smart Love Into an Existing School
- Starting a Smart Love Preschool
- Teacher Questions and Answers
- Curriculum Suggestions
- Certification as a Smart Love Teacher

GLOSSARY

Addiction to Unhappiness: A learned need for painful, uncomfortable, self-defeating or self-destructive experiences.

All-Powerful Self: A normal developmental phase for preschoolers that embodies children's unrealistic beliefs that they have enhanced powers, both physical and cognitive, and which will be outgrown naturally as children's cognition matures.

Aversive Reaction to Pleasure: Reactive need to make oneself unhappy in some way after a success or a period of feeling happy. A characteristic of psychopathology, that is, of the addiction to unhappiness.

Caregiving Motives: Teacher's caring, positive motives to respond to children in ways that are developmentally facilitative. See *Personal Motives*.

Intrapsychic Humanism: The foundational psychology underlying Smart Love, which includes original discoveries about child development, psychopathology and psychotherapy. The need for the meaning of being loved and loveable is the essence of human consciousness and human existence.[22] See *Smart Love*.

Loving Regulation: Responding to anti-social, resistant, or out-of-control behavior only with kindness and understanding and never with discipline, disapproval, lectures, isolation, or coping mechanisms.

Personal Motives: Personal motives are motives that reflect how teachers themselves are feeling rather than on how children are feeling and what they need. See *Caregiving Motives*.

Play: Activities chosen out of interest and solely for enjoyment.

Playful Learning: Learning playfully is different in a Smart Love preschool. It truly builds on children's interests as expressed in play. There are no formal worksheets, testing, learning centers for children to rotate through in groups, rewards, or directed play that is solely determined by teachers. Teachers join children in play and use that opportunity to introduce learning content in a fun way that children enjoy and build on. Children get help as requested and effort is prioritized over the right answer. If teachers do suggest a project and children don't seem interested, teachers simply offer another idea. The goal is always to preserve and enhance creativity, curiosity and enthusiasm.

Scaffolding: Helping children acquire a skill and then removing help when children are themselves capable of enacting that skill. In effect scaffolding punishes children for success in learning, and asking for help may simply be about wanting/needing closeness with a teacher.

S.M.A.R.T.: Stay Positive, Model Kindness, Acknowledge and Accept Feelings, Regulate Behavior, and Time With.

Smart Love: An original and empirically tested psychology, which includes a unique understanding of child development and leads to an optimal approach to children's social-emotional needs, motivated learning, classroom management, parenting, and the role of the teacher. See *Intrapsychic Humanism.*

Social-Emotional Learning: Children learn social-emotional skills most effectively by imitating important adults rather than by lectures, disapproval, or various forms of discipline.

Notes

1.	Pieper, M. H., & Pieper, W. J. (2011). *Smart love: The comprehensive guide to understanding, regulating, and enjoying your child* (Revised ed.). Smart Love Press.

2.	Meltzoff, A. N., & Williamson, R. A. (2013). Imitation: Social, cognitive, and theoretical perspectives. In P. D. Zelazo (Ed.), *The Oxford handbook of developmental psychology, vol. 1: Body and mind* (pp. 651–682). Oxford University Press.

3.	Meltzoff, A. N., & Prinz, W. (Eds.).(2002).*The imitative mind: Development, evolution and brain bases.* Cambridge University Press. *https://doi.org/10.1017/ CBO9780511489969*

4.	See Appendix for follow-up comments from parents of older children who attended the Preschool.

5.	Pieper, M. H., & Pieper, W. J. (2019). *Addicted to unhappiness: How hidden motives for unhappiness keep you from creating the life you truly want, and what you can do* (2nd ed.). Smart Love Press.

6.	Szalavitz, M., & Perry, B. D. (2010). *Born for love: Why empathy is essential — and endangered.* New York: William Morrow.

7.	When children live in places in which violence or natural disasters of any kind are a constant presence, their fright is more apparent to them and more overwhelming. It can be hard to know what to say to them. Perhaps the most helpful approach is to give them the chance to tell you what worries them, let them know that their fears are understandable, that it's very unfair because no children should ever have to worry about these things, and that you will do everything you can to keep them safe at school.

8.	The all-powerful self is a discovery made by Martha Heineman Pieper and William J. Pieper as part of their reconceptualization of child development. It is described more fully in *Intrapsychic Humanism* and *Smart Love.*

9.	Kohn, A. (1999). *Punished by rewards: The trouble with gold stars, incentive plans, A's, praise, and other bribes.* Houghton Mifflin. Also, Mueller, C. M., & Dweck, C. S. (1998). Praise for intelligence can undermine children's motivation and performance. *Journal of Personality and Social Psychology, 75*(1), 33–52. *https:// doi.org/10.1037/0022-3514.75.1.33*

10.	Kohn, A. (2016, September 7). On punishment for bullying — and punishment as bullying. *Education Week.*

11.	Stone, A. (2018, January 5). Is your child lying to you? That's good. *The New York Times.* This article explains that lying is normal in young children and an indication of intelligence.

12.	Miller, E., & Almon, J. (2009). *Crisis in the kindergarten: Why children need to play in school.* Alliance for Childhood.

13.	Brown, S., & Vaughan, C. (2009). *Play: How it shapes the brain, opens the imagination, and invigorates the soul.* Avery.

14.	Friedman, S., Bredekamp, S., Masterson, M., Willer, B., & Wright, B. L. (Eds.). (2021). *Developmentally appropriate practice in early childhood programs* (4th ed.). National Association for the Education of Young Children.

15   School Zone, et al. (2017). *Get Ready for Kindergarten Workbook - 256 Pages, Ages 5 to 6, Alphabet, ABCs, Letters, Tracing, Printing, Numbers 0-20, Early Math, Shapes, Patterns, Comparing, and More*. School Zone Publishing.

16   Science, Technology, Engineering, and Math

17   Pieper, M. H. (2012). *Mommy, Daddy, I Had a Bad Dream!* Smart Love Press. p.6.

18   Sullivan, R. M., Landers, M., Yeaman, B., & Wilson, D. A. (2000). Good memories of bad events in infancy. *Nature, 407*, 38-39. In a relevant animal study, young rats who get shocked when smelling an odor develop an attraction to that odor, whereas older rats develop avoidance behavior.

19   For more information on aversive reactions to pleasure and the addiction to unhappiness, see Pieper, M. H., & Pieper, W. J. (2019). *Addicted to unhappiness: How hidden motives for unhappiness keep you from creating the life you truly want, and what you can do* (2nd ed.). Smart Love Press.

20   Foundation for Child Development..

21   Pieper, M. H. (2012). *Mommy, Daddy, I Had a Bad Dream!* Smart Love Press.

22   Pieper, M. H., & Pieper, W. J. (1990). *Intrapsychic humanism: An introduction to a comprehensive psychology and philosophy of mind*. Falcon II Press.

Bibliography

Benforado, A. (2023). *A minor revolution: How prioritizing kids benefits us all.* Crown Forum.

Boyack, C. (2016). *Passion-driven education: How to use your child's interests to ignite a lifelong love of learning.* Libertas Press.

Brown, S., & Vaughan, C. (2009). *Play: How it shapes the brain, opens the imagination, and invigorates the soul.* Avery.

Christakis, E. (2016). *The importance of being little: What preschoolers really need from grownups.* Viking.

Christakis, E. (2016, January/February). The new preschool is crushing kids: Today's young children are working more, but they're learning less. *The Atlantic.*

Copple, C., Bredekamp, S., Koralek, D., & Charner, K. (Eds.). (2013). *Developmentally appropriate practice: Focus on preschoolers.* National Association for the Education of Young Children.

Davies, S. (2019). *The Montessori toddler: A parent's guide to raising a curious and responsible human being.* Workman Publishing Company.

Decety, J., & Meltzoff, A. N. (2011). Empathy, imitation, and the social brain. In A. Copland & P. Goldie (Eds.), *Empathy: Philosophical and psychological perspectives* (pp. 58-81). Oxford University Press.

Elkind, D. (1987). *Miseducation: Preschoolers at risk.* Knopf.

Elkind, D. (2006). *The hurried child: Growing up too fast too soon* (25th anniversary ed.). Da Capo Lifelong Books.

Engel, S. (2015). *The hungry mind: The origins of curiosity in childhood.* Harvard University Press.

Friedman, S., Bredekamp, S., Masterson, M., Willer, B., & Wright, B. L. (Eds.). (2021). *Developmentally appropriate practice in early childhood programs* (4th ed.). National Association for the Education of Young Children.

Gartrell, D. (2004). *The power of guidance: Teaching social-emotional skills in early childhood classrooms.* Delmar.

Gartrell, D. (2013). *A guidance approach for the encouraging classroom* (6th ed.). Wadsworth Cengage Learning.

Goodwin, B. (2020). *Building a curious school: Restore the joy that brought you to school.* Corwin Press.

Gopnik, A. (2016). *The gardener and the carpenter: What the new science of child development tells us about the relationship between parents and children.* Farrar, Straus and Giroux.

Hirsh-Pasek, K., Golinkoff, R. M., Berk, L. E., & Singer, D. G. (2008). *A mandate for playful learning in preschool: Presenting the evidence.* Oxford University Press.

Hirsh-Pasek, K., Golinkoff, R., & Eyer, D. (2003). *Einstein never used flash cards: How our children really learn and why they need to play more and memorize less.* MJF Books.

Katz, L., Chard, S., & Kogan, Y. (2014). *Engaging children's minds: The project approach* (2nd ed.). Praeger.

Kirp, D. L. (2007). *The sandbox investment: The preschool movement and kids-first politics.* Harvard University Press.

Kohn, A. (1992). *No contest: The case against competition.* Houghton Mifflin.

Kohn, A. (1999). *Punished by rewards: The trouble with gold stars, incentive plans, A's, praise, and other bribes.* Houghton Mifflin.

Kohn, A. (1999). *The schools our children deserve: Moving beyond traditional classrooms and "tougher standards."* Houghton Mifflin Harcourt.

Kohn, A. (2011, April 27). Poor teaching for poor children … in the name of reform. *Education Week.*

Kohn, A. (2016, September 7). On punishment for bullying — and punishment as bullying. *Education Week.*

Kohn, A. (2020, January 21). Autism and behaviorism: New research adds to an already compelling case against ABA. *Education Week.*

Koplow, L. (2021). *Emotionally responsive practice: A path for schools that heal.* Teachers College Press.

Lansbury, J. (2014). *No bad kids: Toddler discipline without shame.* JLML Press.

Masterson, M. L., & Bohart, H. (Eds.). (2019). *Serious fun: How guided play extends children's learning.* The National Association for the Education of Young Children.

Meltzoff, A. N., & Moore, M. K. (1994). Imitation, memory, and the representation of persons. *Infant Behavior and Development 17*(1), 83-89.

Meltzoff, A. N., & Williamson, R. A. (2013). Imitation: Social, cognitive, and theoretical perspectives. In P. D. Zelazo (Ed.), *The Oxford handbook of developmental psychology, vol. 1: Body and mind* (pp. 651–682). Oxford University Press.

Miller, E., & Almon, J. (2009). *Crisis in the kindergarten: Why children need to play in school.* Alliance for Childhood.

Mueller, C. M., & Dweck, C. S. (1998). Praise for intelligence can undermine children's motivation and performance. *Journal of Personality and Social Psychology, 75*(1), 33–52. *https://doi.org/10.1037/0022-3514.75.1.33*

Paley, V. G. (2004). *A child's work: The importance of fantasy play.* University of Chicago Press.

Perry, B. D., & Szalavitz, M. (2011). *Born for love: Why empathy is essential – and endangered.* William Morrow Paperbacks.

Pieper, M. H. (2012). *Mommy, Daddy, I Had a Bad Dream!* Smart Love Press.

Pieper, M. H. (2017). *Jilly's terrible temper tantrums: And how she outgrew them.* Smart Love Press.

Pieper, M. H., & Pieper, W. J. (1990). *Intrapsychic humanism: An introduction to a comprehensive psychology and philosophy of mind.* Falcon II Press.

Pieper, M. H., & Pieper, W. J. (2010). *Smart love solutions in early childhood: A handbook for parents, teachers, and caregivers.* Smart Love Family Services.

Pieper, M. H., & Pieper, W. J. (2011). *Smart love: The comprehensive guide to understanding, regulating, and enjoying your child* (Revised ed.). Smart Love Press.

Pieper, M. H., & Pieper, W. J. (2012). *Smart love solutions for school-age children and teens: A handbook for parents, teachers, and caregivers.* Smart Love Family Services.

Pieper, M. H., & Pieper, W. J. (2019). *Addicted to unhappiness: How hidden motives for unhappiness keep you from creating the life you truly want, and what you can do* (2nd ed.). Smart Love Press.

Reissland, N. (1988). Neonatal imitation in the first hour of life: Observations in rural Nepal. *Developmental Psychology, 24*(4), 464–469. *https://doi.org/10.1037/0012-1649.24.4.464*

Robinson, K., & Aronica, L. (2015). *Creative schools: The grassroots revolution that's transforming education.* Penguin.

Scheinfeld, D. R., Haigh, K. M., & Scheinfeld, S. J. P. (2008). *We are all explorers: Learning and teaching with Reggio principles in urban settings.* Teachers College Press.

Siegel, D.J., & Bryson, T. P. (2014). *No-drama discipline: The whole-brain way to calm the chaos and nurture your child's developing mind.* Bantam.

Stone, A. (2018, January 5). Is your child lying to you? That's good. *The New York Times.*

Sullivan, R. M., Landers, M., Yeaman, B., & Wilson, D. A. (2000). Good memories of bad events in infancy. *Nature, 407*, 38-39.

Van der Horst, F., & and Van der Veer, R. (2008). Loneliness in infancy: Harry Harlow, John Bowlby and issues of separation. *Integrative Psychological & Behavioral Science, 42*, 325-335.

Wolfe, J. (2002). *Learning from the past: Historical voices in early childhood education* (2nd ed.). Piney Branch Press.

Index

Index